D0426045

Fortunes of Change

Fortunes of Change

The Rise of the Liberal Rich and the Remaking of America

David Callahan

WILEY

John Wiley & Sons, Inc.

Published by John Wiley & Sons, Inc., Hoboken, New Jersey
Published simultaneously in Canada

For general information about our other products and services, please contact our Customer Care Department within the United States at (800) 762-2974, outside the United States at (317) 572-3993 or fax (317) 572-4002.

Wiley also publishes its books in a variety of electronic formats. Some content that appears in print may not be available in electronic books. For more information about Wiley products, visit our web site at www.wiley.com.

Library of Congress Cataloging-in-Publication Data:
Callahan, David, date.
Fortunes of change : the rise of the liberal rich and the remaking of America / David Callahan.
    p. cm.
Includes bibliographical references and index.
ISBN 978-0-470-17711-2 (cloth); ISBN 978-0-470-60652-0 (ebk);
ISBN 978-0-470-60653-7 (ebk); ISBN 978-0-470-60654-4 (ebk)
  1. Fund raisers (Persons)—United States. 2. Rich people—United States.
  3. Liberals—United States. 4. Pressure groups—United States. I. Title.
HV41.9.U5C35   2009
305.5'2340973—dc22

2009041792

Printed in the United States of America

10 9 8 7 6 5 4 3 2 1

Contents

The New Class Traitors

I F YOU WANTED TO TRAVEL TO Barack Obama's inauguration by private jet, you needed luck and maybe a prayer to find a parking space within fifty miles of the capital. Any number of billionaires and millionaires, it seemed, had the same plan: to zip into Washington on their Gulfstreams or Lears—or maybe even their customized Boeing 767s—to savor a day of history and a night of exclusive parties. Hundreds of people had contributed the maximum amount to the Inaugural Presidential Committee, which was $50,000, and many were promised prime seats at the swearing-in and invitations to the best balls. By flying private to D.C., they could enjoy these perks without suffering the indignities of commercial aviation. Granted, the new president was sure to use the inauguration to repeat his pledge to curb greenhouse gas emissions. But no worries: many of his biggest donors fancied themselves to be "green" jet-setters because they bought carbon offsets for each private jet flight they took.

The only problem, then, was where to land—and park. Reagan National Airport hadn't allowed private jets since September 11, 2001, so that was out. Washington Dulles International closed one of its runways to handle private jet traffic, making one hundred parking spaces available. But there were more jets flying in for the inauguration than the airport could handle. According to aviation authorities, the D.C. area had never before experienced as large an influx of private jets as it did when Obama took office—nearly six hundred jets in total, or double the number for George W. Bush's second inauguration.[1]

A few months earlier, when Obama was running for president on a liberal platform that included tax hikes for the rich and health care for all, he drew enthusiastic backing from the usual Democratic suspects. Labor unions poured tens of millions of dollars into his campaign and mobilized an army of field organizers to win key swing states. African American and Latino activists registered record numbers of voters. MoveOn.org ran television ads that, among other things, featured a stuffed moose fretting about Sarah Palin. Liberal bloggers—the "netroots"—rallied behind Obama's campaign, and the Internet crackled with viral Obamania. The *Nation* ran a cover story that pronounced Obama the "left's best chance" to bring to "fruition a new progressive majority."[2] Even the street artist Shepard Fairey got excited about Obama, creating the instantly iconic *Hope* poster of the candidate. Rarely in memory had a Democratic nominee received such heartfelt support from the party's base.

But the defeat of John McCain in November 2008 was also helped along by a less likely set of supporters, a group that *Forbes* dubbed "Obama's billionaires." Among them were some of America's wealthiest hedge fund managers, including Thomas Steyer, Kenneth Griffin, Paul Tudor Jones, James Simons, and—predictably—George Soros, who was the single largest donor to the Democratic push in 2008. These men backed Obama even as the candidate pledged to more than double taxes on hedge fund profits, a move that could cost some of these donors millions of dollars a year. Several tech titans also threw in their lot with Obama, including the CEO of Silicon Valley's hottest company—Eric Schmidt of Google—who hit the campaign trail for the candidate. In Hollywood, Obama secured early backing from three of the biggest moguls in town, the DreamWorks trio Steven Spielberg, David Geffen, and Jeffrey Katzenberg. Warren Buffett, the perennial number two on the Forbes 400 list, also came in early. He reached out to Obama shortly after his famous 2004 convention speech and threw a fund-raiser for him in Omaha. Buffett didn't write the big campaign checks that others did, but he provided something far more valuable, as this revered wise man of business emerged as a trusted adviser to the young candidate. Another billionaire—the hotel heiress Penny Pritzker—chaired Obama's finance committee, an operation that mobilized scores of wealthy bundlers, who, in turn, raised tens of millions of dollars from some of the nation's richest people.

When it was all over, Obama had raised more money than McCain in eight of the ten wealthiest zip codes in the United States and had outraised him in any number of industries, including hedge funds, venture capital, private equity, corporate law, investment banking, and high tech. In a first for Democratic presidential candidates, Obama even raised more money than McCain did from commercial bankers.

Obama didn't break every fund-raising record on the books merely because he had armies of small donors—in truth, he raised about the same percentage of funds from such donors as Bush had in 2004—it was also because he inspired surprising support from upper-class America. That was evident on Election Day, when Obama won eight out of ten of the wealthiest counties in the United States.[3]

A century ago, as Theodore Roosevelt veered to the left, he commented that "the great bulk of my wealthy and educated friends regard me as a dangerous crank." His cousin Franklin would draw even more hostility, as *Time* noted in 1936: "With few exceptions, members of the so-called Upper Class frankly hate Roosevelt."[4]

Today, both men would find plenty of company in their liberal politics among fellow swells. Many super-rich Americans donate exclusively to Democrats; more corporate executives are embracing causes such as gay rights and environmentalism; prominent billionaires have publicly called for tax increases on high earners; and the mega-rich have begun to bankroll liberal organizations with unprecedented sums of money. Meanwhile, the traditional politics of class are turning upside down in many places as America's most affluent communities throw new support to the Democratic Party—a party that has tacked notably to the left since the Clinton era. In August 2009, Gallup released a list of the most liberal states as measured by the percentage of residents who self-identify with this label. Among the top ten were six of the wealthiest states in the nation.[5]

Liberalism in the upper class is nothing new—the phrase "limousine liberal" was coined back in 1969—but it's far more widespread than ever. What is going on?

Just to be clear, the liberal leanings of the wealthy are anything but universal. The rich in red states still vote solidly Republican. Nationally, Obama won voters who earn more than $200,000 a year, according to exit polls, but he lost upper-income voters in every state that went for McCain. And Obama drew far more support overall from the lower classes than from the upper classes. Voting data over the past few decades show that the Democratic Party actually lost some ground among affluent whites between 1976 and 2004 and that, more broadly, income became a slightly greater predictor of voting behavior. Upper-income whites shifted somewhat toward Republicans during this period; lower-income whites moved toward the Democrats. The past two elections, 2006 and 2008, have interrupted this trend as a growing number of affluent voters have gone for Democratic candidates. Still, it is crucial to recognize a paradox: wealthy liberals have emerged as a larger force in political life, even as they have remained a small minority of their class and affluent voters overall have backed the Republican Party. As political scientist Larry Bartels reminds us, "traditional class politics is alive and well."[6]

Yet although rich liberals remain a small minority of their class, their ranks are growing—along with their influence. This shift reflects the changing sources of wealth creation, with the rise of the knowledge economy and what Richard Florida calls the "creative class." People who already trend liberal—like super-educated coastal professionals—make up an ever larger slice of the rich. Most of the big money is being made these days in blue states, not in red states. There are other trends at work, too, such as rising pressures on the upper class and corporations to become more socially responsible; the growing liberalism of elite schools where the rich and the future rich are educated; the radicalization of the Republican Party; and the changing priorities of longtime wealthy people who are turning their focus away from making money to solving social or global problems.

All of these trends have been emerging for years and now have achieved critical mass. With the Democratic capture of Congress in 2006 and Obama's election in 2008, U.S. politics moved more sharply to the left than at any time in nearly half a century. This shift remains historic despite the subsequent conservative backlash and Democratic losses in elections in 2009 and 2010. Various factors account for the shift, and many agents of change can claim a share of the credit. But the liberal rich have played an indispensable role.

If all of this comes as a surprise to you, join the club. Only a few years ago, I certainly never imagined that I'd be writing a book like this. In 2004, I published *The Cheating Culture*, which chronicled the pervasive greed and corruption found in the "winning class" of the Enron era. The book was filled with stories of rich people who saw themselves as above the rules—or who had rigged the rules in their favor.

This bad behavior hasn't disappeared, and I don't pretend that it has. Greed and corruption at the top endure, even after the financial crash. Wall Street is quickly returning to its old ways, executive compensation is still out of control, and corporate lobbyists are working overtime to block reforms that would benefit ordinary Americans at the expense of the well-heeled. Plenty of large fortunes remain arrayed behind conservative think tanks and candidates. Buffett once remarked of our era, "There's class warfare all right, but it's my class, the rich class, that's making war." This remains true today.

Paradoxically, though, liberalism has spread in the upper class in recent years, even as large swaths of this class have grown more self-interested and predatory. As a result, the wealthy are divided as never before, and the fiercest battles over elections and public policy now pit billionaire against billionaire.

Rich is a hard word to define in the United States, where even wealthy people may self-identify as middle class. I define the rich as people who can afford a certain lifestyle and level of influence in society.

The rich have enough money to live in America's wealthiest neighborhoods, send their kids to private schools, give generously to charity or political candidates, belong to exclusive clubs, fly on private jets, vacation at the most exclusive resorts, and leave an inheritance to their children. Because the cost of all of this varies by place, I don't offer a dollar threshold to define the rich. Also, this book is really about two different classes of the wealthy: I explore the changing beliefs of the ultra-affluent class as a whole—those in the top 1 percent of households—which is quite a large group, but also the political activism and philanthropy of the mega-rich, a much smaller group of people who have personal fortunes of hundreds of millions or billions of dollars.

The ranks of both the ultra-affluent and the super-rich have soared in the last fifteen years and remain very large today, despite the financial crash. According to the authoritative *World Wealth Report*, there were 2.5 million high-net-worth individuals in the United States at the end of 2008, who were defined as people who each had at least $1 million in investable assets. The report also estimated that 30,600 households in the United States had assets greater than $30 million. These estimates were made after the crash but before the stock market rebounded in 2009. Another estimate, which looked at households rather than at individuals and was released in March 2010 by the Spectrum Group, estimated that 7.8 million U.S. households had liquid assets greater than $1 million and 980,000 households had assets of $5 million or more.[7]

The number of billionaires has also fallen since the crash, but it remains large. When the Forbes 400 list was first published in 1982, it included only thirteen billionaires. In 2010, there were more billionaires than could fit on the list. In 1982, at the dawn of the long boom, the Forbes 400 had a combined net worth of around $100 million. Now that amount is greater than $1 trillion.

Why are there so many rich people? Easily available capital is one reason. Before the crash, there was far more money sloshing around the world than ever before, which meant that people could borrow big piles of cash to start new ventures or engage in heavily leveraged trading. Another reason is that as the United States and the rest of the world have gotten richer, the market for goods and services has drastically expanded, so if you come up with a great product, you can sell it to many more people. Technological innovation has been another driver of great fortunes.

And, of course, our leaders in Washington have made it much easier to get rich. Taxes on high earners have been far lower since the early 1980s than they were for the previous half-century, and laws designed to share the wealth with workers or protect shareholders from executive greed have been weak. On Wall Street, lax oversight gave rise to profitable but highly risky practices.

The economic pie didn't just grow greatly during the long boom; it was also radically resliced. In 1980, the top 1 percent of families took home about 10 percent of all income earned in the United States. By 2007, these lucky families—with incomes higher than $398,900—took home 24 percent.[8]

It's hard to open a glossy magazine without reading something about the rich, and this group has been ubiquitous in the second Gilded Age. Yet although we know all about Donald Trump's love life or Warren Buffett's stock picks, surprisingly little is known about the political and social beliefs of the upper class. Many books probe inequality and corporate excess or profile titans of business. Few explore ideology at the very pinnacle of the income ladder, and there are good reasons for this void. Survey data about the views of the rich are in short supply, because most polls don't gather information from people with incomes above $150,000.

Some surveys of the rich do exist—these are often conducted by wealth-management or luxury marketing firms—and I draw on these data at different points. I also make use of two major public opinion studies to gain insights into how the wealthy may think: the American National Election Studies (NES), which has collected data on the voting behavior and the political and social views of Americans since 1948, and the General Social Survey (GSS), which has polled Americans on a wide range of topics since 1972. Neither of these surveys breaks out and reports on the individuals who make more than $150,000 or $175,000 a year. In addition, I have drawn on various other polls that have similar income cutoffs.

Anyone who lives in an expensive city knows that a low-six figure income doesn't have anything to do with being rich. But these polls can still offer hints about how income tends to correlate with political and social views. I use these data cautiously.

Campaign finance records offer sharper evidence of the political views of the rich. These records provide a trove of information going back to the late 1970s on donations by individuals, by zip code and state, and by industries and companies. I have mined these data heavily and cite them throughout the book. In addition, I draw on public records of charitable donations, which are found in the 990 tax forms that all foundations are required to file with the Internal Revenue Service. (I do not footnote figures on campaign or charitable donations, because readers can easily access all of these numbers from the Center for Responsive Politics and its OpenSecrets.org database, or from the Foundation Center, which maintains many 990s in electronic form.)

I also examine voting behavior in various ways. I look at exit polls that have surveyed affluent people in recent elections, both for elective office and for ballot initiatives, as well as vote tallies from America's wealthiest counties. And I examine the ideology of congressional members who represent the nation's richest congressional districts. All of this information is illuminating—up to a point. The income cutoff for exit polls is $200,000 or more, while election results for a wealthy county or congressional district don't tell you how the very richest people within that county voted.

Finally, this book draws on interviews with wealthy liberals, as well as those who advise them. Not everyone discussed in the book agreed to talk with me, but many did, and such conversations proved invaluable in understanding the motives of people who have made or inherited wealth and used it to advance change. I don't include citations for quotations drawn from my interviews; quotations drawn from secondary material do have citations.

The views of the wealthy described in this book fall along a broad spectrum. Some affluent people are overtly ideological and are working to mobilize power on the left; others are liberal in some areas but centrist in others. Many might not even describe themselves as liberal or progressive but rather would say they are pragmatic and focused on solutions. Someone like Bill Gates would fall into this category. Ultimately, though, labels matter less than actions, and my focus throughout this book is on wealthy people who are embracing or promoting core liberal ideals. I look at six in particular: more broadly shared prosperity; social inclusion; environmental sustainability; greater responsibility on the part of business; an active role for government in promoting the common good; and global humanitarianism.

Although these aren't the only liberal ideals that matter, they have been at the center of modern liberalism during the last forty years. And now, thanks in part to deep-pocketed new backers, these ideals are gaining stronger traction in American life.

This may sound like great news if you care about rebalancing U.S. politics after years of conservative dominance. But there's a catch that I explore in the pages to come, which is that the outsized wealth—regardless of its political stripe—is bad for representative democracy.

Whatever our ideology, we should all be worried about the record sums of money flowing into politics from the wealthiest zip codes and the pivotal role this money plays in electoral outcomes. We should be worried about how big-time philanthropists increasingly chart policy in fields as diverse as public education and global health. We should be worried as ever more rich people tap great fortunes to buy their way into elective office, bulldozing veteran public servants in the process. Ironically, a growing sense of public purpose in the upper class can serve to magnify its power as rich "super-citizens" push into every last corner of America's civic space and drown out the voices of ordinary Americans. In this way, the swelling ranks of the liberal rich pose their own special threat to democracy.

The other catch is that at a fundamental level, many rich liberals aren't in the business of dismantling their class privileges. A signature trait of wealthy liberalism is that social and environmental concerns get top billing, while economic inequities are rarely a priority. Some rich liberals are more apt to champion the plight of polar bears than of the janitors who clean their offices at night. This has changed somewhat, with new support emerging for steps to mitigate the

United States' extreme inequality. But the first eighteen months of the Obama administration have seen a lot of business as usual when it comes to class interests: no sooner did the rich help put Obama in office than some started to push back against his boldest proposals.

To cynics, this is precisely *why* so many wealthy people backed Obama: so that they would get their phone calls returned when their perks came under attack—or, better yet, to keep such attacks from emerging in the first place.

I mostly take a different view about motives. If what you want are low taxes and unchecked capitalism, you're a fool to help build the power of today's Democratic Party, which has moved steadily to the left since the Clinton years.

Still, the ultimate question is whether even the most liberal members of the upper class are truly willing to challenge how wealth and power are distributed in the United States. I do my best to answer that question in the pages ahead.

EDUCATED, RICH, AND LIBERAL

AFTER LEAVING THE WHITE HOUSE, George W. Bush moved into a sprawling, five-bedroom ranch house in one of the most affluent neighborhoods in Dallas: Preston Hollow. Bush had lived in the area earlier, before he became governor of Texas. It is the kind of neighborhood where big money and conservative politics have long mixed, and a number of GOP stalwarts own mansions not far from Bush. His neighbors include T. Boone Pickens and Harold Simmons, both whom had spent millions financing the Swift Boat ads against John Kerry in 2004, which helped ensure Bush's reelection. Dallas's Republican mayor also lives in Preston Hollow, as does Roger Staubach, the former Dallas Cowboys star quarterback and big-time GOP donor. After a rough ride in the White House, noted the *Dallas Morning News* in December 2008, "Mr. Bush can take comfort in knowing his new precinct is overwhelmingly Republican."[1]

Or *was*, anyway.

Things have changed in Preston Hollow since Bush lived there last. The houses have gotten bigger and more expensive. The richest residents have gotten much richer. And there are also more Democrats. Although Preston Hollow is still strongly Republican, the balance is shifting, and, in 2008, Barack Obama raised more money in Bush's new zip code than John McCain did.

How could it be that a liberal African American from Chicago could outraise a Sun Belt Republican war hero in an area like Preston Hollow? At least one explanation is clear: lawyers. The neighborhood is crawling with them—affluent partners in downtown Dallas law firms. These people are loaded, and most of them are Democrats. Fred Baron, who had made a fortune litigating asbestos cases and had given a big chunk of it to the Democrats, most notably to John Edwards, was a longtime resident of Preston Hollow before his death in October 2008. Not far from Bush lives Les Weisbrod, who advertises himself as the "pitbull" of Texas's medical malpractice bar and is among the larger Democratic donors in Texas. Other major Democratic donors in Preston Hollow include Charles Siegal, a partner at Waters & Kraus; Terrell Oxford, with the liberal firm of Susman Godfrey; and Steven Baron (no relation to Fred), with Baron & Budd.

A few hundred miles away, in the richer and more famous Texas neighborhood of River Oaks, Houston, the picture is much the same. Although the Enron executives who once lived in River Oaks are long gone, either dead or in prison, prosperous Republican oil men such as Robert Mosbacher still live here. But so do well-heeled lawyers, and they give generously to the Democratic Party—so much so that Obama raised nearly as much money in River Oaks as McCain did, a stunning feat in a historically conservative neighborhood once known for its deed covenants restricting home sales from blacks and Jews.

Among Obama's big donors from River Oaks was Stephen Susman, who founded the boutique litigation firm of Susman Godfrey. Susman is Texas born but Yankee educated; he got his BA at Yale University. He has long seen himself as a friend of liberal causes, and his latest specialty—once pure heresy in a place like Houston—is global warming litigation. Susman and his partner, Lee Godfrey (another Yale man), hire lawyers who share their politics and often their Ivy League backgrounds. Though small,

Susman Godfrey was ranked among the top twenty law firms in its 2008 political contributions, with 97 percent of those funds going to Democrats. The firm is rolling in money from a number of big settlements, and partners often pull in several million dollars a year, which goes a long way in Texas.

Lawyering is the prototypical knowledge-economy profession, albeit one that is less new and trendy. As a lawyer, you don't make anything and never will. You earn a living with your brain alone. First you need a Juris Doctor (JD) degree, which requires that you spend three years mastering all sorts of arcana. If you go to one of the top ten law schools, you will spend that time in a heavily Democratic city such as Boston, Chicago, New York, or Berkeley, and on a campus where liberal values are dominant—for example, Yale, Harvard, Columbia, or Stanford. Your professors will be Democrats by a big margin. If you join a top firm, you will be staying on in blue America, because most of these firms are located in liberal cities. The big firms aren't bastions of left-wing politics by any means, and some are quite conservative. Corporate lawyers in particular make their living defending powerful private interests. Still, this world is way more liberal than one might suppose, and many of your new colleagues will be people who once wanted to make the world a better place before realizing they had six-figure student loans to repay and, later, jumbo mortgages. During the 2008 election cycle, lawyers made up the single largest industry backing the Democratic Party, giving $235 million. Three-quarters of all political contributions by lawyers went to Democrats, a ratio that hasn't changed much in twenty years. If you want to rise at a major firm, it might be a good idea to start giving to Democrats yourself. But mainly your success will hinge on analyzing information and manipulating specialized knowledge. Cognitive muscularity is a definite asset for those hoping to become partners.

Lawyers don't make the really big money in the knowledge economy, but the pay is still good and has soared in the last fifteen years, dramatically expanding the ranks of rich lawyers. In 2008, seventy-five law firms had profits per equity partner of more than $1 million, and such profits were greater than $3 million at the top five firms.

This is way up from a decade ago, when only seventeen firms had profits per equity partner of more than $1 million.

Most lawyers who make a few million dollars a year are in firms that mainly do corporate work. If you want to get seriously rich, you need to be on the other side of the fence, suing corporations and insurance companies. Top plaintiff lawyers can make tens of millions of dollars a year. The richest tort lawyer in the United States is Joe Jamail, with a net worth of $1.5 billion in 2010. Jamail lives in Houston and has donated tens of thousands of dollars to the Democratic Party.

Texas now has seventy thousand lawyers. In addition to the local firms such as Susman Godfrey, more big national firms have opened offices in Houston or Dallas. And as more lawyers in these cities have shared in the swelling riches generated by their firms, they are buying into neighborhoods such as Preston Hollow and River Oaks and changing the political makeup of the moneyed Texas elite.

That elite is also being reshaped by the new wealth created in finance and high tech. Technology is now the top industry in Dallas, and that city has one of the biggest concentrations of techies in the United States. Most of them work in the Telecomm Corridor north of the city, where companies such as Nortel, Ericsson, and Alcatel are based. Finance is booming in Dallas, too, or at least it was before the crash. Among the biggest Democratic donors in Bush's neighborhood is Laurence Lebowitz, who is the chairman and managing director of HBK Capital Management, one of the largest hedge funds in Texas. In River Oaks, Obama drew support from John Arnold, a thirtysomething hedge fund whiz who has built a $4 billion fortune through energy trading. Arnold got his start at Enron, where he had earned an $8 million bonus in 2001 for Internet-based trading, just before the company collapsed. Raised in Dallas by a lawyer dad and an accountant mom—typical parents for a new-economy billionaire—Arnold and his wife, Laura, gave more than $120,000 to the Democratic Party in 2008. (Laura is not the kind of wife you would have met in River Oaks in earlier times; she holds degrees from Harvard, Yale, and Cambridge and left a high-powered law career to focus her philanthropic energies on poor kids.)

Houston is still the capital of the U.S. energy industry, but finance and services now account for a larger share of the city's economy, and this is where much of the Democratic money is coming from—not to mention many of the votes. Harris County (where Houston is) went for Obama in 2008, as did Dallas County. In 2009, Houston elected a lesbian Democrat as mayor. Even the oil rich in Houston aren't as Republican as they used to be. The city's recent mayor, Bill White, made a fortune prospecting for gas and oil in the Caspian Sea and is a prominent Democrat. He has been chair of the Texas Democratic Party and has worked in the Clinton administration. He's not your typical good old boy. Of course, these politics aren't so surprising when you consider White's background: he went to Harvard University before returning to Texas to get a law degree and become a plaintiff lawyer at Susman Godfrey. Only later did he enter the energy business.

Farther to the west, Austin has long been an island of blue in a sea of red. There was a time when the city's liberalism was primarily due to its high concentration of government workers, college professors, and pot-smoking twenty-somethings who hung around town for the music scene. More recently, the city has emerged as a center of the new economy and a popular destination for go-getters with fancy degrees. Besides computer-related industries, Austin has scores of biotech firms. The number of patents coming out of Austin jumped from seventy-five in 1975 to two thousand in 2001. The "People's Republic of Austin" used to be a middle-income city. Now it is seriously affluent.[2]

Texas is still a conservative place, and the state's richer residents, overall, remain strongly Republican. In 2004, exit polls showed that Bush won an extraordinary 92 percent of Texans who earned more than $200,000 a year. McCain also won this group, as well as beating Obama among the state's most educated voters. The day may soon come when Texas is flipped into the Democratic column by an alliance of educated metro liberals and ever more numerous Latinos— Obama lost the state by only 9 points—but it's not here yet.

The story is much the same in other Southern states. Although the number of Democrats in the South's most well-to-do neighborhoods is rising, liberals are a long way from taking control of the country club.

Things are different in the North. Here, the movement of ultra-affluent voters into the Democratic Party is well along and says much about the new politics of class.

A few decades ago, the prosperous precincts of Connecticut, Long Island, and Westchester County were strongly Republican. These were the bedroom communities for CEOs, Wall Streeters, and white-shoe lawyers, and come election time, vote tallies reflected their class interests. The same crew still lives in these places—in places such as Greenwich, Connecticut, and Bedford, Scarsdale, Rye, and Oyster Bay Cove in New York—only they are far richer than they used to be. And far more liberal.

Campaign contribution data offer one indication of the Democratic leanings of the rich in these areas. In Greenwich, the wealthiest town in the United States with a population greater than fifty thousand, Democrats outraised Republicans in the 2008 campaign cycle by 59 percent to 41 percent. McCain did well in Greenwich, pulling in $2.5 million—but Obama raised more, netting $2.7 million from Greenwich residents.

Richest Zip Codes and Political Giving: 2008 Election Cycle

Community	Percentage Democrat	Percentage GOP
Jupiter Island, FL	19	81
Aspen, CO	79	21
Sea Island, GA	22	78
Palm Beach, FL	65	35
Centre Island, NY	51	49
Mountain Village, CA	91	9
Hillsborough, CA	79	21
Rancho Santa Fe, CA	91	9
Upper/Old Brookville, NY	57	43
Ross, CA	88	12

Source: Center for Responsive Politics.

Democrats did even better in the super-rich towns of Westchester County. In Bedford, home to some of the county's wealthiest residents, Democrats received 84 percent of all political contributions in the 2008 election cycle. In Scarsdale, Democrats got 73 percent, with Obama hauling in nearly half a million dollars. Out on Long Island, in wealthy East Setauket, Democrats took in 86 percent of all political contributions in the 2008 cycle. These places have been trending Democratic for years, but Obama ignited particular passions, and that is not surprising: he is more like affluent East Coast professionals than any presidential contender in memory, with his meritocratic background, Ivy League credentials and calm, accentless rationality.

Republican fund-raisers do better in the ritzy parts of New Jersey, which historically have been GOP strongholds. But even here, things are changing. Democrats are now outraising Republicans in some of the state's wealthiest towns, such as Short Hills, and are holding their own in Saddle River. This wealthy town was once so Republican that Richard Nixon felt comfortable enough to buy a home there. "He'll be most welcome in Saddle River," the town's mayor had said when it was announced that Nixon was moving in. "We've never had a Democrat serve as Mayor or Councilman since the beginning of time."[3] The town's politics have changed since then, and in 2008 political contributions from Republicans just barely edged out those from Democrats. Saddle River also isn't as white as it used to be: Russell Simmons, the hip-hop mogul—and liberal activist—owns a lavish mansion there.

Money is flowing heavily to Democrats from affluent communities outside the Northeast, too. The wealthiest zip codes in California—towns such as Mountain Village, Rancho Santa Fe, and Hillsborough—give overwhelmingly to Democrats. The same is true for Aspen, Colorado, the second-wealthiest town in the United States, where 75 percent of all campaign donations in the 2008 election cycle went to Democrats

Only in the South and in Florida, in places like Jupiter Island, are the wealthiest towns giving more to Republicans than to Democrats. As it happens, though, most of the rich live in the Northeast and the West.

• • •

Voting patterns also show a shift toward Democrats in upper-class America. Obama won eight of ten of the richest counties in the United States, whether measured by median income or by number of millionaire households. In Virginia, a key battleground state, it wasn't only urban neighborhoods in Richmond and the suburbs of Fairfax that put Obama over the top. It was also Loudoun County, a lushly beautiful place with the highest median income in the entire nation. Loudoun had long reliably voted Republican—before all of the lawyers and the tech executives moved in.

In California, Obama came close to winning Orange County and did win San Diego County, which has more millionaires than Manhattan and has long been a GOP stronghold. Less surprisingly, Obama won narrow victories in Nassau and Suffolk counties, the two wealthiest counties in New York. Historically Republican, these areas had been drifting left for some time. Meanwhile, Obama scored blowout wins in some other prosperous counties, taking Santa Clara County—which covers much of Silicon Valley—by 70 percent and also winning big in places like Seattle.

Obama even won Greenwich, Connecticut, and easily carried the rest of the state overall—among the wealthiest in the nation. Obama's large margin in Connecticut was predictable, given political trends in the state during the last decade. The percentage of registered Republicans has been falling for years in Connecticut and, by 2008, was at its lowest point in a half-century. The steep falloff for the GOP paralleled an explosion of new wealth in Connecticut, fueled by the rise of the state's financial services and insurance industries. The richer Connecticut has become, the less Republican it has voted.

Obama got clobbered among wealthy voters in Douglas County, Colorado, the sixth-richest county in the United States, and also lost badly in extremely wealthy Sun Belt enclaves such as Sea Island, Georgia. In many parts of the country, the link between class and partisanship remains strong. In poorer states, such as in the South and the Midwest, income correlates very closely with partisanship, with richer voters far more likely to vote Republican. But the

2008 Election Results in the Top Wealthiest U.S. Counties, by Median Income

County	Obama	McCain
Loudoun County, VA	53%	45%
Fairfax County, VA	60%	39%
Howard County, MD	54%	44%
Somerset County, NJ	52%	47%
Morris County, NJ	45%	54%
Douglas County, CO	41%	58%
Montgomery County, MD	71%	27%
Nassau County, NY	53%	46%
Prince William County, VA	54%	44%
Santa Clara County, CA	70%	29%

Source: U.S. Census and CNN 2008 Election Results.

pattern is much weaker in rich states, where voters as a whole have gone increasingly to the Democrats and where income has less correlation with voting. Yes, rich people in longtime blue states are more likely to vote Republican than poor people are, but only by a modest margin. For example, in Maryland—now the richest state in America—Obama won 69 percent of the votes of people who earn less than $50,000 per year and 55 percent of the votes of those who earn more than $100,000. In Alabama, Obama won 48 percent of the votes of people who earn less than $50,000 per year and only 24 percent of the votes of those who earn more than $100,000. A study by two political scientists concluded, "In poor states, rich people are very different from poor people in their political preferences. But in rich states, they are not." That's not exactly right, but it is true, as the study also suggested, that the link between income and partisanship in rich states had been growing steadily weaker over the last twenty years.[4]

Fifteen years ago, most of the twenty-five wealthiest congressional districts in the United States sent Republicans to Congress. Now a majority of these districts send Democrats to Congress. It is especially striking to compare the districts of key party leaders. While

Speaker Nancy Pelosi represents wealthy San Francisco—she had more than 21,000 taxpayers in her district in 2006 with yearly incomes higher than $200,000—her GOP counterpart, Minority Leader John Boehner, represents a working- and middle-class district in Western Ohio that had only 4,500 high-income filers. Other key Democratic leaders, such as Henry Waxman, also represent very wealthy districts. Waxman, in fact, has more rich constituents than nearly any other member of Congress—because his district covers some of the richest parts of Los Angeles County, which has more millionaires, many more, than any other county in the United States. Data released in 2007 by the IRS showed that taxpayers in Waxman's district had the second-highest federal tax burden of any district in the United States.[5] They can partly thank their own congressman, because Waxman has a super-liberal record on taxes and has voted for higher taxes on the rich nearly every chance he has gotten since he was first elected in 1974. Most recently, Waxman pushed a health-care proposal that included a special tax of up to 5.4 percent on the wealthiest U.S. households. Waxman gets top ratings from liberal groups such as the Citizens for Tax Justice and dismal ratings from conservative antitax groups, such as Americans for Tax Reform.

How does all of this affect Waxman's ties with his gilded constituency? He hasn't faced a serious electoral challenge in years and typically wins reelection with more than 70 percent of the vote.

The same goes for Carolyn Maloney, who represents another top cluster of the super-rich, on Manhattan's Upper East Side. Maloney has virtually an identical record on taxes to Waxman's, most recently supporting Obama's tax hikes on the rich. In 2007, her constituents led the nation in the percentage of their adjusted gross income going to taxes.

A 2009 study found that Obama's tax plan would take the biggest bite out of households in some of the most Democratic cities in the United States, with New York City getting hit the hardest, Los Angeles and Chicago coming next, and San Francisco not far behind. These are the same places that already pay some of the highest taxes in the United States, and you might assume that congressional representatives would at least waver on tax issues in order to appease their wealthiest and most powerful constituents. Not quite. Nearly every representative from each of these cities regularly gets the lowest possible rating from the conservative National Taxpayers Union: F. Of the ten congressional districts facing the largest tax hikes, the top seven sent Democrats to Congress in 2008—including, for the first time in memory, the district that covers Greenwich, Connecticut. More than half of the fifty districts facing the biggest tax increases under Obama's plan elected Democrats in 2008. Taxpayers in Maloney's district faced the biggest hike under the plan of anyone in the country: an average of $49,420 each.[6] Maloney herself will be paying higher taxes thanks to Obama, given that she is a multimillionaire whose late husband was a former vice president of Goldman Sachs.

Is Maloney paying a political price for her steady record of taxing the rich? Hardly. In 2008, Maloney raised more money than ever and won reelection with 79 percent of the vote; in 2006, she won by 84 percent. What's more, Maloney's constituents—especially those in the fabled 10021 zip code—have given more money to Democrats in recent election cycles than any other group by a huge margin. The most heavily taxed neighborhood in America, it turns out, is a fundraising paradise for a party hell-bent on taxing the rich.

Most legislators from those districts with the greatest numbers of rich people aren't liberal only on tax issues; they are liberal across the board. In 2008, Americans for Democratic Action gave a "liberal score" of between 90 and 100 percent to six out of ten of those congressional members from districts with the largest number of taxpayers who earn more than $200,000 a year. Maloney and Waxman both received 95 percent ratings. Anna Eshoo, who represents much of Silicon Valley, received a 90 percent rating. Nita Lowey, who represents Scarsdale and other swanky parts of Westchester, received a 100 percent rating, as did Chris Van Hollen, who represents some of the wealthiest towns in Maryland. Forty percent of Democrats from high-income districts facing the biggest tax increases under Obama were members of the Progressive Caucus, which places them firmly on the left of the Democratic Party.[7]

• • •

Why are so many rich people voting for liberal Democrats?

The rise of the knowledge economy—which now mints the majority of rich people—is a big part of the explanation. In 1980, manufacturing accounted for 20 percent of GDP; by 2008, it was 11 percent.[8] Other sectors surged as manufacturing declined, and the makeup of the rich has followed this shift. When the Forbes 400 list was first published in 1982, it was dominated by oil, manufacturing fortunes, and old-money families. Of the paltry 13 billionaires on the 1982 list, 5 had made their fortunes in oil. By 2008, nearly half of the billionaires on the Forbes list—190 people—derived their wealth from financial services, technology, and media or entertainment. Only 51 billionaires got rich from oil, gas, chemicals, manufacturing, mining, and lumber.

Many of the new-economy rich are trending Democrat, while the old-economy rich are more likely to be Republican. There are a number of reasons for this.

For starters, these two groups can have different views of wealth creation. If you work in the knowledge economy, you may tend to see wealth creation as a collective enterprise, not as stemming from Ayn Randian individual heroics. The success of your business will depend on your hiring highly educated employees, and you'll rely on public schools and universities to turn out such people. If you own a factory or a chain store, you can get by with high school grads. Not so if you're running a litigation firm or a software company.

Likewise, you'll be attuned to how government investments in scientific research can play a key role in propelling your industry. If you own one of Austin's many biotech firms, you'll applaud every time that the National Institutes of Health ups its research budget and every time a state promises to put money into stem cell research, because some of the breakthroughs from this work may eventually lead to new products and profits at your firm. At a broader level, you will worry about the physical and technological infrastructure that allows goods and services to move around. You will understand the centrality of capital markets in ensuring that you have the money to invest in growth. You will sense the importance of a stable global order in which peace prevails, talented immigrants can move across borders, and open trade is the norm. (The terrorist attacks of September 11, 2001, hurt U.S. firms that rely on skilled immigrant workers, who suddenly found it much harder to come to the United States.) You might even appreciate government regulation for the way it enforces standards and ensures a level playing field.

Martin Rothenberg, who made millions as a software entrepreneur, summed up the collective view of wealth creation this way: "My wealth is not only a product of my own hard work. It also resulted from a strong economy and lots of public investment, both in others and in me. I received a good public school education and used free libraries and museums paid for by others. I went to college under the GI bill. I went to graduate school to study computers and language on a complete government scholarship, paid for by others. While teaching at Syracuse University for twenty-five years, my research was supported by numerous government grants—again, paid for by others." Warren Buffett has made the same point more bluntly: "I personally think that society is responsible for a very significant percentage of what I've earned. If you stick me down in the middle of Bangladesh or Peru or someplace, you'll find out how much this talent is going to produce in the wrong kind of soil."[9]

If you see wealth creation as the product of a collective national effort, you are less likely to resent paying for this effort at tax time. You might even think that you'll get richer over the long term if taxes are raised to support better schools, modernize infrastructure, invest in alternative energy, and expand scientific research. And if you take a longer view, you'll be open to "recycling" some of your wealth through estate taxes to perpetuate the system of supports that made your fortune possible—a view that Andrew Carnegie famously espoused in the late nineteenth century.

The other thing, of course, is that those who get rich in a knowledge economy are—almost by definition—likely to be very educated. The high-tech world is filled with computer whizzes, many of whom have PhDs. Some of the top hedge funds are run by mathematicians and scientists. Investment banks are jammed with MBAs, corporate law firms with JDs. Biotech companies and medical instrument firms are home to MDs-turned-entrepreneurs. Some of the biggest zones of wealth creation in the new economy are near major universities, such as Silicon Valley, which originally emerged from Stanford University, or the Research Triangle in North Carolina, or the Route 128 corridor around Boston. Austin has become a hotspot for biotech companies, in large part because the University of Texas has top-tier programs in bioengineering, nanotechnology, and pharmaceutical research.

Study after study shows that wealth goes hand in hand with high levels of education, and this correlation has grown as the United States has moved into the information age. Someone with a postgraduate degree will, on average, make four times as much money over his or her lifetime as someone with only a high school diploma, and certainly the postgrad will have a better shot at becoming rich.[10] A big reason for the bulging wealth at the top is the rising pay for highly educated professionals who, in earlier times, might have remained upper middle class. Changes in the economy and technology—such as the advent of personal computers and the Internet, new medical devices and procedures, oceans of investable money, and more litigiousness—mean that hordes of these people can now make several million dollars a year. (In turn, conservative tax policy victories starting in the early 1980s have allowed them to keep more of this money.)

In 1982, roughly 50 members of the Forbes 400 had college degrees. By 2006, 244 of those on the list had finished college and at least 132 had graduate degrees—or nearly a third of U.S. billionaires. That some of America's richest people dropped out of college, such as Bill Gates, Steve Jobs, Michael Dell, and Larry Ellison, stands at odds with the broader trend. According to an analysis by Forbes, billionaires in the finance sector were the most educated group among the super-rich in 2006: 55 percent had graduate degrees. Attending an elite university seems to have much to do with getting rich, too. A 2008 analysis by Forbes found that 141 U.S. billionaires had gone to just five top schools for either undergraduate or graduate degrees: Harvard, Stanford, the University of Pennsylvania, Yale, and Columbia. And 1 out of 10 billionaires holds a degree from Harvard University alone. Ninety percent of billionaires in finance with MBAs got their degrees from only three Ivy League schools: Harvard, Columbia, and the University of Pennsylvania.[11]

All of this education has reshaped the culture of finance. Back in the fabled 1980s, the flood of MBAs onto Wall Street was just beginning, and many top earners made do with BAs. Things changed as finance became more complicated—as "quants" found new ways to make money using statistical techniques and algorithms, as automated trading systems came online, and as new financial products for managing risk or structuring debt, such as derivatives, came into being. Top universities spat out PhDs in fields such as mathematical finance and computational finance. Newly created master's programs sprang up in financial engineering. MBA programs bolstered their quantitative offerings. More lawyers went into finance, applying their legal skills to the ever more complex deals that were going on. If finance had long been a haven for jocks, it has increasingly come to rely on geeks.

There are a lot of "pretty high-achieving characters on Wall Street," said Raj Date, who was a senior vice president at Capital One before becoming a managing director at Deutsche Bank Securities. "They have impressive academic credentials and a combination of analytical abilities and facility with language." Date himself fits that profile. He has a law degree from Harvard and was a McKinsey consultant before going into finance, where he made much more money.

Date is a Democrat, who raised money for Obama from his contacts in the finance world. It wasn't hard, even though Obama "was pretty clearly left of center-left." For a crowd of high achievers who had logged years in top universities and prided themselves on their analytical skills, "the increasing anti-intellectual tone of the Bush years was insulting, affirmatively insulting." The message seemed to be that "if you were a high-achieving person, you were somehow inauthentic. That had real power to drive people the other way."

The xenophobic drift of the Republican Party is another big turnoff. "Being well educated and working in global institutions, you're necessarily multicultural," Date said. Date is the son of two Indian-born doctors and exemplifies a key shift under way in finance: a growing number of the younger, most highly educated people in finance are immigrants or the children of immigrants. The Republican Party may be ever more based in the whitest parts of the United States—small towns, newer suburbs, and rural areas—and top Republicans may see political gains from demonizing immigrants as they once demonized welfare queens, but knowledge-economy leaders are headed in the exact opposite direction. If you run a hedge fund, a tech company, or a law firm, you depend on talent that increasingly comes in all colors from all backgrounds and countries. Forty years ago, nearly three-quarters of the graduates of engineering and science doctoral programs were U.S.-born white males; now only a third are.[12] The quants on Wall Street look nothing like Sherman McCoy, the pedigreed WASP protagonist of *The Bonfire of the Vanities*. And, increasingly, the highly educated engineers and computer scientists working in Silicon Valley look nothing like Bill Gates or Steve Jobs. They are as likely to be from Madras as Massachusetts.

The same trend is evident in law. In 2009, the graduating class of Harvard Law School was a quarter nonwhite, and if you were to meet all of the first-year associates at a top firm like Cravath, Moore, you'd see a snapshot of a professional upper class in rapid demographic transition.

To many in the new wealth elite, Obama's race is no big deal. Although African Americans are still scarce within this elite, Obama is otherwise familiar: he's the son of professional parents who attended an elite private school, graduated from an Ivy League university, and got a postgrad degree at yet another Ivy League school. But Obama's most important credential for this crowd is that he is manifestly intelligent. "It was hard to listen to Obama and not be impressed and feel that he wasn't a smart person," said Date.

In his classic 1963 book *The Protestant Establishment*, Dingby Baltzell argued that the WASP upper class could not retain its legitimacy if it failed to overcome a fixation with caste and ethnicity. Back then, the question was whether Catholics and Jews could push their way into elite circles through the sheer force of education and meritocratic achievement. That kind of battle may still be going on in Tulsa country clubs or even in exclusive clubs on Manhattan's Upper East Side, but it is largely over in the wealthiest reaches of the knowledge economy.

Outside the South, the most highly educated people in the United States tend to be Democrats. Obama won voters with postgraduate degrees by 17 points. John Kerry lost overall to Bush in 2004, including among college graduates, but beat him among voters with postgraduate degrees by 11 points. Al Gore also lost college grads overall but won the postgrads in 2000. Increasingly, the most credentialed places in the United States are Democratic strongholds. Obama won the ten states with the highest percentage of residents with bachelor's degrees and eight out of ten of the most highly educated counties in the United States. Kerry won eight out of ten of the most highly educated states and six of the counties.[13] In certain swing states, the support of postgrads proved decisive for Obama. For instance, 63 percent of Colorado voters with postgraduate degrees—who made up more than a fifth of the electorate in 2008—went for Obama, helping to compensate for his loss among voters who had only attended high school or some college. In North Carolina, Obama won only among high school dropouts and voters with postgraduate degrees—which was enough to take the state. A year later, as Republicans swept gubernatorial races in Virginia and New Jersey in 2009, voters with postgraduate degrees stuck with Democrats in both elections.[14]

Beyond the pragmatic reasons for knowledge workers to be liberal, the educated usually trend left for other reasons. In their 2002 book *The Emerging Democratic Majority*, John Judis and Ruy Teixeira describe how professionals have long been the strongest supporters of "civil rights and feminist causes." And there is a reason for this: the more educated you are, the more likely you are to question rigid hierarchy, be tolerant of cultural differences, and reject traditional values. These correlations aren't found only in the United States; they are also evident globally, as the political scientist Ronald Inglehart has shown through the World Values Survey. Although education can obviously open one's mind to new ideas and experiences, Inglehart suggests a deeper underlying dynamic, which is that the educated are more likely to have been raised in economically secure families. As Inglehart tells the story, people who grow up feeling secure tend to focus more on self-expression and worry less about maintaining order. They are "postmaterialist." The insecure, in contrast, worry about their material well-being and are prone to see the world as a precarious place that requires strong authority and traditional values. During the 1960s, it was upper-middle-class college kids taking acid and protesting the war, not working-class kids. Little has changed, and educated, affluent Americans are more liberal on social issues—and are less religious—than members of the working class.[15]

The big difference now is that questioning the status quo can result in serious financial rewards. A few decades ago, the main way that someone joined the upper class was by climbing to the top of a large and centralized industrial company. Back in the era of the "organization man," traits such as creativity and initiative were often less valued than conformity. Success in the knowledge economy, in contrast, often comes by challenging existing systems, thinking outside the box, and taking risks. Here, bourgeois and bohemian values have seamlessly fused—a trend seen elsewhere, too, as David Brooks argued in *Bobos in Paradise*. Entrepreneurs who strike out on their own to "monetize ideas" are heavily represented among the new rich, while certain major knowledge-economy companies are set up to accommodate creative individuals. Google, for instance, has a "20 percent rule," which allows its engineers to devote a fifth of their time to whatever they are passionate about.

All of this helps to explain a paradox about class and income. Even though wealthy people are far more likely *on average* to be Republican, an influx of successful creative types into the upper class has translated into many more rich liberals.

Another factor at work is that the knowledge economy is based in the most liberal places in the United States. Silicon Valley lies in the Bay Area, a birthplace of the counterculture; Hollywood, always a very liberal town, has become an economic juggernaut as the global market for U.S. cultural products has exploded; Seattle, home to companies such as Microsoft and Amazon, ranks as one of the most progressive cities in the United States. Boston was a bastion of Yankee liberalism well before it gave birth to thriving tech, medical, and financial sectors. Austin was liberal well before it became a high-tech center. And, of course, the financial services industry and the corporate law world are centered in New York City, where registered Democrats outnumber Republicans six to one.

It is no coincidence that the knowledge economy has exploded in historically liberal places, because the highly educated are attracted to communities that are tolerant and open-minded. They are seeking nonhierarchical environments where creativity is valued more than conformity or status. In earlier times, a concentration of smarts and sophistication often only meant local coffeehouses with better folk singers and poets, not to mention cab drivers who could quote Nietzsche. Think of Cambridge or San Francisco in the 1970s. Now it means entrepreneurs with a knack for inventing new products and services. The more that people like this congregate in one place, the more economic dynamism there is—as "creative class" guru Richard Florida argues in his book *Who's Your City*.

In a knowledge economy, the breakthroughs that produce wealth emerge from social processes: the exchanging and synthesizing of ideas or discoveries. "The more smart people, and denser the connections among them, the faster it all goes," wrote Florida. In turn, the growth that comes from a concentration of highly educated people draws yet more educated people in search of opportunity. There has been a "mass relocation," Florida said, "of highly skilled, highly educated, and highly paid people to a relatively small number of metropolitan regions." Forty years ago, Americans with college degrees were distributed pretty evenly across the country. Now they are ever more concentrated in a handful of cities—sometimes to an extreme degree. In Seattle, America's most educated city, half of all adults have college degrees and one in five has an advanced degree. Not surprisingly, wealthy people are now more concentrated in these same metro areas, a trend that has sharply accelerated in the last twenty years.[16]

Members of America's affluent knowledge elite are flocking together as never before. And they are ending up in places that have long been quite liberal. Or they are helping turn places liberal, such as the prosperous neighborhoods of Dallas and Houston.

The link between liberalism and high tech has grown notably stronger in the last twenty years. According to data compiled by Bill Bishop and Robert Cushing, high-tech cities were only slightly more liberal than the national average in 1990. That changed dramatically in the 1990s, and by 2000, the twenty-one high-tech areas they analyzed voted Democratic at a rate of 17 percent above the national average. In 2004, they reported, "John Kerry outpolled Bush by more than 5 million votes in the high-tech cities, in an election Bush won by more than 3 million votes."[17]

Because so much wealth creation is now happening in liberal America, the most ambitious young people have little choice but to move to these places. And once there, chances are good that their politics will begin creeping to the left. Psychologists have long documented the effects of social conformity and peer pressure to show how the beliefs of individuals are strongly shaped by the views of the dominant group. A twenty-something Republican who moves to Portland to work for Intel can change the mailing address on his or her *National Review* subscription and keep tuning in to the *O'Reilly Factor* every night. But if this young Republican is living in one of the trendy downtown neighborhoods, he or she will find it pretty hard to meet other Republicans in the flesh, because the percentage of registered Republicans in this age group who live nearby may be less than 10 percent or even 5 percent. Conservatives who move to New York City have long taken refuge on the Upper East Side, but even that neighborhood has changed, and no single zip code in the United States gives more money to the Democratic Party than that which covers the ritziest sections of Madison, Park, and Fifth avenues.

The socializing effects of a liberal metro area are likely to be all the more influential when you consider that many of the talented, super-educated go-getters who are moving to these places have already logged a number of years on the liberal campuses of top universities (more about that later).

The term *self-interest* comes up a lot in conversations about politics. Voters are supposed to vote their self-interests, and when they don't, pundits scratch their heads in puzzlement. But, of course, not everyone defines his or her self-interest by the same criteria. Many of the educated wealthy give priority to social and environmental issues, in the same way that born-again poor whites line up behind a pro-life GOP. The educated wealthy are apt to be cultural liberals not only because of the tolerance associated with education, but also because of the milieus in which they live.

These views can trump financial concerns. More important, though, people who get rich in a knowledge economy are likely to have a nuanced view of their financial self-interests. They may be focused less on which party is going to boost their bank accounts next year with a tax cut and more on which will spur long-term growth in their sectors. By this measure, liberal Democrat politicians who want to spend more money—a lot more—bolstering the foundations of the knowledge economy can look pretty appealing.

A *Wall Street Journal* article, noting the political shifts at the top, commented in 2009 that Democrats need to get used to being "the party of the rich." That's way overstating what has happened—traditional class alignments still prevail in the aggregate—but there is enough change that we need to think differently about class and politics. A look at which Democratic members of Congress stood with President Obama on crucial votes underscores the new reality. Members from the most affluent districts and states mostly backed the White House on its first budget, the stimulus bill, health care reform, and financial regulation. Standing against the president in each of these battles were Democrats from middle-income or downscale areas.

"Corporate Democrats" and special interests—reliable culprits in the left's narrative about stymied reform—are only part of the problem. The antigovernment views held by less educated white voters of modest means now stand as a comparable obstacle to progressive ambitions. As Thomas Frank described in *What's the Matter with Kansas?* many of these voters subscribe to a conservative populism that pits know-it-all liberal elites against the common man. Frank, along with commentators like Robert Kuttner, believes that the key to recapturing these voters is for the Democratic Party to tack left on the economy. That solution may work in some cases, such as in getting tougher with banks or insisting on fairer trade rules. Otherwise, the evidence from Obama's first year is that downscale white voters have been among the lead skeptics of proposals to raise taxes, increase spending, and expand regulation. Even more ambitious liberal plans to expand the role of government aren't going to win back these voters.

In any case, economic populism has become less of an option for a Democratic Party that increasingly relies on affluent voters both for financial and electoral support. Liberal strategists can debate all they want about whether the Democratic Party should eject affluent Americans from the progressive coalition. The truth is that it is too late for that. Class politics has already remade itself, thanks to economic change, and the challenge now is forging an ambitious liberal agenda that capitalizes on this reality rather than fights it.

2

WHAT'S THE MATTER WITH CONNECTICUT?

O<small>N A SPRING NIGHT IN</small> 2007, one of the wealthiest hedge fund tycoons in Greenwich, Connecticut, threw a lavish fund-raiser at his $25 million waterfront mansion for a member of the U.S. Senate.

The host of the evening's bash was Paul Tudor Jones II, a financier worth more than $3 billion. Raised in Tennessee, he had gone to the University of Virginia and is an avid hunter. His lifestyle is replete with the most conspicuous kind of consumption. The waterfront mansion sat on a site where Jones had torn down a previous mansion to build a new and larger home—a place modeled on Monticello but with a twenty-five-car garage underneath the house. In addition, Jones owns three other homes: an estate on Chesapeake Bay, a place in the Florida Keys, and an oceanfront home in Sydney, Australia. To get around, Jones owns three private jets.

Rich guys from Greenwich with roman numerals after their names would seem to fit the Republican archetype to a tee. In fact, though, the event that night was for one of most liberal members of the Senate, a Democrat running for president: Barack Obama. One might suspect that Jones, in feting Obama, was simply making a cagey investment to have a friend in the White House. After all, not long before his Obama fund-raiser, Jones had contributed to John McCain's presidential race, and he had a long history of contributing to both Republicans and Democrats. His political involvements, it might seem, very much mirrored his day job of hedging his investment bets.

But Barack Obama is no Bill Clinton, with solid centrist credentials. Obama was liberal enough that the most left-wing advocacy groups in the United States had often given him their highest rating in analyzing his Senate voting record. Planned Parenthood had given him a rating of 100 percent, as did the AFL-CIO, Citizens for Tax Justice, the NAACP, the National Education Association, the Children's Defense Fund, PeacePac, and the National Organization for Women. Summing up Obama's voting record, *National Journal* had given him a "composite liberal score" of 95.5 percent in 2007—the highest score of any senator that year, including Bernie Sanders, the Socialist from Vermont.

Meanwhile, Obama had gotten consistently low marks from conservative groups. Some of his lowest ratings were from business and antitax organizations. The U.S. Chamber of Commerce calculated that Obama had voted against its interests 67 percent of the time in 2007, and the National Federation of Independent Businesses said that he had been against that organization 88 percent of the time. Grover Norquist's group, Americans for Tax Reform, rated him a 5 out of 100. The National Taxpayers Union gave him an F.

Obama, in other words, was not exactly an obvious friend to the Masters of the Universe set. Indeed, he had vowed that if elected, he would raise taxes on the rich, make it easier to form unions, and slap new regulations on Wall Street. Given these promises, Jones's mansion should well have been empty that night. It wasn't. More than three hundred people showed up, each contributing $2,300. The event included a private reception with Obama for another dozen people who had raised more than $25,000 each for his campaign.

That Paul Tudor Jones would be shaking the Greenwich money tree for Obama is not as odd as it looks. Jones isn't a Gordon Gekko kind of Wall Streeter. He has long been involved in social causes and in more than a passing way. He was a cofounder of the Robin Hood Foundation, one of the largest antipoverty groups in New York City. He personally underwrote many of Robin Hood's administrative expenses, so that the group could claim that 100 percent of the contributions would go directly to help New Yorkers in need. Partly because of Jones's involvement, Robin Hood has turned into one of the hottest philanthropic causes on Wall Street. A stunning $72 million had been raised in a single night during Robin Hood's 2007 fund-raiser, money that was funneled to dozens of community groups working in some of New York's poorest neighborhoods.

Jones is involved in other causes, too. He helped start a commodity investment pool, the One to One Charitable Fund, with the profits going to disadvantaged children, and he sits on the boards of two environmental groups—the Everglades Foundation and the National Fish and Wildlife Foundation.

You might imagine that Paul Tudor Jones II—as an antipoverty advocate, an environmentalist, and an Obama fund-raiser—would be an outlier among the hedge fund set. Not at all. During the 2008 election cycle, Democrats raised nearly twice as much money from the hedge fund industry as Republicans did, and Obama himself raised $1.3 million from hedge fund managers, nearly two times the amount that McCain raised. Obama didn't secure only Jones's backing but locked up support from a range of hedge fund hotshots, including Kenneth Griffin, David Shaw, James Simons, Thomas Steyer, and Stephen Mandel.

Before the crash, hedge fund managers had a reputation as being overly rich, brash, and prone to excess—sort of Tom Wolfe characters for a new age—but they are actually an eclectic lot. And many have exactly the sort of background one might associate with liberal Democratic leanings.

Look at someone like Thomas Steyer, a billionaire whom *Fortune* has called "California's Hedge Fund King" for his leadership of Farallon Capital Management, a multibillion-dollar fund based in California. Steyer grew up in a liberal New York household. His father was a lawyer on Wall Street, while his mother taught in public schools in Harlem. Steyer went to Yale, and even as he later rose in finance, he remained a committed liberal. He became involved in various causes, such as financing a community bank that invests in poor communities, and also started to give tens of thousands of dollars to Democrats. Although Steyer initially backed Hillary Clinton, he switched to Obama after the Iowa caucuses and later organized one of the biggest fund-raisers for Obama's campaign—an event that netted $7.8 million.

Steyer doesn't see any contradiction between being a filthy rich hedge fund manager and favoring a liberal Democrat who planned to raise taxes on the rich. "There is definitely a strain in American capitalism where people believe that they have made the money on their own, basically working single-handedly as an individual to create wealth for themselves," Steyer has said. "I completely disagree. . . . We have to get back to a sense of shared national purpose and that we are connected and responsible for each other."[1]

David Shaw is another good example. Shaw is the founder of the D. E. Shaw Group, a large hedge fund that had $39 billion in assets before the crash and offices on three continents. Shaw started out as an academic, getting his PhD from Stanford University in 1980 and then joining the faculty of Columbia University's computer science department, where he led work on supercomputers. Shaw later moved to the investment world, where he made a killing using advanced quantitative trading methodologies—an approach that led *Fortune* to call him "King Quant."

Eventually, Shaw drifted back to computer science, founded a research firm, and affiliated again with Columbia. But he remains involved with his hedge fund—involved enough to make $275 million for himself in 2008—and avidly pursues his passion of liberal politics. Shaw has been one of the largest hedge fund contributors to the Democratic Party in recent years, giving the party hundreds of thousands of dollars. Employees at D. E. Shaw have also been very generous, and his firm was among the top three hedge funds in terms of their contributions to Democrats during the 2008 election.

Who works at D. E. Shaw? As described in the firm's promotional materials, it sounds like an eggheadish crowd: "Our staff includes a number of Rhodes, Fulbright, and Marshall Scholars, Putnam Fellows, and the winners of more than 20 medals in the International Math Olympiad. Current employees include the 2003 U.S. Women's Chess Champion, a Life Master bridge player, and a *Jeopardy* winner, along with a number of writers, athletes, musicians, and former professors. Over 100 of our employees hold PhDs, almost 40 are entrepreneurs who previously founded their own companies, and approximately 20 percent are published authors whose work ranges from highly technical papers in specialized academic journals to award-winning mystery novels."

This is definitely not the Sarah Palin demographic. With a crew like this, it's no wonder that 94 percent of the firm's political contributions in the 2008 election cycle went to Democrats. Or that Larry Summers chose D. E. Shaw as a place to hang out after being booted from the president's office at Harvard University.

Another brainy hedge fund, Renaissance Technologies, has much the same profile. That firm, whose employees collectively contributed almost half a million dollars to Democrats in the 2008 election—and nearly no one in the firm gave money to Republicans—was founded by one of the most successful quantitative traders of all time, James Simons. In 2008, during the great bear market, Simons earned an almost unbelievable $2.8 billion, and he made nearly that much in 2009. *Forbes* pegged his wealth at $8.5 billion in 2009. Simons has given tens of thousands of dollars to Democrats in recent years, writing $25,000 checks to the Democratic Senatorial Campaign Committee and the Democratic Congressional Campaign Committee, as well as smaller checks to any number of top Democrats, including Hillary Clinton, Nancy Pelosi, Charles Rangel, David Obey, Christopher Dodd, and, of course, Barack Obama. His two children, Audrey and Nathaniel, also write huge checks to Democrats, as does his wife, Barbara.

If you take away what Simons does for a living, his political leanings track logically with his background. Like David Shaw, Simons is an academic by training and spent his formative years in university settings in some of the most liberal places in the United States. He went to college in Cambridge, at MIT, and then spent years in

Berkeley getting his PhD at the University of California. After that, it was back to the East Coast, where Simons taught at MIT and Harvard. He then logged ten years as chairman of the math department at the State University of New York at Stony Brook, where he did groundbreaking work on geometric measurements and won the prestigious Veblen Prize.

Simons decided to put his scientific skills to more profitable use in 1978 and has raked in vast sums ever since. Renaissance uses mathematical models to analyze data on trading patterns worldwide—of stocks, bonds, commodities, and currencies—and identify predictable changes in price. Computers are then programmed to engage in automated trades based on these formulas. "Our trading models tend to buy stocks that are recently out of favor and sell those recently in favor," Simons explained in 2008. During its first eleven years of operation, Simons's Medallion Fund achieved a stunning cumulative return of 2,478 percent. *Fortune* has called Simons the "smartest billionaire," and his firm has come as close as anyone has yet, it would seem, to inventing a money-making machine.

Simons steered far clear of Wall Street in building Renaissance Technologies. The firm operates out of a fifty-acre campus on Long Island, near Stony Brook, and is run by people you'd more likely encounter in a faculty lounge that at a pricey steak house. "We hire physicists, mathematicians, astronomers and computer scientists and they typically know nothing about finance," Simons once explained in a speech. "We haven't hired out of Wall Street at all."[2]

The culture at Renaissance is decidedly casual, and suits are scarce. The same is true of D. E. Shaw, which has no dress code—jeans are common in its midtown office—and lets many employees set their own work hours. Shaw and Simons may be making big money, but they haven't cut their academic roots.

Another common figure in the hedge fund world is the blue-collar kid made good. These individuals may start out narrowly focused on making money, but they develop a social conscience later in life—once big money is in the bank—that leads to liberal politics.

This has been Robert Schulman's trajectory. Schulman grew up in a working-class neighborhood in Brooklyn in the late 1950s and

Contributions from Hedge Fund Employees: 2008 Election Cycle

Company	Total	Dem	GOP
Elliott Management	$1,507,990	1%	99%
Fortress Investment Group	$676,107	88%	12%
Citadel Investment Group	$572,828	68%	32%
SAC Capital Partners	$535,050	80%	20%
D.E. Shaw & Co.	$519,415	94%	6%
Renaissance Technologies	$471,900	95%	5%
Oaktree Capital Management	$363,150	76%	24%
Tudor Investment	$361,200	77%	23%
Paulson & Co.	$329,246	62%	38%
HBK Capital Management	$319,900	58%	42%

Source: Center for Responsive Politics.

the 1960s, the son of a small business owner. His parents were nominally Democratic but conservative. They didn't like unions or taxes. Schulman went to New York University, where he hung around with libertarians, reading and discussing the novels of Ayn Rand. Schulman got excited enough about these ideas to serve as president of NYU's Objectivist Club, which was dedicated to spreading Rand's philosophy.

By his early thirties, after getting an MBA, Schulman was in the finance sector, climbing the corporate ladder at large brokerage firms. Activist movements were roiling the United States, but Schulman didn't pay much attention. "I didn't have social views," he said. "I was out there trying to make money and build a family." He worked largely with people like himself—guys from Brooklyn, Queens, and elsewhere in the New York area. Back then, some traders came directly out of high school. Many others graduated from no-name schools. Schulman got his MBA at Pace, not at Harvard or Wharton. It was a world very different from the WASPy investment banks or the blue-chip asset management firms.

Schulman did well. He started a division of E. F. Hutton in 1982 that specialized in derivatives, futures options, and other exotic financial products. Then he landed a bigger job at E. F. Hutton in 1986 and later, after a series of mergers, held a top job at Smith Barney.

Schulman made a big career change when he left Smith Barney for a tiny hedge fund called Tremont Group Holdings. Hedge funds were still unusual at that time; there were only a few hundred in existence (there are thousands now), and most people didn't know what hedge funds did. Schulman joined Tremont just before the great bull market of the 1990s, and the firm turned out to be wildly successful. In 2001, it sold out to Oppenheimer Funds for $150 million, and Schulman, who had stayed on at Tremont but cashed in his equity stake in the firm, made serious money.

The Bush years would turn out to be the golden age of hedge funds, and Tremont flourished. As it did, Schulman's own fortune grew into the tens of millions of dollars. Yet somewhere along the line, the money started to become less important to him, and, as well, his political views changed.

The shift actually started in the 1990s, after many years of taking home big bonuses as an executive. "Our thinking changed," Schulman said about himself and his wife. "We realized we had enough money. We had an apartment in the city and a big house in Westchester. I was not interested in private planes or private boats. And we decided that for our lifestyle, that we in fact had plenty of money. And that our children and our children's children were not going to want for an education or a retirement."

At Tremont, Schulman was still driven to make more money. A lot more. "That is the way you keep score," he said. But he no longer worried about having enough. "The marginal utility of going from being worth twenty-nine million dollars to being worth thirty million is entirely different from the marginal utility of going from being worth one million to two million," Schulman said. "The marginal utility of going to thirty million is close to zero. It's not going to change anything. If somebody dropped $100 million in your lap, maybe you'd go buy a plane. But going from twenty-nine, which is clearly enough, to thirty? Or thirty-two? It won't change much.

You can only eat in one good restaurant a night. You can eat in the best restaurants you can get reservations in. What, are you going to go to a more expensive one?"

As Schulman acquired wealth, he found himself developing a social conscience for the first time in his life. He and his wife began to give more to charity and eventually started their own charity that helps at-risk youths graduate from college and battered women rebuild their lives. Schulman also shed his old libertarian politics. "I had to go through a process where I realized there are no absolutes. There is no Ayn Rand place in the world."

He came to see society as a place entirely constructed by social policy, with government playing a key role in creating opportunity—especially as the economy grew more complex. And, as Schulman saw it, the United States wasn't doing such a hot job on this front. "I want everybody to have a real chance. If you want everybody to have a real chance, they have to have medical care. And they have to have access to high-quality education. And they have to live in a place that is safe for them to raise their children. They have to be able to get a job on which they can support a family. Otherwise, it really isn't fair. We've had a society that was designed to make educated white males successful. And I have come over a period of time to appreciate that that has to change."

Schulman stopped voting Republican and started to vote Democrat. Then he began to give money to Democrats, which included contributing the maximum amount to Barack Obama. He gave some money to liberal policy groups. And in the autumn of 2008, with his conversion complete, Schulman even went to Pennsylvania and campaigned door-to-door for Obama.

Hedge funds weren't the only corner of the financial world where Obama did extraordinarily well. The banking industry—long a citadel of Republicanism—now includes a great many Democrats. Although nationally Republicans have raised far more money from commercial and investment bankers than Democrats have since 1990, that decisive margin disappears when you look at the most elite banking institutions. Sixty-three percent of contributions from Goldman Sachs since 1990 have gone to Democrats and only 37 percent to Republicans. At other banks—Citigroup, J.P. Morgan Chase, Bank of America, and Morgan Stanley—employees have contributed to Democrats and Republicans in nearly equal measure.

The tide of banking money to Democrats has been rising. In 1992 and 1996, commercial bankers gave to Republican presidential candidates by an overwhelming margin, and the same was true in 2000 and 2004. But in the 2008 cycle, Barack Obama became the first presidential candidate to raise more money from commercial bankers than his Republican counterpart.

Some bankers backed Obama even though he posed a very specific threat to their institutions. Take a man like Robert Wolf, who runs UBS Americas. A youthful CEO in his forties, Wolf was one of Obama's biggest fund-raisers in New York City, securing hundreds of thousands of dollars to support Obama's run for the presidency. He made untold phone calls, threw parties, and otherwise knocked himself out to get Obama into the White House. Wolf acknowledged to *New York* magazine that one motive was his desire to have a friend in the White House and how he was impressed by his early access to Obama. But Wolf was also impressed by Obama's views, and for him one issue that really mattered was Iraq. Wolf liked Obama's strong and early stand against the war. And Wolf liked Obama despite the fact that he had introduced a Senate bill to crack down on offshore tax havens and had promised to go after such accounts if elected president—none of which was good news to UBS, which has been the single biggest target of federal investigators probing offshore accounts.

The shift toward Democrats has been more gradual in other areas of finance, such as private equity firms. Until 2002, private equity firm employees gave most of their money to Republicans. Now most of the money from private equity is going to Democrats. In some recent elections, for instance, Democrats have raised nearly four times as much as Republicans have from the fantastically wealthy staff of the Blackstone Group, even though this firm was cofounded by prominent Republicans Peter Petersen and Stephen A. Schwarzman. Equally notable is the flow of money into Democratic coffers from Bain Capital, the private equity group that Republican presidential candidate Mitt Romney cofounded and led. Bain employees gave to Democrats by a 4-to-1 margin in 2004 and still gave more money to Democrats in 2008 even as Romney ran for president.

Donations to Democrats from the finance industry haven't risen only in absolute terms; they have also constituted a larger share of overall Democratic campaign dollars. For instance, in 1999 the Democratic Senatorial Campaign Committee raised just 5 percent of its funds from securities and investment firms. In the 2007–2008 election cycle, it was 15 percent.

Republicans still dominate many industries, such as energy, agribusiness, and construction, and it is the wealthy from these industries who provided some of the deepest pockets for George W. Bush and then John McCain. Many of these industries are located in the red heartland, where conservative values are strongest.

A common view of why Wall Street and business types give money to the Democrats is that the party has moved to the right and become more congenial to the upper class. As Robert Kuttner argued in his 1987 book, *Life of the Party*, and many others have argued since, Democrats stopped siding with the little guy and sold out to corporate America in return for boatloads of campaign cash. Thus, it should be no surprise that the rich support Democrats.

There are many anecdotal examples to support this view. Exhibit A, until recently, was Senator Charles Schumer of New York, long one of Wall Street's most ardent defenders on Capitol Hill—and among the biggest recipients of its campaign donations. Between 1999 and 2008, Schumer collected nearly $4 million from the financial services industry. When he was a member of the House of Representatives during the 1990s, he raked in more money from Wall Street than any other representative did. During the Bush years, Schumer became chair of the Democratic Senatorial Campaign Committee and vacuumed up cash from Wall Street in even larger quantities. Nobody has done more in recent years to rope wealthy financiers into the Democratic Party.

And, by many accounts, Wall Street got what it paid for. Schumer has taken Wall Street's side again and again on key battles and has convinced Senate colleagues to do the same. He has defended the tax loophole on carried interest income for hedge funds and private equity firms, has sought to cut the fees that Wall Street pays to the Securities and Exchange Commission (SEC), and has tried to block stricter oversight of the credit agencies that rate Wall Street debt. In a 2009 interview with the *New York Times*, John Bogle, the founder of the mutual fund colossus Vanguard Group, said about Schumer, "He is serving the parochial interest of a very small group of financial people, bankers, investment bankers, fund managers, private equity firms, rather than serving the general public."[3] Thanks to friends like Schumer, Wall Street was allowed to blow itself up— and take the economy with it—after an era of risky and unrestrained financial engineering. Schumer also fought reforms that might have prevented the frauds that exploded at Enron and WorldCom. Only in 2010, as Schumer eyed a bid for senate majority leader, did he cease defending Wall Street.[4] Other Democrats, such as Chris Dodd, have also shilled for financial interests, and there is little question that Wall Street money has led Democrats to be less aggressive on regulation. More broadly, it is indisputable that some New Deal ideas about how to create a fair economy have lost traction within the Democratic Party since the 1960s.

Yet the overall narrative about Democrats migrating to the center at the behest of big donors has grown dated, and parts of this story were never true to begin with. The paradoxical truth of recent years is that the Democratic Party has moved to the left even as its take from financiers has soared. The Obama administration may be stacked with protégés of Robert Rubin, with not a single true liberal critic of Wall Street on the economic team, but the centrist Democratic Party of the 1990s is long gone. The Democratic Leadership Council (DLC) has so little juice that it couldn't get even one of the eight Democratic presidential candidates to address its annual event in 2007—in contrast to the leftie Daily Kos convention, which nearly all of these candidates treated as a command appearance.

And long before Democratic presidential candidates started to worry more about the progressive netroots than about the DLC, they had begun to distance themselves from big business. In 2000, Al Gore ran one of the most populist campaigns in memory—"the people against the powerful"—in which he vowed to institute tougher regulations on business and to preserve the Clinton administration's tax hikes on the rich, despite a large budget surplus. Ralph Nader dismissed the differences between Bush and Gore as negligible—"Tweedle Dee versus Tweedle Dum"—when in fact the two candidates could hardly have been more stark in how their policies would affect the bank accounts of the super-wealthy. Bush proposed record tax cuts for the rich, while Gore opposed these cuts as an upward redistribution of wealth. Gore's leftward trajectory as a public figure, from stalwart DLC centrist to a left-wing eco-crusader, is itself a revealing indicator of where the Democratic Party has moved since the 1990s.

In 2004, John Kerry was equally unambiguous in his views on taxes and the wealthy. Kerry, rated by *National Journal* as the most liberal member of the Senate during the year he ran for president, pledged in his presidential race to raise taxes on the rich and lambasted "Benedict Arnold CEOs" who moved jobs overseas. Kerry's running mate, John Edwards, talked about class and inequity with a passion not often heard in presidential campaigns, and he gave moving speeches about "two Americas." Edwards ratcheted up this language when he ran for president a second time, and his evolution from centrist senator to economic populist was yet another indicator of the changing mood among Democrats. The amount of money that Edwards raised for his 2008 race paled in comparison to Obama's and Hillary Clinton's funding, but it was huge in historical terms: $57 million, much of which came from wealthy contributors who gave the maximum amount. The fact that a candidate so openly hostile to corporate America could raise this kind of money says much about the ideological leanings of some of the Democratic Party's largest donors.

Even Bill Clinton was not exactly the corporate front man that some imagine. Although his administration did nix tougher rules for Wall Street, including oversight of derivatives, and pushed banking deregulation, Clinton enacted the biggest tax hike on the wealthy in a generation, a move that cost the richest of the rich millions of dollars during the course of his presidency. He also imposed an executive pay cap in 1993, and his Justice Department filed the biggest antitrust suit in years when it sought to break up Microsoft. And Clinton vetoed a bill that repealed the estate tax and that would have saved America's richest families hundreds of billions of dollars during subsequent decades.

In any case, if Democrats spent the 1990s in an ideological muddle, the same can't be said of the Democratic Party between 2000 and 2008, which moved in a clearly liberal direction. This same period saw a major increase in support for Democrats by the upper class. Indeed, some of the party's wealthiest donors, such as Peter Lewis and George Soros, worked to push the party to the left, as I'll discuss later.

Congressional roll-call votes offer the best evidence of the Democratic Party's leftward move. An exhaustive analysis of such votes, by political scientists Keith Poole and Howard Rosenthal, finds that congressional Democrats have steadily shifted to the left since 1965. One reason for this shift, of course, has been the shrinking ranks of Southern Democrats. As these members have lost their seats, the Democratic Party has become more homogeneously liberal—although, to be sure, the centrist Blue Dog Democrats remain a potent force in the House, with some fifty-two members. (About half of the Blue Dogs come from states that have tended to go Republican in recent presidential elections. Few represent affluent districts.) But realignment in the South doesn't fully account for the Democratic Party's leftward shift. The roll-call data show that northern Democrats have moved notably to the left in recent decades, along with surviving southern Democrats. A parallel change has happened in the Republican Party, only the results have been more drastic. As Jacob Hacker and Paul Pierson note in their book *Off Center*, any leftward movement of the Democrats pales in comparison to how sharply right the Republicans have moved.[5]

Data compiled by Americans for Democratic Action (ADA) also show that congressional Democrats have moved to the left. For decades, ADA has rated each member of Congress on its

"Liberal Quotient," which is based on the percentage of votes cast in support of liberal policies. While the Liberal Quotient for Democratic members hovered between 50 and 60 percent between 1965 and 1980, it ranged from 75 to 90 percent between 1998 and 2008. According to ADA, Democratic House members racked up their highest LQ ever in 2007. House Democrats had an overall LQ of 92 percent in 2007, up from 81 percent ten years earlier. Fifty-three House Democrats scored a perfect 100 LQ rating in 2007.[6]

Yet another measure of the Democratic Party's ideological leanings can be found in surveys of national convention delegates. In 1972, the year that left-wingers supposedly hijacked the Democratic National Convention, about 8 percent of delegates attending described themselves as "very liberal." That percentage had climbed to 22 percent by 2004. (Meanwhile, the percentage of delegates who earned more than $100,000 a year soared from 12 percent in 1984 to 42 percent in 2004.)[7]

While it is often assumed that many congressional Democrats are liberal on social issues but moderate on economic policy, hard evidence of that disjuncture is scarce. On the contrary, analyses of voting records by *National Journal*, which breaks votes down by issue, find that the ideology of Democrats tends to be consistent across areas. Most members of Congress who are liberal on social or foreign policy issues also tend to be liberal on economic issues, and vice versa. ADA's data find something similar.

The Democratic Party's move to the left has not been lost on the public. According to polls, more Americans now view the party as "very liberal" than at any time since the 1960s.[8]

It is an easy game to zing Democratic leaders for selling out on this or that issue, or to charge that the two parties are indistinguishable tools of a plutocratic overclass. But congressional voting data show that the gap on economic policy between Republican and Democratic members of Congress is greater than at any time in memory. And the gap seems to be widening: not a single Republican supported Obama's first budget or his stimulus plan or the financial regulatory bill approved by the House in December 2009. At this point, any half-sentient citizen should know that if you want lower taxes and fewer regulations, you vote Republican. If you want higher taxes and more regulation, you vote Democratic. Moreover, as the political scientist Larry Bartels has shown, the two parties have delivered on their economic promises: since 1945, the rich have done better under Republican presidents than under Democratic presidents, while middle class and poor families have benefited most when Democrats controlled the White House.[9]

All of these facts deepen the puzzle as to why so many of the wealthy—those who stand to lose the most from tax hikes and new regulations—give money to Democrats.

Some insights to the strange new politics of class come from taking a closer look at the Democrats' push to raise taxes on income from partnerships such as private equity firms and hedge funds. This "carried interest" income has long been taxed as capital gains, but in 2007 House Democrats voted to tax it as regular income, walloping some of the highest earners in the United States. Democrats would have used the money to spare middle-class households from the dreaded alternative minimum tax. Wealth redistribution doesn't get much clearer than this plan, which would have appropriated more than $10 billion from a tiny number of super-wealthy financiers and given it to millions of Americans of more modest means.

Among the Senate champions of this specially targeted tax on rich people was none other than Barack Obama. Given that Obama was actively trying to raise money from precisely the wealthy who would have been hard hit by the carried interest tax, you might think that he would have weaved and dodged on the issue—voicing just enough support for the tax to appease his party's left wing, but not so much that his big money backers would see him as truly serious on the issue. Instead, Obama went out of his way to become a cosponsor of the legislation. When the bill died in the Senate, Obama blasted the outcome, saying, "If there was ever a doubt that Washington lobbyists don't actually represent real Americans, it's the fact that they stopped leaders of both parties from requiring elite investment firms to pay their fair share of taxes."[10]

The measure died in the Senate partly because New York senator Charles Schumer worked to kill it. Schumer's role is significant, in that he was running the Democratic Senatorial Campaign
Committee (DSCC) and was taking in large sums of money from
hedge funds and private equity donors. This link would seem to
explain the motives of such donors. "They got what they paid for,"
said Leo Hindery, who leads InterMedia, a private equity group, but
opposed the carried interest loophole. In line with this theory, the
Nation magazine noted that James Simons gave the maximum to
Schumer's committee around the time that the carried interest issue
was before the Senate.

The quid pro quo view surely explains the motives of some
hedge fund and private equity donors, both in 2007 and afterward,
and it fits with Schumer's reputation as a willing handmaiden of
Wall Street. At the same time, hedge fund donors started to favor
Democrats by a large margin in 2000, well before the carried interest
loophole emerged as an issue or Schumer headed up the DSCC. That
pattern held when Republicans controlled the Senate and Democrats
had no prospects for raising anyone's taxes. As for James Simons, it's
hard to know what he was thinking, because Simons (and his family) have for years given large sums to all of the Democratic committees and to a wide variety of candidates. He gave the maximum
to Schumer's committee not only in 2007, but also in 2005 and 2006,
when Schumer led the drive for a Democrat-controlled Congress.

Simons is known as a brilliant man, but if his goal was defending the carried interest loophole, then helping the Democrats take
the Senate in 2006 wasn't very smart. After all, the only reason this
issue even came to a vote was Democratic control. And that's the
thing about Democrats: yes, plenty of them will sell out to Wall
Street and business, but the party also has a populist wing—one that
has gotten notably stronger in recent years—and any funds that help
the Democrats overall can't help but empower these folks. One of the
fiercest liberal populists in the Senate, Sherrod Brown, won office in
2006 thanks in part to Schumer's millions. The DSCC spent more
in independent expenditures to elect Brown than on any other
Senate candidate in 2006. Another populist, James Webb, also got

big cash infusions from the DSCC to win an expensive Senate race in 2006. Both Brown and Webb voted against the carried interest loophole.

Hedge funds and private equity firms paid for a huge lobbying push to hold onto their tax perks in 2007. The single biggest contract for Washington lobbying that year was a $3.7 million agreement that the Blackstone Group signed with Ogilvy Public Relations Worldwide—with the goal of derailing the carried interest tax hike. It made sense that Blackstone would spend so much, given that its partners stood to lose many millions of dollars if the tax hike went through. Just as it made sense that the main hedge fund lobbying group, the Managed Funds Association, would fiercely oppose a tax on carried interest. After all, the way that hedge fund managers made such crazy amounts of money was by taking a 20 percent cut of all of the profits they earned for clients. That money was typically taxed as capital gains, at 15 percent. If Democrats such as Obama got their way, the tax rate would more than double. So, yes, it made sense that lobbyists would work feverishly to kill the tax.

What didn't make much sense is the individual behavior of the people who hired these lobbyists. In 2008, employees at Blackstone contributed nearly as much money to Democratic candidates as to Republicans. Employees at the Carlyle Group, another major private equity firm, gave 67 percent of their political contributions to Democrats. Overall, Barack Obama raised 45 percent more money from private equity firms than did John McCain—a candidate who stood against the carried interest tax hike. Obama did even better among hedge fund managers, as mentioned, besting McCain with this group by a 2-to-1 margin.

Steve Sleigh, who is a principal at Yucaipa Companies, a private equity group backed by the billionaire Ron Burkle, thinks that the higher taxes promised by Obama weren't troubling to many in his industry because they were already resigned to the fact that "taxes were going to go up. They had to, with the deficit. There was no way around it." Also, this is a crowd that understands that it takes money to make money and that "we need basic investments to make the economy grow and work." Before joining Yucaipa, Sleigh had spent most of his career in labor unions, which typically view things in a "class warfare mind-set." Now that he's on the other side of the fence, working for a very rich and very Democratic businessman, Sleigh sees change under way. "There are more progressive and open-minded wealthy who understand that things need to be done differently."

Bob Schulman saw nothing very surprising about Obama's success with hedge fund managers, despite his promising to raise their taxes and regulate them more heavily. Some in the industry, Schulman included, never believed in the carried interest loophole to begin with and didn't take advantage of it. Rob Johnson, who was a managing director at Soros's operation, thinks there is no great mystery either. "A lot of guys in the hedge funds world thought that loophole was just plain wrong," Johnson said, but the industry groups fought to keep it because "it was a freebie."

The bigger factor may be that paying more taxes is not necessarily such a huge deal to top hedge fund managers and not as important as other concerns. "I find very few people once they get into their fifties, who have money, making decisions just based on what it costs them," Schulman said. "They are thinking about what the right thing is. They are thinking about the legacy they would like to leave to their children." It's a different story for younger people, those not yet fully established. "People who are trying to make it are worried about the taxes," he said, mentioning his thirty-something son-in-law in finance who is more conservative. "People who have already made it, in most cases, feel 'I've got enough money. I can afford to give some back.'"

"My goal is not to pay less taxes," top hedge fund manager and Obama fund-raiser William Ackman said during the campaign. "My goal is to elect an incredibly smart and capable guy."[11]

There is a long history of industries trying to buy off their Democratic opponents with campaign cash. Or, more subtly, donors trying to influence the worldview of Democratic politicians to get a more sympathetic hearing. The problem is not so much blatant quid pro quo, as much as it is influence that occurs when candidates spend a lot of time with rich people, which is required of anyone who wants to finance a modern campaign. A longtime Democratic fund-raiser, the venture capitalist Alan Patricof, once said, "I can tell you honestly that in all the time I've been involved, I have never had anyone ask for something or even discuss with me anything that interested them in exchange for them giving money. It just never even occurred."[12] That may be so. In many cases, what happens is a quieter, more insidious form of corruption, and the payback can be difficult to measure. "The access issue is always there," said Mike Lux, who has worked with many wealthy donors and also in the Clinton White House.

Obama wrote about this in *The Audacity of Hope*, describing what happened after his star began to rise in politics: "Increasingly, I found myself spending time with people of means—law firm partners and investment bankers, hedge fund managers and venture capitalists. As a rule, they were smart, interesting people, knowledgeable about public policy, liberal in their politics, expecting nothing more than a hearing of their opinions in exchange for checks. But they reflected, almost uniformly, the perspectives of their class; the top 1 percent or so of the income scale that can afford to write a $2,000 check to a political candidate. They believed in the free market and an educational meritocracy; they found it hard to imagine that there might be any social ill that could not be cured with a high SAT score. They had no patience with protectionism, found unions troublesome, and were not particularly sympathetic to those whose lives were upended by movements of global capital. . . . I know that as a consequence of my fund-raising I became more like the wealthy donors I met, in the very particular sense that I spent more and more of my time above the fray, outside the world of immediate hunger, disappointment, fear, irrationality, and frequent hardship of the other 99 percent of the population—that is, the people I'd entered public life to serve."[13]

Obama wrote these words before he started to raise really big money from Wall Street. It is hard to imagine that the influence of these donors hasn't had an impact on his worldview. In February 2010, amid red-hot public anger at Wall Street and murderous unemployment, Obama seemed to shrug at the multimillion-dollar bonuses paid to the heads of Goldman Sachs and J.P. Morgan Chase.

"I know both these guys; they are very savvy businessmen."[14] To be sure, the financiers who helped elect Obama are getting a big tax hike, but this may matter less to their bottom line than the gift he gave Wall Street shortly after his election: a moderate economic team that didn't include a single populist liberal.

Yet even as Obama has shamefully compromised himself through his ties to Wall Street, one thing is clear: he's been a lot tougher on the Street than McCain would have been. The administration has been famously cozy with Goldman Sachs, for instance, yet this didn't stop Obama's SEC from charging Goldman with fraud in April 2010.

After Obama's election, it may seem that his victory was inevitable and that canny donors were simply going with a winner. But his victory was never assured: not over the undisputed front-runner Hillary Clinton back in 2007, when Obama first started to draw substantial hedge fund support, and not over McCain in 2008. Obama is an African American who ran for president with the thinnest of résumés and the most liberal of Senate voting records. McCain was, until not so long ago, one of the most admired figures in U.S. politics. He had a shot at winning the election before the financial crash, and polls showed him briefly ahead of Obama after the Republican convention.

There are other reasons to doubt that Obama's donors were motivated mainly by self-interest and that, more generally, super-wealthy donors who contribute to Democrats are after influence. If you give money to politicians to advance your self-interest, your pattern of giving is likely to be bipartisan. You will give money to whoever is in a position to help you or your industry, regardless of party affiliation. When Democrats hold the reins of power, you'll give money to Democrats—and vice versa when Republicans call the shots. This is how most PACs operate.

Yet giving by many wealthy individuals is exactly the reverse of this pattern. An analysis of donations by some of the nation's biggest campaign contributors finds these donors to be ideological purists, more or less, and reveals that they give mainly to one side or the other, regardless of who is in power. Political scientists Keith Poole and Howard Rosenthal have documented this phenomenon as part of their research into the growing polarization of U.S. politics. Another team of political scientists reported similar findings in an article titled "Limousine Liberals and Corporate Conservatives: The Financial Constituencies of the Democratic and Republican Parties." Studying a thousand campaign donors, the authors concluded "that the most active donors hold the most ideologically extreme political views."[15]

So it is, for example, that many of the biggest donors in the banking industry give almost exclusively to either Democrats or Republicans. You see this at the deep-pocketed firm of Goldman Sachs, where those few partners who favored Republicans gave upward of 99 percent of their campaign contributions to the GOP, while the majority of Goldman employees who favored Democrats gave hardly anything to Republicans—not even when the firm's former chief served as Bush's treasury secretary and made decisions that hugely affected Goldman. Of the top donors at Goldman Sachs who have made more than $50,000 in campaign contributions in recent years, none came anywhere close to spreading their wealth evenly between the two parties.

The picture was much the same at Citigroup, where that firm's biggest single donor over recent years, Joseph Plumeri, has given 91 percent of his money to Republicans, while its biggest Democratic donor, Lyndon Olson, has given 99 percent of his contributions to Democrats. What's more, donations from financiers to members of Congress seem only partially targeted at members who could help their firms. During recent years, Goldman employees gave more than ten times as much to senators on the Health, Education, and Labor Committee as to senators on the Finance Committee. The pattern was largely the same for Citigroup donors.

Public records of campaign donations are available dating back to the late 1970s, and they show how some of Wall Street's top people have stuck with Democrats through good times and bad. Jamie Dimon, the CEO of JP Morgan Chase, has been derided as an access donor of the first order, but the record of his campaign giving suggests something different. Dimon has been making campaign gifts since 1991 and has given some $600,000 during a period when Democrats often were out of power and Republicans made the rules governing his industry. Still, only 8 percent of Dimon's money has gone to the GOP.

Dimon gave the most money to Democrats during their darkest days in exile, in 2002 and 2003, when Karl Rove was talking about a permanent Republican majority. Hedge fund managers also started to up their giving to Democrats during this same period of exile. Hedge fund employees gave more to Democrats by big margins in 2000, 2002, and 2004—years in which Democrats lost elections and had little sway over financial policies.

Fixating on a stark dichotomy of motives—access versus ideology—may ultimately miss how wealthy donors really think. In truth, many probably give money for *both* reasons. They may be liberal enough to back Democrats even if it means taking a financial hit, yet at the same time, they may want the kind of access that can soften the hit.

This would explain Obama's experience with big-money donors. When he was a candidate, they saw him as "the One"—a smart, pragmatic, Ivy League–educated man much like themselves—and showered him with praise and cash. In this affection, they were sincere. But the minute that Obama won office, they began to work the system to slow down his boldest reforms to redistribute wealth and regulate business. And here, as well, they were sincere.

The relationship between financial elites and liberal Democrats is still very much in a trial period. It's one thing to bankroll a party in exile. But now the Democrats are in charge and finally have the power to shift wealth down the income ladder. If Democrats fail to use that power to aggressively challenge historic high levels of inequality, this will answer the question of what's the matter with Connecticut: *nothing*—the moneyed class bankrolling the party will have gotten what they paid for.

And if Democrats do use their new power to reslice the economic pie and curb business, we will get the answer to another question: will wealthy donors stick with a Democratic Party that tacks in a truly populist direction? My guess is that the answer—for many donors, anyway—would be no. Which means that the Democratic Party now finds itself in a bind: its new power and muscle have been made possible by upper-class money, but a good chunk of that money could disappear if the party really gets serious about helping the middle and working classes.

Democrats aren't the party of the rich—Obama won his biggest margin among America's poorest voters. But the Democrats' debt to the rich is larger than ever.

3

THE ECO RICH

Not long after the Google Guys spent millions on a new corporate jet in 2005, they discovered that there was a problem with the plane. It wasn't a mechanical problem. The jet was a Boeing 767, long a reliable workhorse of commercial aviation, purchased used from Qantas Airlines.

The problem was the environmental impact of the plane. A 767 is a very large airplane. It is designed to carry 180 passengers, and it is nearly twice as long and three times as heavy as a more typical private jet such as the Gulfstream V. Google cofounders Larry Page and Sergey Brin, along with CEO Eric Schmidt, found plenty of uses for the extra space. They shelled out millions of dollars to renovate the plane's interior to include two private staterooms (one each for Brin and Page), an executive lounge (for Schmidt), and seats for fifty passengers. "It's a party airplane," Schmidt said about the jet at one point. They also spent $1.3 million a year to park the 767 at an airport near Google's headquarters that is owned by NASA—paying about five times the amount it would have cost to keep the plane a bit farther away, at San Jose Airport.

Reactions to the jet were not kind. Critics pointed out that aviation emissions contribute about 3.5 percent of all greenhouse gases, and that a 767 puts out ten tons of carbon per hour of operation. Flying in an ordinary private jet for one hour generates about as much carbon as driving for a year. With a 767, the amount is far greater.

What could the Google Guys have been thinking? No other major company in the United States has so clearly staked out the moral high ground on climate change. Both Brin and Page owned Toyota Priuses and were so keen on "sustainable transportation" that Google offered $5,000 in cash to any employee who bought a hybrid vehicle. More ambitiously, Google had announced that the company would seek to be carbon-neutral in a few years through such steps as using solar panels at the company headquarters in Mountain View—the "Googleplex"—and using a dam to power its Oregon computer center. Google also invested in carbon offsets, funding things such as a project to generate electricity from manure in Brazil. The company's charity arm, Google.org, had made alternative energy and fuel efficiency two major priorities of its investments, saying that one hope was to create a car that got 100 miles per gallon.

"So much for fighting global warming," sniffed one blogger about the 767. Another blogger, castigating "jet-setting hypocrites" on the National Association for Manufacturers Web site, said, "It's just such a classic case of 'do as I say, don't do as I do' for these self-righteous and sanctimonious sods."

Brin and Page defended themselves, saying that all of the extra space on the Google jet would be put to good use. Page said that "part of the equation for this sort of machinery is to be able to take large numbers of people to places such as Africa. I think that can only be good for the world." He also commented, "We've worked very hard to make sure our [net] impact on the environment is positive."[1]

There are now ten thousand private jets zipping around in the United States, nearly twice the number a decade ago. And while the financial crash means that more of the formerly rich are taking off their shoes in security lines, the long-term trend of flying private has been sharply upward for years. Fractional jet ownership has allowed more people to fly private without the cost of owning their own planes, and who wouldn't enjoy the perks? The jet leaves when you want, and you drive up to a luxurious private terminal or right onto the tarmac itself—there are no barking TSA guards, no crowded waiting areas, no flight delays. The onboard cuisine might include food prepared by Wolfgang Puck, whose catering operation supplies the Avion Private Jet Club, a service that bills itself as "a country club in the sky." All of this for a price that large numbers of Americans can afford even after the crash. It can cost as little as $2,500 an hour to fly on a small private jet such as a Cessna CJ3, while going in real style on a Gulfstream 550 costs more like $7,500. Of course, many fliers don't pay this tab themselves, and most private jet flights are taken by business executives (and are tax-deductible).

Alas, private jets became more accessible just as they became naughtier, with climate change concerns hitting mainstream consciousness. The Google Guys aren't the only ones who have dodged flak aimed at private jets. In 2006, Aspen's jet set came under collective attack when a study revealed that private planes accounted for nearly a fifth of all greenhouse gas emissions generated by the town. The aerial comings and goings of the rich generated almost as much carbon as all of the electricity used in Aspen by its fifteen thousand full-time residents. (Another study of Aspen revealed that the monstrous vacation homes of the rich produced 12 percent more carbon than the homes of year-round residents, even though many of these mansions were occupied only a few weeks out of the year.)

Meanwhile, the actor John Travolta emerged as something of an environmental pariah for his private jet addiction. Travolta owns five private jets, including a Boeing 707 (weighing 70 tons) that he flew to Europe in late 2007 for a publicity trip for his movie *Wild Hogs*. Travolta attracted ire during the visit when he said that everyone should "do their bit" to combat global warming. Yeah, right, responded the British press, which reported that he was the sole passenger on the flight across the Atlantic in his 707 and calculated that Travolta's carbon footprint was a hundred times greater than that of the average Briton.[2]

Then there was the flap around the 2007 Davos meeting, where climate change was high on the agenda. Scores of private jets swarmed into Davos for the event, which included a dissection of such matters as whether a carbon tax would be better than a cap-and-trade system at saving the planet. The Google Guys flew in on their 767 and then sparked nonstop gossip at the conference about who would get to fly back with them to Silicon Valley. (Facebook founder Mark Zuckerberg was among the lucky who were chosen.) NetJets Europe, the continent's largest private jet operator, booked no fewer than fifty flights to Davos to handle all of the demand for the conference. These flights were a small fraction of the sixty-five thousand private trips the company operated in Europe in 2006—the equivalent to a plane taking off or landing every eight minutes.

When the CEO of NetJets Europe, Mark Booth, was criticized for spewing so much carbon into the air around the Davos event, he scoffed at the naïveté of such attacks. "The question is, do you want CEOs sitting around in airports trying to connect to aircraft?" Sure, his clients were concerned about global warming, but that didn't mean they would give up their private planes. "We are working with people who really make economies hum. We are talking about the leaders of business around the world. . . . It's not going to happen," Booth said. "If you cut down on people flying, you cut down on economic growth, you cut down on quality of life."[3]

A few years ago, Booth would have had nothing more to say on this matter. The Masters of the Universe set—and those who serve them—hadn't previously paid much heed to environmental critics. Now they do, in part because those critics include their peers. Thus, Booth went on to explain that NetJets Europe was actually hard at work developing a plan to offset its carbon emissions and that the company was committed to doing the "right thing" when it came to climate change. The plan, which was revealed later in September 2007, raised the fees on NetJets' clients between $4,000 and $5,600 a year to offset the carbon dioxide emissions from their flights. "People want to know we are doing the right thing and every month our customers will be reminded of that in their management fee," Booth explained.[4] Two years later, NetJets announced that it was on track to become carbon neutral by 2012.

NetJets wasn't the first jet charter service to make carbon offsets mandatory for all flights. Cerulean Jet, based in Austin, Texas, beat NetJets by a few months in taking this step when it announced that it would buy carbon offsets for all of its flights. Ken Starnes, the CEO of Cerulean Jet, commented that "offsetting our carbon footprint is good for business and good for the environment, ultimately increasing our ability to help in the global warming fight."

Times are certainly changing when private jet companies decide that they need to be on the front lines of the "global warming fight" (or when corporate leaders justify their private jets by saying they want to help Africa). But given just how fast norms of acceptable environmental behavior are shifting among the super-rich, Ken Starnes and Cerulean Jet probably didn't feel that they had much choice. It is risky for any private jet company to get tarred as the laggard in offsetting carbon emissions—a stigma that could diminish market share for years to come. That's why 2007 and 2008 saw other private jet companies, such as Jets.com and V1 International, also start carbon offset programs. In a few years, or perhaps even before these words appear in print, it is likely that all jet charter companies will be doing the same thing, and many major corporations will also be buying carbon credits to offset the private jet use of their executives. Carbon-neutral jet travel not only feels good, but it is relatively inexpensive. According to one analysis, most private air travelers can fly carbon-neutral for only 1 percent of the total flying costs. Although private jet flying can run between $2,000 and $13,000 an hour, carbon offsets range from $7 to $60 an hour, and with more services popping up to assuage the ecoguilt of jet setters, calculating your carbon output and purchasing offsets are easier than ever. The only catch is that many experts say that carbon offsets are an illusory solution to climate change that can actually create perverse incentives to pollute. In November 2009, Responsible Travel, an early leader in offsets, canceled its offset program, citing a report by Friends of the Earth that likened carbon offsets to a "medieval pardon for us to carry on behaving in the same way or worse."[5]

Environmentalists have kept up the pressure on jet-setters, for example, with a June 2009 protest in which activists in pinstriped suits and bowler hats chained themselves to a private jet at London

City Airport. The activists were part of Plane Stupid, a group that works the aviation side of the climate change fight and focuses special attention on private jets. "In an age where we face potentially catastrophic climate change, this is no longer an acceptable form of transport," said a spokesperson for the group. "It's time that private jets were grounded for good."[6]

Where does Plane Stupid get its money? From the super-rich, of course, most notably from a cosmetics tycoon named Mark Constantine.

It's not just private jets where the race is on to go green; it's also mega-mansions. Exhibit A of this trend is a newly constructed ocean-front estate known as Acqua Liana near Palm Beach. The main house is 15,000 square feet and features 8 bedrooms, 11 bathrooms, a theater, 24-foot indoor waterfall walls, 2 elevators, and so on. The luxuries of Acqua Liana are run-of-the-mill for the Gold Coast of Florida, as is the $29 million price tag. What's unusual is that the estate was built in accordance with green building principles. It includes enough solar panels to meet many of the estate's electricity needs, reclaimed wood, motion-activated light switches, high levels of insulation to preserve the air-conditioned coolness, super-efficient cooling and heating systems, and a system for catching rainwater and using it for the gardens and the grounds.

Acqua Liana was built as a "spec" house by a Boynton Beach developer named Frank McKinney. McKinney has made a fortune building huge waterfront mansions. With large amounts of borrowed money on the line, his livelihood depends on figuring out what the super-rich want and giving it to them in excess. For years, that meant erecting standard mega-mansions with all the bells and whistles. Now McKinney thinks it means turning his focus to green building, and he sees homes like Acqua Liana as part of a larger shift toward what might be called sustainable luxury. McKinney's "green giant" mansion has received an enormous amount of press attention, and he's convinced that it will help further fuel a national trend toward green building. "The trend always starts at the top," McKinney has said, which is a debatable point.[7] But there is no question that the rich have helped to accelerate the green building movement, because they can afford the extra costs involved, and their green homes are often quite high-profile.

Another new green mansion that's getting a lot of attention is EcoManor, built in Atlanta by Laura Turner Seydel, Ted Turner's daughter, and her husband, Rutherford Seydel. EcoManor incorporates numerous cutting-edge techniques for both saving energy and avoiding toxic building materials. A Web site touting the home says that one goal in building EcoManor was to use it as a "tool to illustrate the opportunities and benefits of earth-friendly, energy-efficient homes." Just as important, though, the home purports to illustrate how the rich can have it all, because it is the first mansion larger than 5,000 square feet to be certified with LEED (Leadership in Energy and Environmental Design) status by the U.S. Green Building Council, the main nonprofit group that sets green building standards. In fact, the Seydels are quite upfront in stating their desire to convert their fellow rich to green building, and they advocate changing the rules around LEED status, so that larger homes aren't automatically penalized. "That shouldn't be the case," Rutherford Seydel told *Fortune.* "People who can afford to build stately homes tend to adopt revolutionary technologies early. These are the people who can make a huge impact."[8] Any number of wealthy people are now building eco-mansions, including Google's Larry Page and U2's Leo Dickman.

Seydel is right about the effect the rich can have, but experts question the very concept of an "eco-mansion." Such mammoth homes, for all their green features, have a much larger carbon footprint than more modestly scaled dwellings. Still, even as the liberal moneyed class resists real downshifting to save the planet, attitudes in this group are changing fast. During the 2004 election, Teresa Heinz Kerry, the billionaire wife of Senator John Kerry, made wry humor out of her SUV ownership. When asked at a campaign event how she could defend owning an SUV, Heinz corrected the questioner by noting that she owned *five* SUVs (presumably, one for each of her mansions, among which she traveled in her Gulfstream V).

Such a comment would be unlikely today. In 2007, Kerry and Teresa—who met on Earth Day 1990—published a book together about the environment. In promoting the book, Kerry took a more serious view of their personal energy consumption. "We now are buying carbon offsets for the things that we do," he said. "And we should. When we fly on the airplane, or when we are in our cars."[9] Kerry also mentioned that they were switching their cars—their many cars—to hybrid vehicles. "I have a hybrid here in Washington, we have a hybrid in Massachusetts, we have a hybrid at a home in Idaho." As for the Gulfstream, Teresa promised to fly less. "That's hard for me, but that's where I'm trying to make improvements."[10]

In the space of only a few years, large numbers of very wealthy people have pledged to turn green. Why is that?

At some level, the answer is simple. The rich are influenced by the broader culture, just like the rest of us, and that culture has recently become obsessed with environmental sustainability. Far from being an insulated class, somehow impervious to social pressures thanks to all of their money, the rich are very much susceptible to those pressures. They may be even more susceptible, given their high visibility and the frequent media attention paid to how they live. Most ordinary people don't find their lifestyle choices splashed across the pages of *Gotham* or *Forbes*. Beyond our immediate circle of friends, family, and coworkers, nobody is paying attention to what we drive or to the square footage of our homes. If ordinary people wish to practice hypocrisy, we can do so in privacy. The rich have to contend not only with the judgment of those closest to them, but also with the broader public. All of this is occurring at a time when the luxury items that are associated with wealth—private jets, mega-yachts, and mansions—have emerged as symbols of planetary destruction. The rich are an easy target for the opprobrium of environmentalists.

Yet it's also true that the rich have historically been concerned about the environment, going back to Theodore Roosevelt, the first environmentalist president of the United States. Early rich environmentalists include the wealthy Edward Harriman and, of course, the Rockefellers, whose huge land acquisitions made possible such national parks as Acadia in Maine and Grand Teton in Wyoming. As the political scientist Ronald Inglehart has argued, affluence is a leading predictor of environmentalism. When people—or societies—are poor, the overriding focus tends to be on survival and economic well-being. But once your material needs are met, you can turn your attention to other concerns, like maybe saving the sperm whales or the Amazon. "Postmodern values give priority to environmental protection and cultural issues," Inglehart wrote, "even when these goals conflict with maximizing economic growth."[11] Affluent people also have more time and energy to sink into endeavors that aren't simply about making ends meet.

Inglehart bases this conclusion on forty years of research through the World Values Survey, which has tracked changing values in more than eighty-one countries. His findings have consistently shown that rising incomes and more wealth lead ineluctably to an embrace of environmentalism. Richer countries have stronger environmental movements than poorer ones do, and the modern environmental movement in both the United States and Europe was born during an era of mass affluence in the 1960s.

Environmentalism has long been stereotyped as a pastime of well-to-do white liberals. This is not entirely true, of course, and the recent emergence of a strong environmental justice movement in communities of color belies the stereotype. In these communities, which are often dumping grounds for toxic waste or sites for incinerators, activists have organized to press for a cleaner environment—typically without much help from mainstream groups such as the Sierra Club, which have been more worried about redwood trees than about inner-city kids with asthma.

Opinion polls confirm that low-income Americans are often just as concerned about the environment as other income groups.[12] Still, it remains the case that wealthier Americans are more apt to be on the forefront of environmental efforts. This was dramatically on display in 2006 when Californians voted on Proposition 87, the controversial ballot initiative that would have taxed oil companies to fund alternative fuels. The initiative—which was largely financed by the Los Angeles multimillionaire and movie producer Steve Bing—won in higher-income counties, like Marin and Alameda, while losing by huge margins in some of the state's poorest counties. In Modoc

County, a rural white area with the lowest household income in California, only 24 percent of voters supported the initiative, compared to 72 percent in prosperous San Francisco County. More evidence of the environmentalism of the rich can be found by looking at the voting records of members of Congress from the ten wealthiest districts. In 2008, half of these representatives got perfect scores of 100 from the League of Conservation Voters, one got a score of 92 percent, and two got scores of 62 percent.

Although the rich have long had the luxury of worrying about the planet, another dynamic is now under way: the shift to a knowledge economy means that many corporate leaders are no longer natural antagonists to the environment. Those capitalists who make their money in pollution-intensive ways constitute a shrinking minority of the wealthy overall. An analysis of the Forbes 400 list underscores this point: In 2008, nearly half of the billionaires on the list—190 people—derived their fortunes from financial services, technology, and media or entertainment, compared to just 51 billionaires on the list who made their money from oil, gas, chemicals, manufacturing, mining, and lumber. By comparison, when the Forbes 400 list was first published in 1982, the list was dominated by oil and manufacturing fortunes. These days, in other words, the "clean" rich now greatly outnumber the "dirty" rich.

A look at the Fortune 500 shows the same pattern. In 1955, the top twenty companies on the list included seventeen companies engaged in heavy industry. In 2010, the Fortune 500 included just six such companies in the top twenty.

There may be no such thing as a truly eco-friendly industry, and even the high-tech sector is well known for its environmental shortcomings. That's why one day in July 2009, employees at Hewlett-Packard's headquarters in Palo Alto looked out their windows to see Greenpeace protesters climbing the walls outside. The protesters got to the roof, where they spray-painted the warning "Hazardous Products" to draw attention to the toxic chemicals in HP products.

Still, HP is no GM. Whereas manufacturing wealth is created mainly by converting natural resources into products, often on a large scale—such as steel or automobiles—the great fortunes of the new economy emerge from a different process. Vast piles of money in the financial sector are often raked in by Wall Streeters who make winning bets with borrowed money, a process that involves no real material products. Internet companies, such as Google, can use significant amounts of energy, but their products exist mainly as pixels on a screen. Software companies such as Microsoft or entertainment companies such as Disney do create products, but the physical properties of these products are modest—typically, a compact disc and its packaging. Cell phones and BlackBerrys aren't that much bigger. Computers, which are among the more sizable products of the information age, typically weigh a few hundred times less than an automobile.

During the 1960s, corporate America was largely unified in viewing the rising environmental movement as a grave threat to its profits. That made sense, given how big business made its money. The push for clean air, for example, had huge repercussions for smokestack industries. Now there are plenty of corporate leaders who either aren't worried about environmentalists or actively support them. A place like Google isn't going to take a huge hit if the United States signs on to a bold global climate change treaty. The company might even benefit, given its investments in alternative energy.

The changing sources of wealth have shifted the values of the upper class even in places once dominated by the dirty rich. Take Colorado, where great fortunes used to be made from oil or mining, and where members of the state government—along with the state's representatives in Washington—were often creatures of these industries and were not friendly to the environmental movement. Now the state's super-rich are a very different breed and include the satellite TV mogul Charles Ergen, Quark founder Tim Gill, medical instruments heiress Pat Stryker, software inventor Rutt Bridges, and the dot-com entrepreneur Jared Polis. The oil and mining money isn't gone entirely, but the *Dynasty* types, with their ethos of resource plunder, conspicuous consumption, and conservative politics, have been eclipsed by the clean rich. During the 2004 election, after years of Republican dominance in the state, the Democrats won control of the Colorado legislature. Pivotal to this turnaround was an influx of millions of dollars into state politics from the so-called Gang of Four—a group that included Polis, Gill, Stryker, and Bridges.

The chief goal of the Gang of Four was to change Colorado's harsh economic policies and break the Christian right's grip on social policy in the state. But there was another important focus: to strengthen Colorado's environmental protections. In fact, the 2004 Colorado Democratic Party platform devoted more attention to environmental issues than to any other area, laying out twenty-four different goals, including "Developing renewable and alternative sources of energy sufficient to supply 60% of Colorado's power needs from renewable sources by 2010" and "Efforts to require manufacturers to produce street vehicles that achieve mileage rates of 40 mpg." Other platform goals were directly targeted at the mining companies and the developers who had once wielded so much power in Colorado. In 2006, the clean rich continued their sweep of Colorado politics when Democrat Bill Ritter was elected governor. Ritter went on to be voted America's "greenest governor" by the environmental living guide *Greenopia*.

Texas is no longer dominated by the dirty rich the way it once was, either. In 2008, less than half of those Texans on the Forbes 400 list had made their money in oil or energy—a major departure from earlier patterns. The wealthiest Texan today is no longer an oil man; it is Alice Walton, of the Walmart fortune, followed by Michael Dell, the computer entrepreneur. Dell doesn't live in either of the traditional oil money cities of Houston or Dallas; he lives in Austin, a city that has grown more influential in the state's cultural and political life as it has become home to numerous well-off high-tech entrepreneurs. Dallas still has plenty of conservative oil money, but the city's economy is now powered by high tech, finances, and services, as mentioned earlier. If *Dallas* were remade today, J. R. Ewing would probably be a telecom magnate.

The power shift has been even more dramatic in the Pacific Northwest. Back in the early 1980s, the only Forbes 400 member from that region was a timber baron, and many of the rich in Washington State made their fortunes in this same fashion or from shipping or manufacturing. Now, none of the Forbes 400 members from Washington are in the timber business; instead, nearly all are high-tech entrepreneurs.

Meanwhile, at the national level, the political clout of the dirty rich has been diluted by the rising power of clean-wealth elites. Data on campaign contributions during the last two decades tell the story. In 1990, individuals from the communications and electronics sector—including media, computers, and so on—contributed $7.3 million to politicians and parties, while individuals from the energy and natural resources sector contributed $6.5 million. In 2008, campaign contributions from those in energy and natural resources had soared to $76.4 million, but donations from those from communications and electronics had increased to more than twice that amount, to $139.3 million. Contributions from mining, one of the dirtiest industries in the United States, were a paltry $6.3 million in 2008. (Microsoft employees alone contributed $4.2 million.) Lobbying data underscore the same point. The energy and natural resources sector is one of the top five spenders on lobbying in Washington, but it ranks well behind the health-care industry and often behind communications and electronics.

When the Forbes 400 was still dominated by oil men, pleasing the most prosperous people in the country meant being nice to the energy industry. Today there are many other baskets to put your eggs into. Although energy firms enjoyed an unusual degree of clout during George W. Bush's presidency, given both Bush's and Cheney's ties to the oil industry, the larger trend demonstrates this sector's waning relative influence. Other pollution-intensive industries are fading fast as well. The steel industry stopped being a powerhouse in Washington long ago, and the auto industry doesn't even have the juice to secure a decent bailout. In a telling power shift, carmakers lost their best friend in Congress when Henry Waxman ousted Representative John Dingell from his chairmanship of the House Energy and Commerce Committee. Waxman is one of the top environmentalists in Congress—and, not coincidentally, represents one of the most liberal and affluent congressional districts in the United States.

None of this means that the dirty rich will go away any time soon. Energy and natural resource interests spent a staggering $408.8 million in 2009 as climate change legislation came before Congress. That's real money, maybe enough to melt half of the Arctic, and there is plenty more out there. Dirty rich billionaires David and Charles Koch are two of the wealthiest men in the United States. The brothers own Koch Industries, an industrial firm that refines oil and makes chemicals and fertilizers, and they have fortunes of $16 billion each. Koch Industries is notorious as one of the worst environmental offenders in the United States, and it has repeatedly tangled with the Environmental Protection Agency (EPA), incurring both criminal and civil charges. For decades, the Koch brothers have used their money to underwrite efforts to weaken or block environmental rules. Together, they have funneled tens of millions of dollars into conservative think tanks such as the Heritage Foundation, the Reason Foundation, and the CATO Institute, which Charles Koch helped to found.

These groups have mounted a fierce attack on environmental regulations, calling for the abolition of the EPA and a rollback of major environmental laws. One of their greatest successes has been to slow efforts to address global warming. Right-wing scholars on the payroll of the Koches and other dirty money donors argued for years that global warming was simply a "theory" and that no immediate action was needed. They have stuck with this argument even as the polar ice caps and mountain glaciers have begun to melt.

The big money behind anti-environmental efforts is no secret. What's new today is that environmentalists can put up a real fight, thanks in large part to wealthy donors.

The story behind this influx of funds goes back to the early 1970s, when the modern complex of environmental groups came into being. Among them were the League of Conservation Voters and the Natural Resource Defense Council (NRDC), both founded around 1970 and now two of the most powerful environmental groups in the

United States. The rise of these organizations says much about how massive amounts of liberal money have been mobilized behind all things green.

The League of Conservation Voters was conceived by a young congressional staffer named Marion Edey, who thought that the environmental movement needed a political arm. Edey came from inherited money—her maternal grandfather, ironically, had made a fortune in oil pipelines and refineries—and she grew up on a sprawling estate on Long Island. Edey spent her childhood years exploring the fields and woods around the estate, only to watch in distress later as much of this land was developed. Her connection to nature, she said, was "very basic and visceral from a young age." She worried not only about trees and plants as a child, but about poisons in the air and the water. If a delivery truck idled in front of the mansion, Edey would climb into the cab to turn off the engine.

Edey traveled an education path that would become well worn for children of the well-to-do. She went to a liberal prep school, the Putney School in Vermont, which had been founded as an experiment in progressive education. Then it was off to another super-liberal institution: Reed College in Oregon. After college, Edey went to Washington to fight for environmental causes, only to find that most members of Congress didn't care about the environment—including her own boss, a Democrat from Long Island. She came to see "that sweet reason will not win the day." Only votes and money counted. Edey came up with the idea for the League of Conservation Voters because when she was a teenager, she had watched her mother write checks to the Council for a Livable World, a group that focused on electing members of Congress who supported nuclear disarmament efforts. Edey's mother, an active philanthropist, stressed to her the importance of pressuring the politicians to achieve change.

Edey not only had the idea for the first environmental PAC, she also had the money—her own money. She had inherited more than $1 million at the age of twenty-one and could afford to quit her job on Capitol Hill and support herself as she formed the League of Conservation Voters. Edey used her fortune to cover her own living expenses, as well as many of the League's operating costs, such as direct mail. During her sixteen years of running the group, she never drew a salary. "I was an employee in every way but one," she said.

The League was almost immediately successful, and in 1972 it scored a huge victory when it helped knock out the anti-environmental Democratic congressman from Colorado, Wayne Aspinall. Aspinall was reviled for giving away Western land to oil companies, and his defeat signaled a major shift in Democratic politics. (Among other things, Aspinall disparaged his critics as "overindulged" and "aristocrats.") By the 1980s, the League was a potent force in politics that tracked congressional voting records and channeled money to numerous races. The sums kept getting larger and larger.

Big donors to the League included fourth-generation members of the Rockefeller family, who continued their family's environmentalist tradition—only in a more hard-hitting fashion. "I was never focused on land conservation," said Alida Rockefeller Messinger, the daughter of John D. Rockefeller III. "I was always interested more in the activist political side because it leads to long-lasting change." The League was certainly activist with its power to pay for attack ads and end political careers. Messinger started off with modest gifts to the League. But in recent years, she has become one of its most generous donors, giving the League $1.5 million between 2004 and 2008 to help fund attacks on Republicans such as Rick Santorum, George Allen, and Ted Stevens.

Like Edey's, Messinger's connection to nature started on family lands. She grew up in New York City, but her father owned a hobby farm not far from the Rockefellers' famed Pocantico estate in Westchester. She spent every weekend at the farm, being around animals and walking in the fields and the woods. She first turned to environmental activism in college at Stanford University, backing the Save the Redwoods League, as loggers threatened to fell some of the most majestic trees on Earth. Messinger continued giving to environmental causes after college, helped by Wade Greene, a former journalist who advised many of the cousins on their philanthropic giving. Greene was highly respected in environmental circles and helped Messinger get involved with the League and other groups.

Everything changed in 1978, when her father was killed in a car accident and Messinger came into a full inheritance at the age of twenty-seven. (*Forbes* would estimate her fortune at $200 million in 1985.) Messinger started to ramp up her philanthropy, but, wary of trying to give away so much money herself, she formed an advisory committee to help devise a strategy. Wade Greene was on the committee, as well as Lenny Conway, who directed the Youth Project and advised other heirs who gave to liberal causes, and Shelly Korman, who worked with the Ms. Foundation for Women. Another member was John Adams, who was the cofounder and executive director of NRDC, which used lawsuits and other legal tactics to advance environmental goals such as clean air.

Messinger liked NRDC's strategic approach and became an important backer of the group. One big focus was trying to shut down nuclear power plants in the wake of the accident at Three Mile Island in 1979, and Messinger gladly opened her checkbook to fund this work. "I supported several lawsuits against nuclear power plants," she said. She also gave money to advocate for alternative energy when this issue first emerged during the Carter years.

The growth of NRDC illustrates how and why the environmental movement has become so powerful. In the years after NRDC was first started, with funds from the Ford Foundation, it was almost entirely dependent on foundation money. Gifts from wealthy individuals were "small potatoes," recalled James Gustave Speth, a cofounder of the group with Adams. "It was not part of the culture in those early days."

During the 1980s, though, Ronald Reagan's environmental policies created alarm among many Americans, including those in the upper class, and NRDC started to receive more money from individuals. By 1987, only 40 percent of its money came from foundations. The group stepped up its focus on individual donors in the 1990s, as the great boom of that decade got under way, and began to pull environmentally minded corporate leaders onto its board. These included people such as Frederick A. O. Schwarz, a partner at the august law firm of Cravath, Swain, and Moore, and an heir to the FAO Schwarz toy fortune; Robert Fisher, of the Gap; and Alan Horn, the president of Warner Bros.

By the time George W. Bush was elected, NRDC was getting 70 percent of its money from individuals and, as the Republicans set about dismantling environmental protections, its budget skyrocketed—more than doubling by 2008 to top $80 million a year. John Adams, who led the group until 2006, had an uncanny knack for finding super-wealthy people with deep ties to nature and getting them to open their checkbooks in a big way. "A lot of people have been brought into this movement who had some interest but developed a powerful interest," said Speth, who sat on NRDC's board during its most significant growth period.

Adams did especially well in Hollywood. Robert Redford had been involved with NRDC since its earliest days, but the organization didn't start to raise truly big money in Hollywood until the late 1990s, when Alan Horn and director Rob Reiner spent three full days taking Adams around to visit all of the heads of major Hollywood studios. Soon the contributions were rolling in. Reiner also arranged for Adams to meet Laurie David, who was married to Larry David, the mega-rich producer of *Seinfeld* and *Curb Your Enthusiasm*. David became an ardent fan of NRDC and a prominent donor. She joined the board of directors and shook other money trees around town. In 2004, David put together a star-studded fund-raiser for the group that brought in celebrity donors such as Tom Hanks, Leonardo DiCaprio, and Michelle Pfeiffer. The event raised $3 million in a single night. DiCaprio also joined the board. Maybe the most generous Hollywood donor of all to NRDC has turned out to be Steve Bing, who reportedly gave $1.7 million so that NRDC could finish a new, super-green building in downtown Santa Monica.[13]

The Sierra Club's budget also surged during the Bush years—helped along by the largest gift in the organization's history: a $100 million donation from California hedge-fund billionaire David Gelbaum. Over the last decade, Gelbaum has given a reported $250 million to environmental causes, making him one of the foremost environmental donors in the United States.

Gelbaum is a familiar figure in wealthy liberal circles: the geek who struck gold. He grew up in Minnesota, the son of a math professor, and moved to California when his father became the founding chairman of the math department at UC–Irvine. Gelbaum was a math prodigy as a teenager, taking math classes at UC–Irvine while still in high school before he started full-time at the university as a math major. When he graduated, he got a job with a math professor named Edward Thorp who was starting a hedge fund that used mathematical formulas to predict stock prices. Gelbaum worked with Thorp for the next seventeen years. Later he helped start a new hedge fund using mathematical formulas. His business success, he once told a reporter, "was all a matter of chance. It certainly wasn't because I worked 5,000 times as hard as the average person or was 5,000 times smarter than the average person."[14] (It is not clear that Gelbaum ever gave the Sierra Club the full $100 million, since he announced in 2009 that he was suspending gifts to the group after he suffered market setbacks. Gelbaum also stopped gifts to the ACLU that amounted to $20 million a year, or a quarter of the group's budget.)

An even more important wealthy environmentalist—maybe *the* most important—is John Hunting. Hunting was six years old when his father first gave him stock in a small office furniture company he had cofounded in Grand Rapids, Michigan. The company, which became Steelcase, specialized in making fireproof safes and steel wastebaskets. It grew to become the largest office furniture company in the world. Hunting got richer and richer as he grew older, and by his thirties, amid the social upheavals of the 1960s, he began to donate half of his income from his trust to charity and liberal causes—the most he could give away without adverse tax consequences.

One of Hunting's early ventures was to set up the Dyer-Ives Foundation, which worked on youth and community issues in Grand Rapids as that city grappled with industrial decline and poverty. But philanthropy was not Hunting's main passion during his younger years: theater and singing were, and he moved to New York to pursue a career in the performing arts. He didn't enjoy much success and was still living in New York when he became increasingly concerned about environmental issues. In nearly stereotypical fashion, it was the plight of the whales that captured Hunting's attention, around 1980. "I just couldn't understand how the human race could go out and slaughter almost to extinction the largest animals on Earth." Hunting got involved in this issue, attending several conferences.

Around the same time, Reagan took office and appointed an arch-conservative interior secretary, James Watt. As Watt set about turning over U.S. wilderness areas to miners and loggers, Hunting became more galvanized by environmental issues. "I felt I had this clarion call: Those of us who care about the environment better do something about it." He moved to Washington, D.C., and set up the Beldon Fund in 1982 to handle his charitable giving in this area. (The name was borrowed from the Old English word meaning "from the beautiful valley.") The fund was small at first, supported by income from Hunting's trust, and worked closely with the Sierra Club, fighting Reagan's policies.

Marion Edey recalled that when she first met Hunting, she thought he was simply a staffer at the Dyer-Ives Foundation. "I had no idea he had money," said Edey. "He was the most egoless person I had ever met."

Hunting thought that his sojourn in Washington would be temporary. "I thought I would go back once we got rid of these people," he said. But by the late 1980s, it became clear that environmental problems were much more severe than anyone had imagined, as new evidence emerged that the Earth's climate was starting to warm because of human activity. Hunting talked up the issue every chance he got. He also decided to stay on in Washington. Not long before Bill Clinton came into office, Hunting bought a red-brick townhouse in the Capitol Hill neighborhood of Washington to be closer to the political action and have a greater impact. "I bought a house near the Capitol so when we have fund-raisers, members of Congress can come over and their beepers can get them back in time for votes," he said.[15]

Hunting also turned the townhouse into a cutting-edge show-case for green building, long before this was a trendy topic. He spent some $500,000 renovating the house, putting in insulation and dry-wall made of recycled newsprint, paper, and gypsum and installing a system on the roof to collect rainwater for the toilets and the gardens. The roof also had solar panels to power the hot water heater.

All the while, Hunting held on to the Steelcase stock that his father had given him. And in 1998, after the company went public, Hunting came into his full inheritance: $130 million. Finally, he had serious money to put into environmental issues, and he immediately transferred $100 million to the fund. He also decided that the fund would spend that money in ten years, as opposed to existing in perpetuity like so many foundations. "I believe that it is immoral to hoard money when global warming is on the verge of destroying the ecosystems we depend on," he explained at one point. "Global warming is coming like a freight train. It is serious. It is going to be the most destructive event in the history of the human race. We need to spend the money now to prevent this destructive event from taking place."[16]

Beldon was one of the few foundations dedicated solely to environmental causes, and it was unafraid to back hard-hitting activists. It supported major groups such as NRDC and the Sierra Club, but also smaller operations like Green Corp and Earth Justice. And it pumped money into any number of state-level environmental battles from Vermont to California. Beldon is widely credited with building the power of environmental coalitions, as well as helping curb environmental health hazards—such as toxic chemicals in consumer products. It closed its doors in 2009, having spent about $120 million. During this same period, Hunting also put millions into campaigns to back politicians who were friendly to the environment—including more than $1 million into the League of Conservation voters. In Edey's words, Hunting was "the patron saint of the environmental movement."

John Hunting's big spending on environmental issues has become less and less unusual since he started Beldon. There is not only David Gelbaum's giving, but also Robert W. Wilson's, who made his fortune with a hedge fund that specialized in short-selling. In 2006, Wilson gave $147 million to a number of environmental groups, including the American Bird Conservancy, Environmental Defense, the Nature Conservancy, and the Wildlife Conservation Society.[17] Wilson is an example of why there has been so much cash pouring into liberal causes in recent years. He rode the bull markets for years during the great boom that started in the early 1980s and eventually, in his older age, got bored with making money. "A lot of rich Wall Streeters really can't be bothered with thinking about giving it [money] away when there are so many opportunities to make it," Wilson said in 2007, not longer after he made his big gifts. "But I'm eighty years old, and I haven't been active in the market for twenty years. I don't have that distraction of making money anymore. I have other people who are making money for me, but I myself am not making it. So I can concentrate on this."[18]

Gelbaum and Wilson, as well as Hunting, have given serious money to green causes. But these sums pale in comparison to what Intel cofounder Gordon Moore and his wife, Betty, are spending. Moore piled up a fortune revolutionizing the computer chip industry, and his foundation is one of the largest in the United States, with assets greater than $6 billion in 2008. He has focused much of his giving on an ambitious global effort to preserve wildlife and fragile ecosystems. In 2001, Moore made the largest gift ever to an environmental organization, when he pledged $261 million to Conservation International to scale up its efforts to slow the rate of species extinction. The money is funding acquisition of species-rich land on a vast scale—mostly in remote parts of South America, Africa, and Asia. During the first five years of operation, the Gordon and Betty Moore Foundation sank $479 million into conservation efforts, making Moore the largest environmental philanthropist in history.

But more money is on the way. Much more. Moore is spending $235 million to protect the Amazon River basin, $146 million on marine conservation, $190 million to preserve salmon ecosystems in the North Pacific, and $145 million to study ocean microorganisms. Moore has also spent more than $85 million to protect land around the San Francisco area and on the Pacific Coast. His conservation efforts are on such a large scale that the effects can be seen from outer space.

Moore isn't alone in using his money to preserve vast tracts of wilderness. Ted Turner is now the largest individual landowner in the United States, owning nearly 2 million acres of property, including a 588,000-acre ranch in New Mexico and a 113,000-acre ranch just north of Yellowstone National Park. Many of Turner's fifteen ranches are in ecologically important areas of the United States and will be permanently protected from development. Some, such as the spectacular Flying D Ranch in Montana, have already been protected through deals with open spaces groups. Turner has been obsessed with nature since he was a child and read books about animals in Africa and marine life. One of his first major moves as a philanthropist was to establish the Turner Foundation in 1990 to support environmental activism. Turner is best known for giving $1 billion to UN-related causes, but he's also up there with the biggest environmental donors in U.S. history. He's given more than $300 million to these causes since 1990. When he eventually turns over his land holdings to permanent conservation, that amount will be much greater.

Brad Kelley, who became a billionaire through selling discount cigarette brands, is doing much the same thing that Turner is—buying up land and preserving it for conservation. The little-known Kelley now owns 1.7 million acres, and he is buying more all the time. Among other holdings, he owns hundreds of thousands of acres in West Texas, where Amazon's Jeff Bezos has also bought a reported 300,000 acres.

Roxanne Quimby, the founder of Burt's Bees, has bought up thousands of acres in northern Maine, the largest virgin wilderness east of the Mississippi. Quimby first came to Maine in a Volkswagen microbus as a back-to-nature hippie in the 1970s and started making candles out of leftover beeswax. Eventually, she pocketed several hundred million dollars from the sale of Burt's Bees and began to bankroll a dream that has tantalized environmentalists since Henry Thoreau's day: protecting the great forests of Maine in perpetuity. So far, she has bought more than 100,000 acres.

The fashion entrepreneur Doug Tompkins, who founded North Face and Esprit, owns more land than anyone, only it's mostly on the tip of South America. During recent years, Tompkins—a left-wing former climbing and skiing bum—has used his private fortune to amass two million acres of some of the wildest and most ecologically sensitive land in the Western Hemisphere. Tompkins's approach has been to acquire large, strategic tracts of wilderness with the goal of eventually turning the land over to national park systems, ensuring that these lands stay wild. His greatest creation so far is Pumalín Park, a 750,000-acre nature conservancy in southern Chile consisting of rugged shoreline, inlets, rain forests, and mountains. An even more stunning swath of Chilean wilderness, on the island of Tierra del Fuego, has been forever protected, thanks to Hank Paulson, of all people. Goldman Sachs became the owner of the tract, 680,000 acres, roughly equal to the size of Rhode Island, when it took possession of the assets held by the Trillium Corporation, a failed U.S. company. Trillium had planned to lease parts of the land to logging companies. But Paulson, then Goldman's CEO and a strong conservationist, pushed to donate the land to the Wildlife Conservation Society in December 2003.[19]

So many rich people are trying to save the planet these days that it can be hard to keep them all straight. Beyond staggering new investments in environmental philanthropy, the rich are spending unprecedented sums on political campaigns to further green causes. In 2006, for example, Steve Bing spent $49.6 million backing Proposition 87. This stands as the largest amount of money that any individual has ever spent on a ballot campaign. The campaign also attracted financial support from Google's cofounders and CEO; Gap chairman Robert Fisher; Nathaniel Simons, the son of hedge fund manager James Simons; Jeff Skoll; Qualcomm chairman Irwin Jacobs; Warner Bros. president Alan Horn; and John Doerr.

The effort failed, but that didn't stop another super-rich environmentalist from backing another clean energy ballot initiative two years later, in 2008. This time, the money came from Peter Sperling, the billionaire son of John Sperling, who made the family fortune in for-profit education by founding the University of Phoenix. (The elder Sperling, also a liberal, has spent heavily on ballot campaigns to decriminalize marijuana.) Peter Sperling's initiative, Proposition 7, would have mandated that the California utilities buy half of their energy from renewable sources by 2025. Sperling spent more than $7 million on the initiative campaign, which failed to win over a majority of voters.

Even bigger money has gone to Al Gore's Alliance for Climate Protection, which is the most ambitious environmental advocacy effort ever mounted. In early 2008, the Alliance began a three-year, $300 million advertising campaign aimed at rallying Americans behind efforts to reduce carbon emissions. Even before the first ad aired, the campaign had reportedly raised half of its estimated budget—most of it from super-rich anonymous donors.[20]

It is tempting to think that the current environmental craze will not last and that as the "green bubble" deflates, the eco rich will move on to other fads. This has happened before: environmentalism and alternative energy were very trendy in the 1970s, only to fade in the 1980s.

A repeat of that cycle seems unlikely. The major drivers of environmentalism among the moneyed class aren't going away. The shift from a manufacturing to a knowledge economy is not yet complete, and this will be an ongoing trend in coming years. The ranks of the dirty rich will shrink further, along with their influence, and the clean rich will grow more numerous. Meanwhile, the vast intergenerational transfer of wealth in coming years will mean ever-expanding ranks of young heirs who take economic security for granted and are free to focus on postmaterialist concerns. And there are few such concerns that have galvanized GenXers and Millennials more than the environment and climate change. As one leading young organizer, Jessy Tolkan, has said, "The fight for a clean and just energy future is the defining issue of our time and the defining issue of this generation."[21]

Quite apart from economic and demographic trends, the ever more alarming news about climate change is likely to draw more wealthy people to this problem. Except for Gordon Moore, none of the truly mega-rich has made the environment the overriding focus of his or her philanthropy, and Moore has generally steered clear of advocacy. But if it's true that the climate crisis threatens all human endeavors, this is likely to change in coming years. After all, what's the point of funding a new wing of MoMA if New York City is going to be underwater in a century?

John Hunting had a huge effect in catalyzing environmental activism with a $120 million fortune spent out over a decade by the Beldon Fund. That's pocket change for many of the Forbes 400, and all it would take is a few massive new donors to reshape the politics around environmentalism. If one of the Google founders decides to focus on green causes, for instance, that money could be a game changer.

In other words, the influence of the eco rich is probably just beginning.

4

WEALTH AND THE
CULTURE WAR

IMAGINE GROWING UP as a gay teenager in a place like Kalamazoo, Michigan. It's the 1970s, and you don't know a single person who is gay. Your Republican parents tell you that God made you and Jesus loves you. A woman named Anita Bryant is on television regularly, crusading against homosexuality. Although your grandfather is a big deal in town, you feel alienated and angry because there is a part of you that must be kept buried, a part that you're told is wrong.

You go to a tough, mostly black high school at a time when the civil rights movement is still in the air, and you feel a natural affinity for minorities who are shut out. You're one yourself, after all.

You stay in the closet during your twenties, even in Berkeley, where you go to graduate school to train to become an architect, and where most of your friends are gays and lesbians. You get married and have two children. You stay in your hometown, inherit an unbelievable amount of money, and become a prominent citizen, joining boards and charities. You keep your secret, and although you've lived in Kalamazoo since you were a kid, you still don't know anyone there who is gay.

Then something changes. At thirty-six, you finally decide that you can't keep living a lie. Your marriage is over. The fortune you have inherited is big and keeps getting bigger—so big that you'll eventually end up on the Forbes 400 list. Bill Clinton is in the White House, and he is the most gay-friendly president in history. Gay rights issues are everywhere, fiercely contested, and you feel an obligation to join the fight. So you come out, finally, as a gay man. "I'm probably one of the wealthier gay men in this country, and I felt I had a big responsibility," Jon Stryker would later tell a reporter.

Stryker, as in the medical technology goliath. The firm was started in the 1940s by Homer Stryker, Jon's grandfather, a doctor who invented the mobile hospital bed and went on to patent numerous other devices. Jon Stryker inherited a piece of the company, as did his sisters, Pat and Ronda. In 2009, they were each worth about $1.5 billion. Pat and Jon are both huge donors to the Democratic Party, but Jon has made a bigger mark with his money by supporting the rights of gays and lesbians.

Before Stryker came out, his philanthropy had been scattershot. He donated to civic organizations and gave to causes when his friends asked for help. After coming out, he became much more strategic. "I quickly realized that there was very little funding for LGBT [lesbian, gay, bisexual, transgender] communities, and that LGBT rights was a niche that was not only personally important to me, but also an area where I could have a big impact as a donor," he would say later.[1] Matthew Shepard's brutal murder in 1998 dramatized the urgent needs of gays and lesbians who battled isolation and discrimination across the United States.

Stryker started locally, in Michigan. He knew what it was like to grow up gay and alone in a state that wasn't very tolerant, and he wanted to do something about it. He gave money to the Kalamazoo Gay and Lesbian Resource Center and to As We Are, which provided faith-based support to LGBT youths in western Michigan. Other early grants went to the Lesbian and Gay Network of Western

Michigan, to a new LGBT center in Lansing, and to the Triangle Foundation in Detroit, the leading LGBT civil rights group in the state. This local giving would increase in the coming years, amounting to millions of dollars to numerous groups, as if the sheer application of cash and determination could root out homophobia in the state of Michigan.

Stryker started to give at the national level, too. He put money into the push for gay marriage in Vermont and California, and he backed an organization that worked with gay soldiers who had been drummed out of the military by the "Don't Ask, Don't Tell" policy. He gave money to the National Gay and Lesbian Task Force in Washington, D.C., which pressed an LGBT agenda across a range of areas. He supported the ACLU's work on gay and lesbian rights, the Family Pride Coalition, and PFLAG, the family support group. But with only one employee at the new foundation he created, Arcus, his efforts were limited and the grants were small. In the wake of the demonization of gay marriage by the Republican right during the 2004 election, Stryker stepped up his national efforts. He hired a program officer from the Ford Foundation, an expert on LGBT issues, Urvashi Vaid, to run an expanded operation. Stryker quit working as an architect to devote himself full-time to philanthropy.

The grants got bigger and bolder. In 2005, he gave $3 million to the National Gay and Lesbian Task Force, the most generous gift in its history. He expanded support for gay marriage advocacy to more states: to Maryland, New Jersey, and Iowa. Stryker's national giving jumped from less than half a million dollars in 2003 to $6 million in 2006. He started a special program devoted to increasing tolerance for gays and lesbians within the faith world, backing projects that preached tolerance among Episcopalians, Lutherans, Muslims, Jews, and the United Church of Christ. He underwrote protests of the Catholic Church's homophobia when the pope visited the United States in 2008. He gave money to fight antigay prejudice among African Americans and to promote LGBT rights among Latinos. The foundation also underwrote the creation of the National Queer Asian Pacific Islander. Other grants went to help gay and lesbian prison inmates, as well as immigrants. In addition, Stryker gave large chunks of money in support of LGBT youths, seeking to reduce the bullying of gay kids in schools and helping gay runaways and homeless teenagers.

Still, Stryker wasn't done. He and the foundation's staff realized that the most intense battles for gay and lesbian rights were not in the United States but in other countries. And so Arcus began an international program and pumped several million dollars into these efforts to start with. "People don't realize that there is just one country in Africa where homosexuality is protected by the constitution," Stryker said. "They don't know that there are seven countries in the world where homosexuality is punishable by death." In many countries, LGBT groups operate in secrecy and members fear for their lives. Stryker hoped to change that.

Stryker started to show up on lists of the most generous Americans, such as the Slate 60, as he transferred more of his personal assets over to the Arcus Foundation. In 2006, he gave the foundation $73 million, and by 2008, its assets were greater than $100 million. Arcus is by far the largest donor to LGBT causes in the world.

One evening in 2008, Stryker found himself standing before twenty-one thousand LGBT activists in Washington to receive the first-ever Creating Change Award from the National Gay and Lesbian Task Force. He was still a quiet billionaire who'd spent nearly his entire life in Kalamazoo and was not used to the spotlight. He read carefully from a prepared text. "I think I owe everyone an apology for being so late," Stryker said. "I was so late coming out and joining this movement. . . . I am trying to make up for lost time." Apparently so.

David Bohnett is another wealthy activist who has moved aggressively in recent years, giving tens of millions of dollars to support gay and lesbian rights. Bohnett didn't spend nearly as much of his life in the closet as Stryker did—he came out in his twenties—but his personal experiences as a gay man had a searing impact on him and have driven his activism.

Bohnett grew up in an affluent suburb of Chicago, the son of Republican parents. His father was a business executive, his mother a housewife. Bohnett was interested in business from a young age, selling Amway products and delivering newspapers. "I thought I would make money and be successful," he said of his life aspirations. Starting in seventh or eighth grade, he also realized that he was different—that he liked boys more than girls and that this wasn't okay. It was something to be suppressed. There were no openly gay people in his high school. "I didn't know anybody else like me."

The public high school had a computer science course where Bohnett learned BASIC, an early computer programming language. He loved it. He chose the University of Southern California for college because it was one of the few schools with a computer science program. During college, he had his first gay romance, with a student at Notre Dame whom he had met while working at a summer job. The relationship was intense, but it ended abruptly in his senior year when his boyfriend—Michael Lyons—hung himself. Lyons was from a large Catholic family in a small Indiana town. "He just couldn't reconcile his religious beliefs with his homosexuality," Bohnett recalled. "And I just thought I'd do whatever I could to make sure that other people don't go through this same tragedy." It was 1978, the year Harvey Milk—the first openly gay elected official in the United States—was assassinated in San Francisco.

Bohnett became active in gay rights issues when he was in graduate school at the University of Michigan. He worked at the gay and lesbian student center, manning the "gay crisis hotline." Back in Los Angeles, he stepped up his activism when he began a relationship with Rand Schrader, who was eleven years older than him and one of the first openly gay judges in California. Bohnett became involved in the Gay and Lesbian Alliance Against Defamation (GLAAD), which worked against the negative portrayal of gays in the media. He reveled in being in an openly gay relationship with a prominent gay leader and finally came out to his parents. He and Schrader entertained often at their Los Feliz house, connecting with a wide variety of gay activists. The goals of the gay rights movement back then were modest. "I thought what was possible was to create an environment where there was much less stigma around homosexuality and it was easier to come out," Bohnett said. Beyond this cultural battle, there were fights to stop discrimination against gays in housing and the workplace.

Then AIDS came along. It devastated the gay community, as well as Bohnett's own life. Numerous friends died during the 1980s and, in 1993, the epidemic claimed Schrader. They had been together for ten years. But even though they were life partners, Bohnett was entitled to none of Schrader's assets, such as his judicial pension. And he had to sell the house they lived in because the IRS—then as now— didn't recognize the transfer of assets from a deceased person to a same-sex partner and taxed Schrader's estate. "It was just so unfair," Bohnett said.

Stripped of income and wealth that should rightly have been his, Bohnett found himself living in a one-bedroom apartment. He quit his job and took six months off to travel and think about his plans. He had been involved in various software ventures, but after Schrader died, Bohnett wanted to do something that would draw from the activist side of his life and have more purpose. Around this time, he started to read with excitement about a new thing called the World Wide Web. "I had to be part of it," he said. "*Had to.*"

In 1994, Bohnett created a site that allowed Internet users to make their own Web pages, connect with others, and express their passions online. The site was briefly called Beverly Hills Internet until it was renamed GeoCities.

Bohnett put everything he had into the business, and it took off. "I got tremendous satisfaction out of giving people a voice," he said. By June 1997, GeoCities was the fifth most popular Web site on the Internet. In 1998, GeoCities went public. And in 1999, with GeoCities now the third most visited site on the Web, Bohnett and his partners sold out to Yahoo for $3.57 billion. Bohnett walked away with a reported $267 million for five years of work.

He didn't wait long to put this money to work. In fact, he had long been thinking about the day when he could cash out and turn his full attention to activism. He immediately created the David Bohnett Foundation, as well as a political action fund. Both were directed by his friend Michael Fleming, who had led media work at the ACLU's Southern California office. Bohnett also used his new wealth to splurge a bit, such as buying Gary Cooper's old house in Los Angeles and restoring it to its original splendor. The project involved buying adjacent properties and tearing them down, and the cost ran into eight figures. He also bought and restored a home in Southampton, New York.

Bohnett wrote big checks to national organizations such as GLAAD, Family Pride Coalition, and Human Rights Campaign, but his real passion was for more local work aimed at supporting gays and lesbians and reducing the stigma around homosexuality. "The foundation of my activism is to create an environment which destigmatizes homosexuality," Bohnett said. "Everything comes from that. You just have to wait." The way to reduce the stigma, Bohnett believes, is to get more people to come out sooner in their lives. This means more open gays and lesbians who are part of every community and more people who know and accept them.

Bohnett focused money and energy on building community centers for gays and lesbians in various cities. The vision was to create safe havens to be gay, as well as places where young people could find real resources, such as computers and the Internet. Like Jon Stryker, Bohnett knew what it was like to grow up in America's heartland gay and isolated. "I had no role models," he said. Now his money was changing that. By 2010, his foundation had supported LGBT centers in nearly every corner of the country: Atlanta, Baltimore, Buffalo, Cleveland, Dallas, Denver, El Paso, Houston, Jersey City, Kansas City, Las Vegas, Orlando, Salt Lake City, San Antonio, and Tampa, and the list goes on. Stryker and other donors channeled money to the same centers, quietly creating a large national network to support gays and lesbians in even the most conservative of places. These centers not only fostered the kind of openness that helped people come out earlier, they also served as a nexus for organizing across a variety of issues: anti–gay bashing efforts, health services, and marriage equality.

Meanwhile, Bohnett has used his money to nurture gay and lesbian political leaders and to create an environment that is receptive to the push for LGBT rights. He funds fellowships at Harvard's John F. Kennedy School of Government that help train gay elected officials, government executives, and public officials. Bohnett also tries to make sure that these people have the money they need to win campaigns. When a gay politician runs for office, such as Sean Maloney in New York, who ran for state attorney general in 2006, he can count on generous support from Bohnett and other major gay donors. Maloney received more than $45,000 from Bohnett, $50,000 from Jon Stryker, and $35,000 from Tim Gill—big money for a little-known candidate running for a state office. (Maloney lost to Andrew Cuomo.)

Bohnett gives to plenty of nongay politicians, too, but in a very strategic fashion. For years, he has been supporting local candidates and elected leaders who are fighting to reform the maze of laws that hurt gay families on issues such as employment, housing, health care, and adoption. From the start, he saw all of this giving as laying the foundation for a long-term national push to achieve marriage equality. Bohnett has been a major supporter of marriage equality work in a number of states. In 2008, he was the single largest donor to efforts aimed at blocking Proposition 8, the California ballot initiative to ban gay marriage. He spent $2 million. The initiative passed, but Bohnett wasn't worried. "I'm an impatiently patient person," he said. Long-term, the political, social, and generational trends all point to success in achieving marriage equality. "It's simply inexorable," he said.

The ability of the rich to make change in the world is one very big way in which they are different. It is an example of what the scholar Paul Schervish has called "hyperagency." As Schervish has written, with colleague Andrew Herman, "The wealthy are uniquely endowed with material resources and cognitive dispositions that enable them, both as a group and as individuals, to shape the rules, practices and positions of social structure. Wealth grants special capacity for *empowerment*."

Schervish's analysis of hyperagency is based on extensive interviews conducted during a four-year study on wealth and philanthropy. Many of his interviewees talked of their personal efficacy and ability to set their own agenda—as well as that of society.

The "wealthy, it turns out, 'make history' for themselves and others," Schervish and Herman wrote. "While the non-wealthy generally reside within structure, the wealthy construct it."[2] Fran Lebowitz once made a similar point, without the jargon: "To us the world is a museum; to them it's a store."

Both Jon Stryker and David Bohnett are living out a fantasy that surely every closeted gay or lesbian has at some point in his or her life: that they could part with their fear and shame, emerge as their real selves, and wave a magic wand to banish homophobia.

Antigay sentiments are still powerful in the United States, but the gay rights movement has made huge strides in recent years, and big money has been pivotal in this fight. In fact, it is hard to think of another area where such a small handful of wealthy donors have had so much impact.

These donors have found plenty of allies among the straight wealthy, as the upper class has grown dramatically more gay-friendly in recent years. This is especially true in places like Los Angeles and New York City, where many of the super-rich actively support gay rights. The power of this backing was vividly on display on an October night in 2008, when supermarket magnate Ron Burkle threw a fund-raiser at his baronial Beverly Hills estate, "Green Acres," which raised $3.9 million in last-minute emergency funds to defeat Proposition 8. The host committee for the event included Steven Spielberg and other straight industry heavyweights. A few weeks earlier, Brad Pitt had donated $100,000 to the battle to stop Proposition 8. And days before the event, Steven Bing had announced a $500,000 donation. He would ultimately spend $1 million. Up in Silicon Valley, Google founders Sergey Brin and Larry Page put $140,000 into the campaign, while Apple contributed $100,000. All told, opponents of Proposition 8 would raise $45 million—among the largest amounts of money ever mobilized to stop a ballot initiative. (Supporters of the proposition raised $40 million from deep-pocketed conservatives such as John Templeton, a haul that served as a reminder that gays and lesbians still have plenty of powerful enemies.)

It's not only California where the wealthy are friendly to gays. Leading corporations across the country have embraced gay and lesbian workers to the point that a majority of Fortune 500 companies now offer domestic partnership benefits. In 2008, the affluent congressional district covering Boulder, Colorado, elected an openly gay congressman, Jared Polis. The other two openly gay members of Congress—Barney Frank and Tammy Baldwin—also represent affluent districts.

The country club homophobe is an enduring stereotype, and not without reason. In the older WASP world, homosexuals were in the same boat as blacks and Jews: feared deviants who threatened to corrupt the purity of a white and Protestant world.

That was then. The upper class has grown more gay friendly as wealth has become more closely correlated with education and the rich are more heavily concentrated in liberal metro areas. Also, a younger cohort of moneyed Americans is emerging that sees being gay as perfectly normal. And the linkages go deeper than these recent shifts. Worldwide, wealthier people and prosperous societies tend to be more secular, rationalistic, and tolerant—all of which are characteristics linked to more acceptance of homosexuality. Cross-national polling finds that some of the richest countries, such as Denmark, Sweden, and Switzerland, are among the most gay friendly.

That affluent Americans are more gay friendly than other income groups is now well documented. For instance, a 2008 survey by the Center for American Progress found that Americans earning more than $100,000 a year were less likely by half than those earning less than $20,000 a year to agree that "homosexuality is unnatural and should not be tolerated by society."[3] Surveys on same-sex marriage find a sharp divide in views based on income. A May 2009 poll of New Yorkers found that people with incomes greater than $100,000 supported legalizing same-sex marriage by 14 percentage points more than those who earned less than $50,000 a year. Exit polls in California in 2008 found that the voters who earned more than $200,000 a year voted against Proposition 8 by the highest percentage of any group.[4] Three-quarters of the voters in Marin, the wealthiest county in the state, voted against Proposition 8, while nearly a similar percentage in Modoc, the state's poorest county (which is rural and largely white), voted for Proposition 8—a remarkable spread of 50 percentage points. In Arizona, 57 percent of the voters who earned more than $100,000 a year voted against the 2008 gay marriage ban, even as the ballot initiative passed by a healthy margin. In Florida, every single income group voted for a 2008 gay marriage ban by a wide margin—except for voters who earned more than $200,000 a year, 60 percent of whom voted against the ban. In contrast, two-thirds of the poorest voters in Florida voted for the ban.

The big income gap on gay marriage votes in 2008 was new. Four years earlier, voters in eleven states had passed ballot initiatives banning gay marriage, and exit polls showed that voters in all income groups had supported such bans with nearly equal enthusiasm. These results and other polls suggest that although public opinion around homosexuality has been changing fast, it is higher-income people whose views are evolving most rapidly. Meanwhile, members of Congress from some of the wealthiest districts have been key allies of gay rights groups in Congress. Seven out of ten of those members representing the very richest districts received voting scores of more than 85 percent in 2008 by the Human Rights Campaign.[5]

Gay rights is only the latest battle in the culture war where the rich have been pivotal supporters of greater equality. The reproductive rights movement has been backed by the rich since the days of Margaret Sanger, and among its largest contemporary donors is Warren Buffett, who has poured millions into support for Planned Parenthood. Whenever an abortion issue comes up on a ballot initiative, the votes by class are predictable. For instance, the highest margin of opposition to a 2008 ballot effort in California to require parental notification for abortions was among voters earning more than $200,000 a year. The same year in Michigan, higher-income voters provided the biggest margins of support for a law that would allow stem cell research.

Civil rights has also been a cause célèbre among the wealthy at times. The civil rights movement didn't draw in only upper-middle-class northern college kids; it also attracted serious liberal money starting in the early 1960s. Among the movement's biggest funders were Stephen and Audrey Currier, forgotten figures today but perhaps the richest and most glamorous liberals of their time. (They both died in a plane crash in 1967.) Stephen was the stepson of Edward

Warburg of the Kuhn, Loeb banking family, while Audrey was the granddaughter of Andrew Mellon and an heiress to one of the largest fortunes in the United States. The couple established the Taconic Foundation, which gave more than a million dollars to civil rights causes between 1960 and 1963. Stephen Currier organized a famous New York fund-raising event in 1963 that brought in $800,000 from other wealthy donors and foundations. The Curriers were important funders of the Student Non-Violent Coordinating Committee and Freedom Summer, the 1964 push to increase voter registration. Other wealthy liberals, such as Philip Stern of the Stern Family Fund, also channeled serious money to civil rights organizations.[6]

Liberal money has kept flowing into work for racial equality since the 1960s. George Soros, for instance, has put millions into reforming drug laws that disproportionately hurt communities of color, and, more recently, he has begun to bankroll a three-year project on black male achievement. Herb and Marion Sandler have been among ACORN's biggest donors, a group that works heavily with low-income people of color. They've also contributed to the Center for Responsible Lending, which has focused much of its attention on predatory lending practices that hurt poor Americans. Two of the biggest philanthropists in the United States, Bill Gates and Eli Broad, have pumped more than $2.5 billion into urban education in one of the biggest philanthropic ventures of our time. Nearly all of this money is going to schools that are primarily nonwhite. The single largest gift that Bill Gates has given to date is $1.5 billion, to the United Negro College Fund in 1999.

In New York City, there are few more fashionable causes nowadays than the public schools, which have attracted tens of millions of dollars in private donations, even though the rich don't send their kids to these schools and only 14 percent of the students are white. Big donors include people such as the media mogul Mortimer Zuckerman and Barnes and Noble chairman Leonard Riggio, who led an effort to raise more than $20 million for Brooklyn Technical High School, his alma mater. (Riggio himself gave $5 million to the school.) A similar pattern holds in other cities. In 2007, the California real estate developer Richard Lunquist and his wife, Melanie, pledged $50 million to the Los Angeles public school system. The Lunquists had both gone to L.A.'s public schools, but today only 9 percent of the students in that system are white.

Affluent people care more about kids of color in bad schools than maybe ever before. But don't be fooled: civil rights isn't one of the passions of the current liberal rich. A major civil rights issue of our age—the large-scale incarceration of African Americans, many for drug offenses—attracts few philanthropic dollars. And although the Sandlers have given generously to ACORN, groups that focus on building power in communities of color typically have few wealthy donors. Worse, there are plenty of examples of well-to-do liberal bastions doing their best to keep blacks and Latinos far away. In August 2009, New York's Westchester County settled a federal lawsuit that charged that the county was lying about its efforts to promote fair housing, while pocketing millions of dollars in housing assistance. Westchester has pledged to build low-income housing targeted at minorities in its whitest towns—and you can bet that residents in even the most liberal of these towns will oppose such projects.[7]

The movements for greater social freedom, which exploded in the 1960s, have been a key factor in scrambling the politics of class. These movements drew in many affluent Americans, while triggering fear and reactionary responses among working-class whites. Much has been made of how Democrats alienated their blue-collar base by siding with the left in the culture war, which cost them elections, but this stance turned out to have a major upside. Democrats picked up new support among well-off Americans just as this group began to dramatically expand amid boom times. That support has deepened in recent years as Republicans have grown more conservative on social issues, fighting high-profile battles on Terri Schiavo and stem cell research.

A tolerant Democratic Party has attracted large swaths of the upper class—although still only a minority of this group—even as the party has grown more populist, vowing to hike taxes on the rich and better regulate business. Those Democrats who actually represent the rich are no exception: Most of the congressional Democrats who are very liberal on social issues are also very liberal on economic issues. That pattern is evident in the voting records of members who represent the ten wealthiest districts in the United States: These members get nearly the highest possible ratings from watchdog groups that focus on gay rights, civil rights, and abortion—and extremely low ratings from conservative groups that worry about taxes and regulation. Every Democrat from one of the wealthiest districts who received 100 percent ratings from the Planned Parenthood Federation of America and Human Rights Campaign also received an "F" rating from the National Taxpayers Union.

It turns out that "values voters" who put their morals ahead of their financial self-interest don't exist only in places like Kansas or Kentucky. There are also plenty of them in Manhattan and Malibu.

Yet the biggest dividend to Democrats from the culture war may come less in the form of votes in high-income districts than from large checks that are written to the party by donors who are deeply concerned about social issues. And few such issues have mobilized more new money for Democrats since the early 1990s than gay rights.

Long before people such as Jon Stryker and David Bohnett came along, David Mixner was the maestro of gay money in politics. In 1988, Mixner set out to raise a million dollars for Michael Dukakis but was told that the campaign would not accept the money. Things had changed by 1992, and Mixner became a major fund-raiser for his old friend Bill Clinton as that campaign actively curried the support of gays and lesbians. Mixner organized one event for Clinton where more than seven hundred gays and lesbians, including many celebrities, packed into a Hollywood dance club. "I have a vision of the future, and you are a part of it," Clinton told the crowd. After Clinton was elected, Mixner estimated that gays had contributed $3.5 million to his campaign.[8]

Clinton turned out to be an uncertain friend to gays. He watered down his promises about gays in the military, leading to the "Don't Ask, Don't Tell" policy, and he signed the Defense of Marriage Act, which was a major blow to marriage equality efforts. He appointed a White House AIDS czar and spoke often about the epidemic, but his overall record on AIDS was mixed.[9] Still, Clinton and Al Gore were the best friends that gays ever had in the White House, and wealthy gay donors continued to back the Democratic Party.

Bohnett was one of those funders. In the first year after selling GeoCities, he gave the national Democratic Party nearly half a million dollars, helping to finance Gore's run for president. Stryker also made some large gifts, as did other donors.

These substantial donations to the national party have not continued at the same pace, however. Instead, the richest and most influential gay donors have turned their attention to state and local races, while stepping up their giving. Bohnett talks of this shift as a result of a learning curve. Even at his level of giving, it was hard to see the impact at the national level on the issues he cared about. Top Democrats, including Barack Obama, have resisted getting behind marriage equality, even as they pocketed millions from gay donors. "My sense of satisfaction comes from state and local races," Bohnett said, "where you can either knock somebody out who is bad or put somebody in who is good, and my contributions have a direct impact on that." Stryker has come to the same conclusion, and Bohnett and Stryker have both looked to one man for inspiration and guidance in their local political giving: Tim Gill.

Gill is one of the biggest-spending activists to have emerged from the tech world. And perhaps nobody has done more to advance gay rights in recent years.

The son of a plastic surgeon who majored in computer science and math at the University of Colorado in Boulder, Gill felt lonely and alienated growing up gay in the affluent suburbs of Denver in the 1970s. When he came out to his parents, during freshman year of college, his mother was appalled and told him, "If your father's colleagues ever find out, his career will be at an end."[10]

Gill started a software company, Quark, out of his apartment in 1981. The company—which created QuarkXpress—was a huge success, landing Gill on the Forbes 400 list at the age of forty-three in 1997. Three years later, when tech stocks were still riding high, Gill sold his stake in the company for more than $400 million. He put nearly all of the money straight into the Gill Foundation, which works on LGBT issues.

Gill is a prime example of the firepower that now stands behind liberal causes. Here's a guy who cashed out of business with a vast fortune at an age when most people are hitting their peak profession-ally—when they're still young enough to have tremendous energy and drive, yet old enough to have deep experience and judgment. In Gill's case, hitting the jackpot didn't mean it was time to jet off to Tahiti. Instead, he shifted his focus from making software to making change.

Andrew Carnegie turned to large-scale philanthropy at the age of sixty-six and was dead eighteen years later. Tim Gill could well spend three or four decades giving away his money. The same is true of other younger liberal donors who have emerged from the tech world, such as Rob Glaser, Jeff Skoll, Andy Rappaport, and David Bohnett. Quite a few of these people will probably still be shelling out money in the 2020s and 2030s.

The other thing about Gill, which again can be found in other tech donors, is that he is extremely smart. He emerged out of a cul-ture of entrepreneurship that stresses finding gaps in the marketplace and leveraging comparative advantage. He is the antithesis of the passive donor who is content simply to write checks. Paul Schervish has called people like Gill "producers rather than supporters of phi-lanthropy, underwriters rather than just contributors."[11]

Gill started his most significant giving well before either Stryker or Bohnett did, and the flood of money from his foundation has had a huge effect on the gay rights world. It helped national groups scale up, while also spreading the fight to numerous states. Nearly every LGBT and AIDS group in the United States has gotten money from the Gill Foundation, and Gill money has been especially pivotal in bankrolling the push for marriage equality.

But for all of his philanthropy, Gill came to feel during the Bush years that he wasn't having enough impact. Change wasn't happen-ing fast enough, and the right was gaining the upper hand by pass-ing antigay measures in the states. Along with his political adviser, Ted Trimpe, Gill took a long hard look at how he could leverage his fortune to turn the tide. What they discovered is that many antigay measures came out of state legislatures that were dominated by conservatives. "The strategic piece of the puzzle we'd been missing—consistent across almost every legislature we examined—is that it's often just a handful of people, two or three, who introduce the most outrageous legislation and force the rest of their colleagues to vote on it," Gill told the *Atlantic* in 2007. "If you could reach these few people or neutralize them by flipping the chamber to leaders who would block bad legislation, you'd have a dramatic effect."

Going back to the early 1980s, right-wing groups such as the American Legislative Exchange Council had spent tens of millions of dollars to elect Republicans at the state level, and those investments had yielded enormous dividends. Not only did the right exercise huge influence in state legislatures, but it used this arena to nurture a farm team of young pols, and many stars of the movement—such as Rick Santorum—started their political careers in backwater state capitals. So the stakes were doubly high: to stop antigay legislation in the states and also take out ambitious conservatives before they could rise to the national stage.

Gill, working out of offices in Denver, put together a sophisticated political operation that targeted key races and legislatures. He would "punish the wicked" and support politicians who were friendly to LGBT rights. Although federal races are awash with big money, state races are far less expensive, and even a few thousand dollars can make a difference. Gill had found his leverage point, and he began to spend millions.

He started in Colorado, teaming up with three other wealthy progressives—Jared Polis, Rutt Bridges, and Pat Stryker (Jon's sister)—to target state-level races in 2004. Antigay conservatives were given special priority. The results were impressive: in a year when Bush won reelection, Democrats won control of both houses of the state legislature for the first time since 1961.

Gill scaled up his giving, creating the Gill Action Fund and donating to races around the country. He emerged as the premier political strategist of the gay rights movement. As important as his own giving was his effort to organize other leading gay donors to strategically target their funds. In 2005, for example, Gill helped coordinate contributions aimed at defeating antigay politicians in

Virginia, channeling nearly $140,000 into state legislative races. That same year, he organized a group called the Cabinet that consisted of himself, Bohnett, Stryker, and several other prominent gay donors: James Hormel of San Francisco, an heir to the Hormel meat fortune; Henry van Ameringen, whose father, Arnold Louis van Ameringen, started an import company that later became International Flavors and Fragrances; Jonathan Lewis, the son of the insurance billionaire Peter Lewis; and Linda Ketner, an heiress to the Food Lion super-market fortune. Since 2005, this group has collectively spent millions of dollars on state races. Besides forming the Cabinet, Gill drew a wider group of funders into his orbit through an annual conference called Out Political Giving.

In 2009, when several states such as Iowa and Vermont moved to legalize gay marriage, the shift may have seemed sudden to some observers, but not to Gill, Bohnett, and other members of the Cabinet, who had been carefully targeting large sums of money in these states. For instance, gay marriage moved forward in New York after Democrats narrowly captured control of the state Senate for the first time in forty-four years. Members of the Cabinet helped that shift along by spending heavily in New York, with Gill leading the way by putting nearly $170,000 into the Senate battle in 2008.

The impressive amounts of gay money flooding into politics have upped the risk of any politician's being an outspoken opponent of LGBT rights. Just ask Sue Kelly, a six-term congresswoman from upstate New York, who voted for the Federal Marriage Amendment in 2004 and later found herself in the crosshairs of Adam Rose in 2006. Rose, a gay man who comes from a wealthy Manhattan real estate family, contributed $500,000 to Majority Action, a 527 (a non-profit group ostensibly set up to advocate for a particular set of issues), with the specific goal of defeating Kelly. The money helped a long-shot candidate, John Hall, to prevail over Kelly by a margin of fewer than 5,000 votes.[12]

The conventional wisdom about money in politics, at least on the left, is that only bad things happen when rich people write checks to politicians. Campaign cash is seen as the great corrupter, the dark force that is forever pulling the United States to the right and, in particular, poisoning the Democratic Party.

Of course, this is simplistic. The more complex truth is that although rich donors do tend to push the Democrats rightward on economic policy, they often push the party to the left on social issues. God help the Democratic presidential candidate who tries to win the "money primary" of raising early contributions, especially on the West Coast, by calling for limits on abortion rights or stronger controls on media content. Before long—maybe sooner than anyone thinks—the liberal litmus test will also include support for gay marriage, and candidates who flunk that test can say good-bye to receiving substantial amounts of early money and thus any real shot at getting nominated.

Is that a good thing? I happen to think so. But I'm also aware of the risks to the Democratic Party when wealthy cultural liberals carry so much clout. Critics have long noted how Democrats have abandoned the working class to suck up to business donors, but these same voters have been alienated by the Democrats' stance on issues like abortion and gay rights. Any honest account of why the Democrats ended up in the wilderness for much of the last forty years must tell this full story.

Are people like Tim Gill leading the Democrats back into the wilderness? That is doubtful, judging by the muted backlash to the gay marriage victories of 2009. The American public, it seems, is coming to view gay marriage as inevitable. More broadly, culture war issues seem to be losing their punch as generational change has moved forward. History is unlikely to be kind to political leaders, including Barack Obama, who hang back in fear on the issue of equality for all Americans, regardless of sexual orientation.

Far from corrupting the Democratic Party, then, some wealthy liberal donors are actually doing the exact opposite: they are helping the party find its moral backbone.

5

THE ONE-WORLD
WEALTHY

IT IS EASY TO IMAGINE the worst about the elites who run U.S. global
policy. The Bush team played to type, as a war cabinet made up
largely of multimillionaires and dominated by three former CEOs—
Bush, Cheney, and Rumsfeld—embarked on imperial adventures.

The Clinton era was quieter but also confirmed populist fears.
An administration heavy with wealthy Wall Streeters, Robert Rubin
most notably, put globalization on a fast track and removed trade
barriers to make the world flatter in ways that benefited corporations
while leaving U.S. workers to be steamrolled by foreign competition.

In the view of critics such as Naomi Klein, the rich have turned
the world into one big zone of plunder, with multinational corporations moving like locusts to suck wealth from developing countries.
All the while, oblivious to the suffering of billions, the wealthy treat
foreign countries as playgrounds, bopping around in carbon-spewing
private jets to places like Cabo San Lucas, Cannes, and Dubai. In any
given issue of *Vanity Fair*, there are stories about Johnny Depp's private island in the Caribbean or photos of George Clooney at his villa

on Lake Como or mention of the billionaire-owned mega-yachts that
trawl the seas. (Paul Allen's 416-foot *Octopus* has been spotted as far
afield as Mombasa, Kenya, while the 453-foot *Rising Sun*, which is
jointly owned by Larry Ellison and David Geffen, has turned up in
Croatia, Sardinia, and St. Maarten.)

But stereotypes of the rich as either neocolonists or jet-setters
gloss over the complexity of attitudes that actually hold sway in the
upper class. This group is anything but monolithic when it comes to
America's role in the world—and never has been.

After World War I, the upper class was bitterly divided over joining the League of Nations. Twenty years later, on the eve of World
War II, the patrician Franklin Delano Roosevelt and the new money
upstart Joseph Kennedy disagreed vehemently about whether the
United States should mobilize against Adolf Hitler. Since the 1960s,
when some of the rich were drawn into the antiwar movement, the
upper class has argued incessantly over the uses of U.S. power, and
that battle continues today.

The Bush administration, with its high-handed unilateralism, did
not speak for many of the wealthy. The cosmopolitan blue-state rich
don't tend to see the world in terms of military rivalries or global
struggles against absolute evil. Rather, they see a world in which
countries are ever more interdependent—enmeshed in a single global
economy and ecology. They are especially attuned to the waning
clout of the United States. The reflex of many knowledge-economy
leaders is not to tally up how many aircraft carriers a country has; it
is to look at how many engineers it is graduating every year and how
fast it is developing the technologies of tomorrow. Far from favoring
efforts to shore up a U.S. hegemony based on military might, some of
the rich have used their wealth to promote a multilateral world order
where Washington gets used to sharing power with others.

But the really striking thing about today's most globally engaged
billionaires and millionaires—what is different and maybe trans-
formative—is their intense focus on combating problems such as
malaria, AIDS, and global poverty. For some of the new economy's
biggest winners, helping the world's poorest people has turned into
an all-consuming passion.

• • •

That is certainly the case for Edward Scott Jr., a successful Silicon Valley entrepreneur. During most of his life, Scott barely gave a thought to the two billion or so people in the world who live without such basics as clean water, vaccines, or education. He was focused almost exclusively on his own career and financial security. When he was young, as a political science major in college at Michigan State and then as a graduate student at Oxford, he thought he wanted to be a journalist like his father, an NBC correspondent. But during the 1960s he ended up in government, working as an aide in the U.S. Justice Department for ten years. Later he became a hotshot in the Carter administration, serving as its youngest assistant secretary with a top job at the Department of Transportation. His time in Washington wasn't infused with great idealism. "During my seventeen years in government I had one motivation," he said, "which was to have a successful career and have enough money to send my kids to college."

Scott eventually came to see that he would never make much money in government, so he embarked on a midlife career switch, going into the high-tech sector and moving to Silicon Valley. He worked for a number of companies, including Computer Consoles, Inc., Pyramid Technology, and Sun Microsystems. "My goal was one thing: make money. That's all I thought about," said Scott. "I was just like everybody else: I was interested in going to work, getting the stock options, and getting the big hit. If anyone had told me to care about something else, I would have said, "Get out of my face. You're crazy.'"

Scott finally had his chance at a major hit when he cofounded a company called BEA Systems with two other former Sun employees. The company was created by purchasing two firms that sold a software system called Tuxedo, which was used in large computer networks. The company raised $50 million in venture capital and used it to buy several other similar Tuxedo-based systems. Soon business was booming, as BEA became a leader in "middleware" programs that allowed different kinds of machines and databases to talk to one another. In 1998, BEA made a huge purchase when it acquired a San Francisco start-up called WebLogic. It moved aggressively in capturing large contracts to build the infrastructure for e-commerce systems, for companies like Amazon. From there, BEA grew by leaps and bounds, adding offices around the world. Scott focused on the sales and the deal-making side of the business, spending a lot of time on airplanes and helping build BEA into one of the top fifteen software companies globally. By 2001, BEA had three thousand employees, offices around the world, and annual revenues greater than $1 billion. (The company would later be acquired by Oracle for $8.5 billion.) Ed Scott was finally rich.

There were other hits in addition to BEA. Scott used some of his winnings from BEA to become one of the earliest and largest investors in StubHub, an Internet ticketing company. StubHub took off and, in 2007, would be acquired by eBay for $310 million. "I made more money, way more, than I ever thought I'd make in my wildest dreams," Scott said. "I was set."

Scott didn't have a voracious appetite for personal spending and extravagant living. He wasn't like his BEA co-founder, Alfred Chuang, who had a thing for Ferraris and collected a dozen of the cars. "I realized that unless you're a very greedy person, you can't actually spend more than ten or fifteen million dollars on yourself." And Scott had way more than that. "Some people, like Warren Buffett, aim to make a bigger and bigger pile," Scott said. "And I gave some thought to that." But this path held little interest to him. So, what to do with his large new fortune?

For personal reasons, Scott got interested in orphanages in Central America and supported several of them. He became a donor to Compassion International, which helps poor and sick children worldwide. "I started to do some discreet things," he said. "And as I did those things, they gave me satisfaction."

His early philanthropic giving also opened his eyes to the miseries of developing countries. "When I was in the business world, I had tunnel vision," he would say later. "I only cared about the company being successful and nothing else. A nuclear weapon could have landed in Kansas City, and I wouldn't have noticed it. Once I left the business, I had to reeducate myself about the state of the world."

In 2000, Scott was watching television when he came upon a documentary on the progressive news channel LinkTV titled *Deadly*

Embrace: Nicaragua, the World Bank and the International Monetary Fund. Because of his interest in Central America, he stopped and watched, finding himself fascinated in a macabre sort of way. He had had no idea that "structural adjustment" had been such a disaster in Nicaragua, helping to explain that country's grinding poverty. "I became interested in debt as a systemic issue, and I began to read more about it."[1]

Scott could see that the crippling foreign debt burdens of poor countries stood as one of the greatest obstacles to their development. And yet when he tried to donate money to an organization dedicated to debt forgiveness, he found that none existed. He also saw a vacuum of expert policy analysis and advocacy on other issues related to global poverty.

Scott made his fortune in Silicon Valley by identifying unmet needs in the marketplace and moving aggressively into these breaches. Now, as he got interested in global development issues, he brought to bear that same kind of strategic thinking. He quickly recognized that individual projects, such as building orphanages or drilling wells, had limited impact and that the only way to make big changes was to redirect the policies of the world's richest countries. This kind of work is done by think tanks and advocacy groups, and Scott decided to put money into such endeavors. Serious money.

In 2001, Scott gave $10 million to start the Center for Global Development, a Washington-based think tank "dedicated to reducing global poverty and inequality and to making globalization work for the poor." The Center quickly became the premier U.S. think tank working on development issues and landed big donations from the Gates Foundation, which gave the Center $10 million in 2006.

"It wasn't like getting a bolt from God," Scott said of his philanthropic career. Rather, it was like any interest that grew rapidly. "The more you get into it, the more you get involved. It totally snowballed."

Scott read everything he could get his hands on and talked to everyone he could. He went from not knowing much about development to becoming "the most well-informed layman you'll find," someone who can hold his own at international conferences. "I just became consumed by it," he said.

It wasn't only an abstract interest. The more he learned about global poverty and health issues, the more he felt a huge sense of responsibility to use his wealth to save lives. "I have a deep-seated conviction that people who have the wherewithal to make a difference have an obligation to do so," he said.

In 2002, Scott helped create DATA, which stands for debt, AIDS, trade, and Africa. The Gates Foundation and Soros were other major funders of DATA, which was founded by Bono and Kennedy heir Bobby Shriver (whose father had created the Peace Corps), along with organizers from Jubilee 2000, a group that called for cancellation of Third World debt. DATA took the same stand on debt, although it mainly focused on the problem of AIDS. DATA later merged with ONE Campaign, a grassroots global antipoverty campaign that was also created by Bono and Shriver. Gates, who often complains that Americans lack awareness of global suffering, clearly saw the benefit of trying to enlist ordinary people in the fight against poverty. In 2004, he put $3 million into the ONE Campaign. During the 2008 election, ONE created ONE Vote '08, aimed at pressuring U.S. presidential candidates to focus more attention on global poverty and disease.

Scott's latest venture is the Center for Interfaith Action on Global Poverty, which he founded in 2008 to help mobilize faith communities behind efforts to help poor countries. And who better to help in this endeavor than yet another wealthy and good-looking Kennedy relative, Tim Shriver, who joined CIFA as its first president?

"All four of the outfits I've funded have the same thing in common," Scott said. "They focus on the behavior of the rich countries in how they deal with poor countries. So the whole concept is leverage—trying to make major, major things happen."

The ranks of wealthy people who want to save the world have been growing fast in recent years, as more people like Scott have cashed out of business and turned to other pursuits. Scott is older than guys like Tim Gill and David Bohnett, but he is part of the same wave of wealth that has been cascading into politics and policy.

Scott is not atypical in the way he came cold into big-time philanthropy, particularly in the international area. Other donors have been just like Scott—people who spent every waking hour building their companies and paying attention to little else. Then one day they find themselves with crazy amounts of money—more than they could possibly spend on themselves—and have to figure out "something useful to do with it," as Scott described the dilemma. It doesn't take much homework to see that helping the poorest of the world's poor offers the most bang for the buck in terms of bettering the human condition. That calculus resonates with people who've spent their lives thinking about return on investment and other concepts of leverage. The other attraction here is the scope of global problems: they are big and daunting but seemingly tractable if the right points of leverage can be found.

Scott is focused on changing policy in rich countries, but other wealthy technologists—such as Greg Carr—are trying out innovative approaches at a more local level. Carr is an interesting figure. After getting a master's in public policy from Harvard University's Kennedy School, Carr made a fortune by selling voice mail services to phone companies. Later, he was chair of Prodigy, an early Internet provider, and sold his stock in the company in 1999, before the dot-com crash. He ended up with more than $200 million.

Carr grew up in Idaho and went to college in Utah. He got his graduate education and built his fortune in Cambridge, one of the most liberal places in the United States. From his base there, he traveled abroad often and became interested in Africa. In 1995, he cofounded a company called Africa Online that aimed to bring Internet service to developing countries.

In 1999, Carr gave Harvard $18 million to establish the Carr Center for Human Rights Policy at Harvard University. He dates his interest in human rights back to college, where he majored in history. "The idea that every human on earth should have basic human rights—I became really excited about that idea," he would say later.[2] Under its founding director, Samantha Power, the Carr

Center quickly emerged as an influential advocate of a moralistic approach to foreign policy, one that places human rights and the rule of international law at the core of America's engagement with the world. Thinkers associated with the Carr Center were loud and persistent critics of U.S. policy during the Bush years. Carr himself was appalled by the administration's arrogance and gave $10,000 to John Kerry's presidential bid. (Carr also attracted attention when he bought the former Aryan Nation headquarters in his home state of Idaho and turned it into a memorial to Anne Frank. Like other rich liberals, he's made something of a project of turning around the politics of his home state.)

Carr saw the Carr Center as fighting for the principles of a more just world and a more enlightened foreign policy. But he also thought in more immediate ways about how to improve the world with his wealth. In 2000, he became focused on Mozambique after meeting that country's UN ambassador. Mozambique ranks among the poorest nations in the world. Half of its population is under the age of fifteen, and life expectancy is slightly longer than forty years. Every year, in this country of 21 million, 110,000 people die of AIDS. The government's budget is around $3 billion a year. But Mozambique also has tremendous assets, such as spectacular natural scenery and a democratic government.

Carr became fascinated by the challenge of turning Mozambique into a successful country, and—after many consultations—he judged that tourism held the key to its economic future, and ecotourism in particular. In 2005, he pledged $40 million to help restore Gorongosa National Park, which had once been among the most spectacular wildlife preserves in Africa before it sank into decay and most of its animals were killed during long years of civil war. With Carr's funds, the great mammals that once inhabited the park, such as zebra, elephants, and wildebeests, are being reintroduced.

Carr's foundation is also spending money to help the villages around the park with new schools and health-care clinics. Already, the park is attracting more tourists to Mozambique. None of this constitutes a solution to Mozambique's manifold woes, but it is something— one area of one desperately poor country that now may have a chance.

Philip Berber thinks much the same way: pick a place and make a difference. Berber is another high-tech entrepreneur who hit the jackpot and is using his money to help a poor country in Africa—in his case, Ethiopia. Berber got rich by starting an online trading company called CyBerCorp.com, which he sold after only a few years—and right before the dot-com crash—to Charles Schwab for $488 million. (He owned half of the company when it was sold.) He lives in Austin and is a regulator contributor to Democratic politicians.

Like Ed Scott, Berber is someone who made a huge amount of money but is not interested in outsized luxury living. In fact, the amount and suddenness of his wealth proved disconcerting to him and his wife, Donna. After an initial feeling of elation, they became anxious from all of the calls and the attention. "We had to change our phone number and get a security system in," Donna recalled. "My biggest fear was that my children would be taken for ransom." Donna's impulse was to get rid of their wealth. "I wanted to give the money away, I wanted to call the media and announce that we were giving it all away." Berber felt similarly. "I have never been attached to money and felt that there was a higher purpose to wealth."[3]

Their focus on Ethiopia emerged because many years earlier, in 1984, Donna Berber had seen searing images on television of children starving in that country during a famine. The image stuck with her. "The calling to do something and make a difference, it was always there," she would recall. "If anything it got louder and louder as my life got quieter and quieter and more comfortable."[4]

Even before Philip sold his company, Donna had visited the Ethiopian embassy in Washington in 1999 and offered to spend $150,000 on an orphanage. The ambassador suggested that she go to Ethiopia first, and she followed his advice. During her first night in Ethiopia, she was distraught by the intense poverty she saw as she rode in from the Addis Ababa airport. She hit the street that same night, distributing blankets and food.

Back in the United States, Donna set in motion a series of activities that eventually would lead the Berbers to create their own foundation—Glimmer of Hope—staffed by Ethiopian development specialists. In plunging into this work, Philip Berber was heavily influenced by a book given to them by their lead Ethiopian adviser, *Lords of Poverty: The Power, Prestige, and Corruption of the International Aid Business*, by Graham Hancock. "It was a pretty damning account of how little of the money was getting to the people in need," Berber said. "People should get locked up for the waste in the international aid business."

The Berbers made an initial commitment of $100 million to their foundation, which takes an integrated approach to combating poverty: funding wells and sanitation, health clinics and schools, and also micro-finance and irrigation. Since 2000, it has drilled more than 1,500 wells, built nearly 200 schools, and created more than 100 health clinics. These projects have benefited more than a million people, mostly the rural poor, and Berber claims they have cost half as much as projects by large aid organizations. This, again, is an example of how entrepreneurs think: it's not enough for them to help people; they also want to find new efficiencies and revolutionize the marketplace. And, of course, there is the relentless focus on leverage. The Berbers' latest venture is a micro-finance project, in partnership with the Clinton Global Initiative, which will provide $2 million in capital for small loans to poor Ethiopians. This effort, said Berber, is about establishing sustainable forms of wealth creation through access to credit.

The Berbers have sunk nearly half of their wealth into the foundation, and most of the rest may eventually follow. Philip Berber is contemptuous of the mega-rich who sit on the sidelines, even as millions of people die needlessly every year. "There are many, many wealthy people, wealthier than us, that choose not to look into their own hearts, who are stuck in a place of fear, fear of losing their money," he said.[5]

Most Americans live in a bubble when it comes to global poverty. We are aware in general terms that a good slice of humanity endures hellish conditions, beset by disease and filth—that some two billion people don't even have basic sanitation—but this knowledge is abstract. We typically haven't seen such poverty firsthand and, anyway, have limited power to change the way things are.

Even people who do have the power to make change don't use it, as Berber points out. But what's interesting is just how fierce the humanitarian imperative can become once the rich take a few initial steps. They can get consumed by what is surely the most profound sense of hyperagency that exists: the ability to save human lives. That's what happened to Ed Scott and the Berbers. It's also what happened to Bill Gates.

Gates imagined that he wouldn't get involved in philanthropy until his fifties or sixties. He moved that timetable up when he started to learn about world health. In 1993, he read the World Bank's annual *World Development Report* on global health, with its mind-numbing statistics about the routine mass deaths in poor countries caused by diseases that, in many cases, could be easily and cheaply prevented. He found the report disturbing and fascinating. "I was, really, like a lot of people, not paying much attention to the conditions in the world at large," he said later. "It was, I think, some-what of a surprise for me to realize how urgent these issues were, and I said to myself, okay I don't want to wait until I'm in my 60s to address things—particularly things that are epidemic, like AIDS, where if you catch it early, the interventions are very dramatic, ver-sus waiting until it's widespread."[6]

At first glance, the vast investments of the Gates Foundation in poor countries do not seem to reflect an ideological agenda. This giv-ing—which totaled more than $2 billion in 2009 and will grow larger as Warren Buffett's money flows in—is focused on specific chal-lenges, such as eradicating malaria and polio and finding a vaccine for AIDS. It seems pragmatic, rather than political, and Gates has often talked in an amazed way about how many lives can be saved with the right investments. "There are thirty million children a year who don't get vaccines," he said at Davos in 2002. "There's a cer-tain amount of money that would cause them to get those vaccines and that would save three million lives a year. Three million lives a year."[7] When Gates made an early grant of $50 million in the 1990s to combat malaria, he was told that he had just increased the amount of money going into malaria research by 50 percent. "And I said, 'That is the most horrific thing I've ever heard. How can that be true?'"[8]

Horrific, yes. But also motivating: Gates realized early on that his wealth had the potential to transform the entire field of global health. And it was here, the most urgent problems of life and death facing poor countries, where he and his wife, Melinda, decided to focus most intensely. Gates would often describe these problems as "market failures," where capitalism falls short because there are no financial incentives to address the health needs of the world's poor. But his foundation has not been out attacking the World Trade Organization or castigating multinational corporations. Although Gates has funded attacks on the way that structural adjustment has imposed crippling misery on indebted poor countries, along with contributing money toward efforts to reform global financial institutions such as the World Bank, he has otherwise not sided with the antiglobalization crowd.

Yet make no mistake: Bill Gates is practicing a radical moralism. The core idea of the Gates Foundation, one that it repeatedly articulates, is that "every life has equal value." Although this may sound innocuous enough, like a throwaway line in a brochure, it is actually at odds with the organizing principle of the nation-state, which is that some human beings—that is, citizens—should get special treatment and protections and others should be excluded from these benefits. Certainly it is at odds with U.S. foreign policy, which has mainly focused on promoting the national interest. It is hard to imagine a U.S. politician—at least, one with any ambition—arguing that "every life has equal value." That is an idea more typically associated with, say, Jesuits than Washington policy makers, and it remains well outside the mainstream, in the lefty world of idealistic dreamers. Yet this is the axiom guiding Gates and now also Buffett, who have harnessed the greatest fortunes of our time to help the poorest people on the planet.

When Gates started with his giving, he said, "I was stunned to find that only about two percent of the philanthropy in the United States has to do with taking resources from the richest country and making them available to the poorest countries." He was stunned because it seemed self-evident to him that this was the right way to distribute charitable resources.[9] "People might ask why I am doing philanthropy that is largely targeting poor countries of the world," Gates said in 2000. "Many of the foundations around the world primarily target the same rich country where the wealth was earned, and although I have no dispute with that—I think it's fine—I think the balance ought to weigh more heavily in favor of the true inequities that exists on a fairly global basis."[10]

Gates isn't alone in this outlook. His brand of one-world moralism is spreading fast in the most rarefied reaches of the upper class. And the force of his example has a lot to with this. Since Gates began to ramp up his giving, the topics of global health and poverty have gone from the margins of elite conversation to its center.

Just look at Davos, where Gates has been a fixture for years. It used to be—before Angelina Jolie showed up—that the World Economic Forum was a venue for neoliberal scheming by business and government leaders. The antiglobalization left so demonized Davos that it repeatedly tried to shut the forum down with protests and created its own global conference, the World Social Forum, to counter Davos's insidious influence.

A funny thing has happened in the last few years, however: Davos is no longer simply a pep rally for global capitalism; it is now also a pep rally for global humanitarianism. Celebrity do-gooders get nearly as much air time at Davos as CEOs and finance ministers do, and many of the forum's ongoing initiatives are focused on issues such as climate change and "sustainable food production." The 2008 meeting featured a number of sessions that could have been held at the World Social Forum. There was a session with Al Gore and Bono on how to merge efforts on climate change and antipoverty work; a panel on the world's water crisis with the UN secretary general and a leader of a top U.S. environmental group; and a conversation cochaired by Emma Thompson that featured six young activists from around the world discussing global problems. There was also a forum on food security and even a discussion led by celebrity chef—and super–Bay Area liberal—Alice Waters on the local food movement.

Gates was also there and used the 2008 meeting to deliver his speech on "creative capitalism," where he proclaimed that the global market economy had failed the world's very poor. A day later, he appeared onstage with other high-profile participants, including Bono, holding a huge banner that called for swifter action to achieve the Millennium Development Goals by lifting more Africans out of extreme poverty, vaccinating more children, and so on. Such spectacles have become pretty common at Davos.

It can be tempting to dismiss people such as Greg Carr and Philip Berber, or even Bill Gates, as Band-Aid providers who aren't tackling the deep structural inequities of the global economy. Humanitarian efforts often don't address the crux of the problem, as identified by Ted Turner, which is that "ten percent of the people have ninety percent of everything."

In fact, though, these donors are working on the deeper inequities, too. The push for debt relief, which has been backed by Gates and Ed Scott to the tune of millions of dollars, has had a huge effect by helping to elevate this issue on the global agenda and also within rich countries. It used to be that canceling Third World debt was a left-wing dream that the *Nation* mused about in Utopian-sounding editorials. Not anymore. Thanks partly to big checks from rich donors, this cause has become mainstream. One of the single largest gifts by the Berbers was $600,000 to the ONE Campaign, which has helped achieve real results on the debt issue. In 2005, leaders of the G-8 countries adopted the Multi-Lateral Debt Relief Initiative, which built on previous efforts to offer 100 percent debt cancellations to the most impoverished countries of the world, based on various conditions. The ONE Campaign has estimated that debt relief is allowing poor countries to redirect $14 billion annually to antipoverty efforts. That is serious money.

It is hard to think about today's global crusaders without comparing them to those of previous eras. But if Gates is a modern-day Rockefeller, who would be the equivalent to Andrew Carnegie, a leading one-worlder who used his fortune to push far-reaching plans for world peace?

The answer is Ted Turner, perhaps the most underrated philanthropist of recent times. Turner came to peace work in the 1980s, a time when many of the wealthy became worried about the cold war and the arms race. He had a quixotic outlook on global affairs, not unlike Carnegie's. At the launch of CNN, in 1980, Turner told reporters that he hoped the network would help bring about world peace. "I'm going to travel around to every foreign country and get the head of the country to show me things he's proudest of about his country. And send it all back by satellite," Turner said. Although that never happened, something else did, which was the "democratization of information," in Turner's words. "For the first time in the history of the world, every world leader, and everybody in the world, had access to the same information at the same time."[11] *Time* magazine would call Turner the "Prince of the Global Village" in naming him Man of the Year in 1991.

In 1985, Turner tapped his cable television fortune to create the Better World Fund, which supported the production of liberal documentaries. These included *Are We Winning, Mommy?* a film sharply critical of U.S. cold war policies, and *Chico Mendes: Voice of the Amazon*, an early exposé of the destruction of the world's largest rain forest. Turner—who once said that every time he sees a Vietnamese person, "I apologize for what we did to their country"—also put on the Goodwill Games in 1986 in an idealistic effort to defuse the cold war with an athletic contest in Moscow after two successive Olympics that either the United States or the Soviet Union had boycotted.[12]

After the end of the cold war, Turner focused his attention on environmental causes and started the Turner Foundation, which quickly emerged as one of the biggest funders of activist groups working on climate change, rain forest preservation, and other issues. Turner's biggest move was his $1 billion gift to support the United Nations, which he announced in September 1997. At the time, it was the largest single donation ever made by an individual, and it was dedicated to an organization that many Americans distrusted. To conservatives and "black helicopter" conspiracy theorists, the UN was a sinister force with an agenda that would curb U.S. sovereignty. One of the ten legislative priorities of the Contract with America was to bar U.S. troops from serving under UN command. (Never mind that the United States has veto power over any military actions by the UN.)

To centrists, the UN was an organization of declining relevance and marginal competence in a world shaped by market forces and U.S. power. At the time of Turner's gift, the United States owed more than $1 billion to the UN—a debt it showed no signs of paying.

The idea that one of America's richest business leaders would choose the United Nations as a focal point for large-scale philanthropy was nearly beyond most people's imagination, and Turner's move was greeted with amazement. *Weird* was among the adjectives chosen to describe the gift by Leslie Gelb, the president of the Council on Foreign Relations.[13] The UN's right-wing detractors employed far harsher language about the gift. Turner explained it all with a shrug, saying he was a long-standing fan of the UN: "I always liked the idea—one for all, all for one." He noted that in August 1997, he had discovered that his net worth had grown by $1 billion in only nine months, to $3.2 billion, as his Time Warner stock soared in value. "So I figure it's only nine months' earnings, who cares?" A few months earlier, Turner had castigated his fellow billionaires for not giving away enough money. "What good is wealth sitting in the bank?" Turner asked at the annual meeting of the Boys and Girls Clubs of America. "It's a pretty pathetic thing to do with your money."

A few years after the UN gift, Turner focused his attention on nuclear weapons and pledged $250 million in creating the Nuclear Threat Initiative. The initiative works to reduce the spread of weapons of mass destruction and also the risk that such weapons might be used. Turner's ultimate goal is to see a world where nuclear weapons are abolished. In his wallet, he carries around Article Six of the 1968 Nuclear Nonproliferation Treaty, the part that commits all parties to eventually move to "general and complete disarmament."

Turner was a strong critic of the invasion of Iraq. "I believe if you go around looking for enemies you'll find them," he wrote in his autobiography, "but if you go out looking for friends you'll find them, too. The United States has so much to offer other countries besides our military might. Instead of sending bombs and missiles to Iraq we'd have been better served by sending doctors, nurses, and teachers."[14]

Back in the 1960s, when he was a conservative Republican running a billboard company built by his father in the South, Turner recalled that he had a "my country, right or wrong" mentality. He disapproved of antiwar protesters, including his future wife Jane Fonda.

All of that changed over time as his wealth grew and he became more deeply immersed in international affairs through CNN. This is a common trajectory for business leaders when they start to operate internationally. And with globalization, more U.S. businesses have a global dimension. Like so many of the rich who now deal daily with the complexities of an interdependent world, Turner came to shed anything that might resemble a traditionalist kind of patriotism. The fact that this outlook remains a centerpiece of the conservative movement is yet one more reason the cosmopolitan rich are fleeing the Republican Party.

By the time Turner was seventy, in the twilight of a long and eventful life, he had nearly fulfilled his commitment to the United Nations and was on his way to doing the same with the Nuclear Threat Initiative.

From the waning days of the Vietnam War until the end of the cold war, the Democratic Party stood clearly to the left of Republicans on issues such as military intervention, human rights, and nuclear disarmament. Wealthy liberals were instrumental in helping to move the Democrats in this direction. For instance, G.M. heir Stewart Rawlings Mott was one of the main financiers of Eugene McCarthy's antiwar candidacy in 1968 and the single largest donor to George McGovern's 1972 campaign. Mott also bankrolled the Project on Military Procurement, as well as the Center for Defense Information, both of which provided ideas for the party's liberal wing. During the 1980s, wealthy donors pushed the Democrats to take liberal stands on the nuclear freeze and Central America.

That clarity is largely gone. Although the Iraq war highlighted sharp differences between the parties, today's Democratic leaders are largely centrist on matters of war and peace, and the two parties are reasonably close on many issues. This is one reason Barack Obama could ask Bush's secretary of defense, Robert Gates, to stay on with barely a murmur of dissent among top Democrats. Bipartisanship has also generally prevailed on one of the biggest hot buttons of the last fifteen years: trade and globalization.

The left wing of the Democratic Party has been anything but inert on foreign affairs, as witnessed by the mobilization against Bush war policies by groups such as MoveOn.org and the Center for American Progress. But the left has lacked big ideas or a grand vision on international policy.

That may now be changing, and—as in the past—liberal money is one reason. Rich one-world moralists are growing more numerous and influential, and they have by far the most compelling alternative vision for U.S. leadership in the world: the belief that this country should lead a great crusade against needless deaths and intolerable poverty in the world's poorest places. Through new think tanks and advocacy groups, rich one-worlders are pushing to recalibrate America's global priorities along these lines. They speak for a small but vocal slice of the U.S. public, and their efforts have begun to move issues such as AIDS, Africa, and women's rights higher on the foreign policy agenda. (At least on paper, Obama has pledged billions more in development aid.)

This is inspiring stuff, and when the United States finally extricates itself from Iraq and Afghanistan, the meta issue of how to reduce vast human suffering worldwide could come to occupy a central place in foreign policy debates. Other big moral ideas, such as the abolition of nuclear weapons, could also get more serious attention. (Obama has embraced this goal, too.)

If the Democrats do move toward one-world moralism, however, get ready for trouble. The Clinton administration's baby steps in this direction during the 1990s, such as its intervention in Haiti, triggered a major backlash from the Republican right. The administration also got zinged by centrist Democrats who derided its foreign policy as "social work."

A bold new humanitarianism could draw the same kind of fire, while costing Democrats support among ordinary Americans who want a greater focus on problems at home. Foreign aid has never been popular with the public at large, and internationalism more broadly tends to be viewed with suspicion. Increasingly, for instance, the public has come to view America's commitment to free trade as a one-way street.

Democrats have been down this path before: their siding with more affluent liberals on foreign policy starting in the late 1960s is one reason they ended up as a minority party. Avoiding a redux means finding ways to convince lower-income Americans that good deeds abroad won't mean hard choices at home. One way to do this is to get serious about dealing with the downsides of globalization, so that workers who lose their jobs due to global trade get real help. If Democrats can show that economic internationalism needn't be a raw deal for the working class, it will be easier to sell other kinds of internationalism—such as a new U.S. humanitarian leadership—and put to rest fears that elites don't really care about America.

6

"Please Raise My Taxes"

W HEN MARIO PROCACCINO first sneered the phrase "limousine liberal" in his 1969 race for New York mayor against John Lindsay, he conjured up an acid image of hypocritical wealthy do-gooders insulated from the negative fallout of their bad ideas. This theme has remained a staple of conservative attacks ever since. Most recently, in his best-selling book *Do As I Say (Not As I Do): Profiles in Liberal Hypocrisy*, author Peter Schweizer berated various wealthy liberals for alleged contradictions between their stated ideals and their personal behavior.

And yet on an issue that hits closer to home than perhaps any other—taxes—rich liberals have often been ready to live their beliefs. That commitment has come across strongly not only in the generous financial support that Barack Obama received from some of the super-wealthy people he promised to tax most heavily, but also in the battles over President Bush's tax cuts that began in 2001. And it's come through clearly in the tax hikes advocated by numerous wealthy Democratic politicians.

Battles over tax policy are often imagined to be a pure form of class warfare, with the wealthy unified in a ceaseless quest to keep their taxes low, chisel new holes in the tax code, and push the burden of funding government onto the rest of us. Former *New York Times* reporter David Cay Johnston has painted a disturbing picture of a plutocratic cabal working to rig the tax system to benefit a tiny slice of America's wealthiest households and "cheat everybody else." His books have been best-sellers in part because they resonate instinctually with what so many Americans believe. Polls have consistently found that a large majority of the public thinks that the rich don't pay their fair share of taxes and that tax laws favor the upper class. It seems logical that if the tax system is rigged to help the wealthy, it is the wealthy themselves who have rigged it.[1]

As well they have. Less obvious, though, is another truth: that the wealthy are deeply divided on taxes, and the battle within the far upper class over what constitutes a fair tax code has at times been as fierce as the battle between income groups. It is a complex contest. The charges leveled at the rich by Johnston and other critics are all too true—some of America's wealthiest individuals really have led a concerted, and often deviously dishonest, attack on progressive taxation. That attack has been under way for more than three decades, it has been extremely well funded, and it has been very successful. The lower tax rates for the rich ushered in by Ronald Reagan saved the top 1 percent of U.S. households trillions of dollars in taxes between 1981 and 2009. All of the revenue lost due to these cuts was replaced by borrowed money—a lasting legacy to future generations.

Polls show that the affluent, on average, are more likely to oppose tax hikes than any other group is. But not everyone in the upper class shares this view. Far from it; many have supported higher taxes on their class. At times, such as in the estate tax fight, these individuals have operated well to the left of public opinion and have intervened decisively to defend tax fairness.

Why some wealthy Americans embrace progressive taxation and others fight such taxes with extraordinary venom explains much about the growing fissures in the upper class—fissures that, in turn, reflect growing changes in who the rich are and how they make their fortunes.

• • •

When Barack Obama addressed the 2004 Democratic Convention, one of the millions of people captivated by the speech was Warren Buffett. After the election, Susan Buffett—Warren's daughter—suggested that they have lunch with Obama, and the senator-elect flew to Omaha for the meeting. That meal opened important doors for Obama as he contemplated his run for the presidency. Buffett soon arranged for Obama to have dinner with his good friend Bill Gates and also invited Obama back to Omaha in November 2005 for a small fund-raiser. It was an unusual move for Buffett, America's second-richest person, who seldom gets closely involved with political campaigns. But, as Buffett told a reporter, "I've got a conviction about him that I don't get very often. . . . He has as much potential as anyone I've seen to have an important impact over his lifetime."[2]

Two years later, with his campaign in full swing, Obama was back in Omaha for another fund-raiser hosted by Buffett. In introducing Obama, Buffett said approvingly that "Barack is here to increase the abundance, but to spread it around a little more so that it is inclusive prosperity." In turn, Obama said that he was getting a lot of advice, but "Warren Buffett is one of those people that I listen to."[3]

Buffett's backing for Obama provided crucial credibility as the candidate sought to expand his backing among the wealthy, and particularly in the financial community. Buffett also helped provide cover for Obama—and perhaps embolden him—in calling for tax hikes on the rich. In *The Audacity of Hope*, Obama wrote that Buffett believed that raising taxes would have no negative effect on economic growth and was the right thing to do. As Obama told the *New York Times* at one point, "If you talk to Warren, he'll tell you his preference is not to meddle in the economy at all—let the market work, however way it's going to work, and then just tax the heck out of people at the end and redistribute it."

This was an unusual specter in recent U.S. politics: one of the most liberal members of the Senate citing the nation's wealthiest and most respected investor to support his case for a tax increase. Yet to anyone following Buffett's statements on taxes, it was not at all surprising. The richer Buffett has gotten, it seems, the more liberal he has become on tax policy.

Buffett began to speak out on taxes in response to Bush policies that slashed rates for the wealthiest citizens. Although he was silent on Bush's first tax cut, in 2001, he was sharply critical of 2003 legislation that cut taxes on capital gains and mainly benefited the wealthiest of the wealthy. "If enacted, these changes would further tilt the tax scales toward the rich," Buffett wrote in a *Washington Post* op-ed, a week after the Senate passed the tax cut. Buffett then went on to compare his tax rate under the plan to that of his receptionist, pointing out that her effective tax rate would be ten times greater than his. Indeed, Buffett said that even without the new tax cut, he paid a lower tax rate than his receptionist did because much of his income came from capital gains—which were already taxed at a lower rate than regular earnings were. Buffett argued that if Congress were serious about stimulating the economy, it should focus on giving tax breaks to ordinary Americans who actually needed the money and would spend it.[4]

Buffett's op-ed sparked a backlash from predictable quarters. Steve Forbes suggested that Buffett's opinion was the result of "guilt" and "misunderstanding," while Republican senator Chuck Grassley argued that the tax bill really would help typical middle-class families and that Buffett failed to appreciate this benefit. Grassley—who himself was worth an estimated $2 million to $4 million—said, "Warren Buffett is one of the richest men in the world and can't have any appreciation for middle-class Americans, for a husband and a wife who work to put food on the table." Of course, though, the raw deal these families were getting was exactly Buffett's point and one confirmed by most analyses of the tax plan. A May 2003 study by the Center for Budget and Policy Priorities, for instance, charged that Grassley and other Republicans used misleading data to describe the effects of the tax cuts. In truth, the study found, "the new law will provide an average tax cut in 2003 of $93,500 to tax filers who make more than $1 million per year. In contrast, most households will get a small tax cut or no tax cut at all."[5]

Buffett's comparison of the taxes paid by himself and his receptionist was a vivid, memorable critique of the shameful way that the tax code had grown twisted to serve the super-wealthy, and it quickly emerged as a staple image in the tax wars. This simple point, offered by a mega-billionaire known for his common sense, resonated in a way that innumerable other critiques of Bush tax policies did not, turning Buffett—incongruously—into one of the nation's most effective proponents of progressive taxation.

Buffett kept up the attack, too. Later in the same year, he pointed out that the property taxes on his $4 million Laguna Beach home in California were $2,200, while those on his $500,000 home in Omaha were $14,000, and that he was paying lower taxes on the Laguna Beach house than were homeowners in California who had more recently bought houses worth just a fraction of the price. Then, in his 2004 letter to Berkshire Hathaway shareholders, Buffett decried the erosion of corporate taxes and wrote, "If class warfare is being waged in America, my class is clearly winning."[6]

Buffett returned often to the example of his receptionist, crunching numbers to compare their taxes in 2006. Buffett found that he was taxed at a rate of 17.7 percent on $46 million of income that year, while his receptionist, who earned $60,000, paid an effective rate of 30 percent when payroll taxes were factored in. In the face of pushback from critics who said that his analysis had to be wrong and even that he was going senile, Buffett said that he would donate $1 million to the charity of choice of any member of the Forbes 400 list if any of those fellow billionaires could show that they paid a higher tax rate than their secretaries paid. The comparison became something of a fixation for him. "Frankly, an economy where my receptionist pays a lot higher tax rate than I do does not strike me as a just economy," Buffett told members of the Senate Finance Committee in 2007.[7] In an NBC interview with Tom Brokaw the same year, Buffett said, "The taxation system has tilted toward the rich and away from the middle class in the last ten years. . . . It's dramatic, and I don't think it's appreciated. And I think it should be addressed."

Buffett made the same pitch at a June 2007 New York fund-raiser for Hillary Clinton before an audience that included more than five hundred Wall Street bankers and money managers. In another era, say, in the 1980s, Buffett's populist appeal—which also mentioned the unfair tax burden on janitors "who clean our offices" and specifically attacked the low tax rate for hedge fund managers—might have met with stony silence from this group. Instead, his points on tax justice elicited loud applause.

"Why are you a Democrat?" Hillary Clinton asked Buffett at the end of the event. Buffett's reply was simple: because the Democrats do a better job of leveling out the playing field for those who have drawn the unlucky tickets in life.[8]

Warren Buffett wasn't the only super-wealthy business leader who publicly supported Obama's plan to raise taxes on the rich. Other billionaires chimed in, as well—such as Thomas Steyer, the California hedge fund king, who told *Fortune*, "The taxes proposed by Obama seem completely consistent with the idea we would actually do something together as opposed to scratching out the most for ourselves as individuals."[9] Obama also received the backing of Google CEO Eric Schmidt, who joined him on the campaign trail and defended his economic policies. Schmidt, who was worth more than $5 billion in 2008, echoed Buffett's point that raising taxes on the wealthy wouldn't have a negative effect on the economy. Another billionaire, Black Entertainment Television founder Robert Johnson, told Fox News that he, for one, wasn't worried about higher taxes: "I mean, people like myself, who can afford to pay more, we are willing to pay more if we know we're getting good management of that investment." What Obama was saying, Johnson said, is that "in order for us to get the country moving again, you have got to have a tax base that is progressive, a tax base that is focused on those who can afford to pay, and then the money is invested in a very smart and prudent way to help those who are in need."[10]

A week after Obama's election, he received yet more billionaire backing for his plan to raise taxes on the rich—this time from individuals who faced a larger tax hike than perhaps anyone else in the United States. During testimony on the financial crisis before a congressional committee, five of the nation's best-paid hedge fund managers—men who had earned between $1.5 and $3.7 billion during 2007—were asked whether they would support taxing carried interest at regular income rates, not at the capital gains rate. This would mean that the hefty management fees earned by hedge fund managers, which were typically 20 percent of returns, would be taxed at more than twice the current rate—a move that would have cost each of the men tens of millions of dollars in 2007. Four out of five of the hedge fund managers— George Soros, John Paulson, Philip Falcone, and James Simons—said they would support such a tax. Only one, Kenneth Griffin, demurred. Watching this episode, the veteran financial observer and *New York Times* reporter Joe Nocera wrote, "I almost fell out of my chair."[11]

Nocera shouldn't have been so surprised, given the large contributions hedge fund managers made to Obama even as proposed exactly this kind of tax hike. The one naysayer of the group, Kenneth Griffin, had himself contributed heavily to Obama.

Once Obama got into the White House, it was inevitable that many of his donors would push to water down his tax pledges. And, in fact, the Obama team quickly announced that it would let the Bush tax cuts lapse in 2011, rather than immediately repeal them, which meant a huge financial windfall for high earners. Obama's full tax plan also went slightly easier on the rich than what he had promised on the campaign trail, proposing a tax burden on the top 1 percent that would be lower than during the Clinton years. Obama stuck with his pledge to close the carried interest loophole for hedge funds and private equity firms, but these groups promptly renewed their lobbying campaign to kill this idea.

At the same time, though, some of Obama's wealthy donors, such as the CEO of Netflix, Reed Hastings, pushed him to raise taxes on the rich even higher. Not long after Obama's inauguration, Hastings published a *New York Times* op-ed titled "Please Raise My Taxes." The article was prompted by proposals to cap executive pay at $500,000, which Hastings thought would have negative unintended consequences. Most CEOs agreed, and most would have left their objections there. But Hastings had another idea: Instead of capping executive pay, Obama should dramatically push up taxes on the super-rich. Hastings advocated going beyond the top bracket of 39.6 percent that Bill Clinton had enacted and called for a 50 percent top federal tax rate for incomes greater than $1 million a year. "Some will tell you that would reduce the incentive to earn," Hastings wrote, "but I don't see that as likely. Besides, half of a giant compensation package is still pretty huge, and most of our motivation is the sheer challenge of the job anyway. Instead of trying to shame companies and executives, the president should take advantage of our success by using our outsized earnings to pay for the needs of our nation."[12]

This suggestion was not surprising, coming from Hastings, who epitomizes today's rich progressives. Like many, he is a second-generation knowledge worker—his father was a big-time lawyer—who grew up in deep-blue America, around Boston. He went to private school in Cambridge; attended Bowdoin, an elite liberal arts college in Maine; spent two years in the Peace Corps; and then got a master's degree in computer science from Stanford. After making a fortune in software during the 1990s, Hastings decided that he wanted to do something important. He gravitated to the field of education and spent $1 million to back a 2000 ballot initiative in California that made it easier for localities to pass school bonds. He was appointed to the California Board of Education by Governor Gray Davis and became its president in 2001. At the same time, Hastings became a major donor to the Democratic Party, writing large checks to the DNC and contributing to statewide campaigns in California.

Like so many wealthy donors, Hastings gave money to elect Obama even as the Illinois senator made it crystal clear that he would raise taxes on the rich. Under Obama's tax plan, Hastings—whose salary was exactly $1 million in 2008 and who is also compensated in stock—faced a tax increase of at least $46,000 a year. Under his own plan, Hastings would see his taxes rise by $150,000 a year and probably much more than that.

The billionaire Edgar Bronfman Sr. chimed in with much the same message as Hastings not long after Obama's election. Bronfman had contributed heavily to the Obama campaign, and he was alarmed when the president-elect indicated that he wouldn't repeal the Bush taxes cuts on the rich immediately but rather would let them lapse in 2011. "Raise my taxes. And raise them now," Bronfman demanded in the Huffington Post. "For the past eight years the wealthy have gotten wealthier. Now it's our turn to pay the piper and help build a more moral America."[13]

In backing higher taxes on the rich, billionaires such as Buffett and Bronfman and CEOs like Hastings spoke for a highly influential segment of the wealth elite. Yet even if this segment seems to be growing, it would be wrong to imagine that the majority of the rich favored Obama's plan to tax them at a higher rate. In fact, this group was deeply divided on the issue of taxes. A survey of nearly five hundred affluent households by Prince and Associates in the fall of 2008 found that more than three-quarters of the voters worth $1 million to $10 million favored John McCain. Only 15 percent said they would vote for Obama. But the picture was nearly the reverse for voters worth more than $30 million, two-thirds of whom favored Obama.

Taxes were the main reason for this difference. Eighty-eight percent of the less affluent rich cited taxes as being an "important" issue, while only 16 percent of their wealthier counterparts said the same thing—instead ranking "social issues" as most important.[14] This disparity might suggest a variation on Senator Grassley's complaint about Buffett wanting to raise taxes: it's not that the super-rich like Buffett have so much money that they are indifferent to struggling middle-class families, but rather they are indifferent to struggling millionaires —those still hoping to afford a decent house in the Hamptons or buy a ski place in Aspen.

Another survey, also conducted during the 2008 presidential campaign, found that Obama-loving CEOs such as Schmidt did not speak for top executives as a whole, and certainly not on the issue of taxes.

The survey of 751 CEOs by *Chief Executive* magazine found that 80 percent supported McCain for president, and only 20 percent planned to vote for Obama. Asked to rate Obama and McCain on a range of issues, CEOs gave Obama an average grade of "D" on taxes—the lowest grade on any of the issues. Asked what the United States needed to do to create the "most high-paying jobs," 95 percent cited lowering taxes as a top priority.[15]

It might seem that anyone with a net worth that was greater than, say, $5 million would have a postmaterialist mind-set and not have a financial care in the world. But even before stock portfolios cratered, thanks to the crash of 2008, survey research found that the rich worried quite a bit about money. In one survey, taken in 2006, nearly half of the respondents—each with a net worth of at least $5 million—said they didn't yet feel economically secure.[16] In 2008, the *New York Times* profiled a number of multimillionaires in Silicon Valley—some with a net worth greater than $10 million—who felt that they had to keep working and earning to be as well off as they wanted.

If you look at the day-to-day finances of seemingly rich people, it's easy to see why they might stress about money. In February 2009, after the Obama administration proposed a $500,000 pay cap at banks receiving TARP (Troubled Asset Relief Program) money, the city's hyper-affluent scoffed at the naïveté about what it costs to live in Manhattan. A *New York Times* story did some math to show how fast the meter runs for the city's more affluent residents: two kids in private schools, $60,000 a year; a mortgage and maintenance on a family-size New York apartment in a doorman building, $192,000 a year; a nanny, $45,000 a year. And then other expenses: a car and driver, a house in the Hamptons, vacations, personal trainers, clothes, and beauty treatments. "Five hundred thousand dollars means taking their kids out of private school and selling their home in a fire sale," said Upper East Sider Holly Petersen, the daughter of billionaire Pete Petersen. The article estimated that the typical lifestyle of a wealthy Manhattanite cost $790,750 a year, requiring a salary more like $1.6 million before taxes. And this is strictly for affluent people at the low end of the scale.[17]

The tax increases proposed by Obama didn't threaten any of the rich fundamentally. But neither were they inconsequential for a crowd that had obscenely high cash-flow needs or for those with a "middle-class millionaire" mind-set. On the other hand, the notion that only the super-rich felt that they could afford Obama's tax increases is plainly wrong. As Raj Date worked to raise money in finance circles for Obama from his perch as a managing director at Deutsche Bank Securities, his experience was that taxes simply weren't a big issue. Before the crash, Obama was running for president at a time when the finance world was rolling in profits and benefiting from years of lower taxes under Bush. "People had made a lot of money, and that took the edge off income tax issues," Date said.

Date was raising money from people like himself: a younger crowd of finance people, many under forty, who weren't becoming billionaires but were doing quite well—enough so that they could easily live with a higher top income tax bracket. "If you're making two or three million a year and you're talking about a five-percent change, it's going to add up to real money," Date said. "That didn't sway anyone's view. If you have that much money, it's not going to make much difference." Mike Tooke, a former investment banker who now finances tech companies, said the same thing: "As far as I'm concerned, if the tax rate goes from 36 percent to 39 percent or 40 percent, I can afford to pay that additional amount of money. Even another five percent beyond that is still marginal."

To many people in finance and elsewhere, the GOP's extreme hostility to taxes makes little sense. They take a more pragmatic view, which is that sometimes the nation can afford lower taxes and other times it can't. "People are realistic that you can't run deficits forever," Date said. "They know that something has got to give. Multiple things have to give." Including the lower tax rates of the Bush-era cuts. "It's hard to make the math work otherwise."

The rich have been squabbling over tax policy for at least a century. But the current fault lines of the debate track back to 1993, when President Bill Clinton submitted to Congress his first budget, which included substantial tax hikes on the rich. On one side, opposing new taxes, were business leaders drawn disproportionately from old-economy industries such as manufacturing, construction, retail, defense, real estate, and energy, as well as wealthy elites from conservative regions of the country. These were the donors to the phalanx of anti-tax conservative organizations that had sprung up in Washington and to the ever-more-libertarian Republicans getting elected to Congress. This group tended to see wealth creation mainly as the product of individual effort and argued that government needed to get out of the way of entrepreneurs and business owners in order to grow the economy and allow more people to get rich.

On the other side were those wealthy who made their living from a burgeoning knowledge economy—which included the high-tech, communications, media, and finance industries. These wealthy elites, many of whom lived in coastal cities and had grown up in liberal parts of the country, often took a communal view of wealth creation and embraced government's role in creating an educated workforce, underwriting basic scientific research, and strengthening the nation's physical infrastructure. They also wanted fiscal responsibility, which they believed would spur growth by keeping interest rates low. In their view, higher taxes were a small price to pay to sustain public investments and reduce the budget deficit; everyone would get richer in the long term.

Although the individualist outlook had prevailed during the Reagan years, when oil and manufacturing fortunes dominated the Forbes 400 list, the communal view was rapidly gaining strength by the 1990s as people like Bill Gates vaulted to the top ranks of the U.S. upper class.

Clinton's tax hikes, when coupled with a big increase in the Earned Income Tax Credit (EITC) to help the working poor, amounted to a major redistribution of national income away from the upper class. No matter. Clinton still got the support of many in this class. In March 1993, the *New York Times* reported, "Since Mr. Clinton presented his economic blueprint to Congress and the nation 12 days ago, he has crisscrossed the country to meet with business leaders and seek their support. And so far, he seems to be getting it—even though the program will inflict pain on many rich business executives and on their corporations."[18] Such corporate support would help ensure the narrow passage of Clinton's budget in Congress. And the unwillingness of even a single Republican in Congress to vote for the plan stood as stark evidence of the growing elite fault line over taxes.

Even back then, Buffett stood clearly on the protax side of that fault line. In his 1993 letter to shareholders Buffett noted that Berkshire Hathaway had paid $390 million in corporate income taxes, and that was just fine. "We work in a market-based economy that rewards our efforts far more bountifully than it does the efforts of others whose output is of equal or greater benefit to society. Taxation should, and does, partially redress this inequality. But we remain extraordinarily well treated."[19]

One influence on Buffett's thinking about taxes was "The Gospel of Wealth," a long essay authored by Andrew Carnegie in 1890 that expressed the fear that America's egalitarian ideals were increasingly threatened by vast fortunes. Carnegie had amassed one of the largest of such fortunes, but he advocated for the taxation of inherited wealth through a progressive estate tax. Carnegie is very much the modern father of the communal story of wealth creation. He argued that large personal fortunes were made possible only because individuals operated within a broader community and that when the rich die, their fortunes should be returned to that community—as opposed to being squandered by heirs. The "best means of benefiting the community," Carnegie wrote, "is to place within its reach the ladders upon which the aspiring can rise." In effect, Carnegie imagined the estate tax as a way to tap great fortunes to recycle economic opportunity for future generations.

Carnegie's view that wealth was the product of communal effort would become a signature idea among the liberal rich, gradually gaining converts during the course of the next century. It is this idea, as much as any other, that divides the liberal rich from those millionaires and billionaires who think they made it big by themselves.

Attitudes about government are pivotal here. Although it's often imagined that the ranks of the rich include only Horatio Alger types who hate government, the picture has always been more complicated. Since the days of Alexander Hamilton, hatred of government has rarely been a natural reflex of credentialed elites who live in cosmopolitan parts of the nation and work in complex economic systems. In fact, starting well before the Clinton years, these elites have often had a long wish list of things that government might do.

In the 1950s, many corporate leaders saw government as a key partner in laying the foundations for growth and prosperity through such investments as the interstate highway system, public universities, and basic research. A good chunk of the business world turned against big government starting in the 1970s, amid fears of a growing regulatory state, which led to the alliance between business and conservatives that remade U.S. politics during the Age of Reagan. Now the pendulum is swinging back. After years of enfeebled government and festering national problems, more business leaders are souring on market fundamentalism and see the need to revive the partnership between the public and the private sector. Bill Gates, for instance, has repeatedly called for a vast increase in spending on scientific research. "In the past, federally funded research helped spark industries that today provide hundreds of thousands of jobs," Gates reminded a congressional committee in 2008. "Countless products and technologies that we take for granted today had their origins in research conducted with federal funds." Gates stressed that business, as well as nonprofits, has a crucial role in technological innovation. But he noted that ultimately "only government has the resources to effect change on a broad scale."[21] Gates called for nearly doubling federal spending on science—a stance that is not even remotely controversial among other super-wealthy leaders from the high-tech world, who have long taken for granted the need for activist government to ensure U.S. competitiveness. Biotech leaders also support billions more for biomedical research—on top of a National Institutes of Health budget that more than doubled between 1998 and 2008. Any number of corporate leaders have called for billions more to be spent on infrastructure or alternative energy.

And, of course, there is a large business constituency advocating for more public spending on education at every level.

This growing wish list helps explain why antitax fervor has subsided in some parts of the upper class. You can't oppose tax hikes if you want more government.

Just as Clinton's tax hikes attracted support from key wealthy quarters, the tax proposals of George W. Bush drew fire from some among the rich. One of the more catchy attacks on Bush's tax cuts came from a group called Responsible Wealth, based in Boston and made up of affluent individuals concerned about rising inequality. Chuck Collins, an Oscar Mayer heir who had given away his inheritance to activist groups in the 1980s, created Responsible Wealth as an offshoot to an earlier group he founded, United for a Fair Economy. Collins noticed that when he gave talks about rising inequality, people would sometimes approach him afterward and say that they were part of the top 1 percent and ask what they could do to help. Responsible Wealth was a way to channel this group's concerns into policy debates.

In 1998, when Congress cut the capital gains tax from 28 percent to 20 percent, a move that mostly benefited the wealthy, Responsible Wealth created a campaign called the "Tax Fairness Pledge." By signing the pledge, members of the group promised to redirect money saved by the tax cut toward organizing for fairer tax policies. By 2001, two hundred members had taken the pledge and had redirected several million dollars. After the Bush tax cuts were enacted, Responsible Wealth renewed its calls for people to sign the Tax Fairness Pledge. Many wealthy individuals responded, and many more also joined a Reject the Rebate campaign, which sought to counter the Bush administration's plan that gave $400 rebate checks to all U.S. households.

Wealthy individuals have also fought against state tax cuts. Any number of prominent business leaders, for example, rose in opposition to state ballot campaigns that would limit taxes. In 1993, Bill Gates made his largest political contribution to date, $80,000, to fight an antitax ballot initiative in Washington State. Gates would oppose similar initiatives during subsequent years. Along with other high-tech leaders, Gates worried that measures to limit taxes and shrink government would undermine public education and thus hurt the state's knowledge economy.

In all, the wealthy went both ways on tax cuts. Whereas super-rich conservatives bankrolled the assault on big government, some of the toughest pushback came from within their own class.

Nowhere did this rift play out more vividly than in the titanic battle over the estate tax. Abolishing the steep tax on inherited wealth had been a dream of wealthy conservatives since the 1920s, when Andrew Mellon tried and failed to kill the tax. It would not be until the 1980s that the estate tax was substantially reduced, thanks to the Reagan tax cuts, which lowered the top rate from 70 percent to 50 percent and created a variety of new loopholes to help the rich pass more wealth to their heirs.

For some of the affluent, though, these reductions didn't go nearly far enough, and a handful of the super-rich began a concerted, well-funded effort in the early 1990s to eliminate the estate tax altogether. This effort would cost millions of dollars in lobbying fees and donations to right-wing think tanks and was financed by families that, in some cases, stood to owe billions of dollars in estate taxes. They included the Mars, Koch, Gallo, and Mayer families. Among the biggest spenders was the Walton family, which reportedly paid Patton Boggs $600,000 for lobbying efforts to repeal the tax. With some $80 billion in assets, the Waltons could one day pay as much as $30 billion in estate taxes.[22]

Republicans in Congress championed these efforts and voted to eliminate the estate tax in the late 1990s, only to be thwarted by President Clinton's veto. It was not until Bush's election in 2000 that this holy grail for antitax forces finally seemed to be within reach. The 2001 tax cuts included a total phaseout of the estate tax by 2010—although the tax would then return when the law lapsed. Making the phaseout permanent became an obsession among some Republicans, who would try several times during the Bush years to permanently kill the estate tax, working in concert with the powerful lobbying and PR infrastructure funded by wealthy families.

Ultimately, though, the repeal failed to win passage in the Senate, losing by the narrowest of margins. Why did this campaign fail? Well, it wasn't because of public opinion. The public has never been enthusiastic about the estate tax, and polls have consistently found during recent years that solid majorities favor repeal. And as the political scientist Larry Bartels has shown, the dishonest campaign against the tax doesn't persuasively explain public opinion. Hostility to inheritance taxes is long-standing in the United States and pre-dates recent conservative efforts to kill the tax. Even in 1935, when antipathy toward the rich was near an all-time high, a poll found that slightly more than half of Americans believed that there should be no limit to the amount of money a person could inherit.[23] During the 2000 campaign, George W. Bush's promise to abolish the estate tax proved to be one of his strongest applause lines—even in front of working-class crowds. Most Americans, it seems, have tended to agree with the conservative argument that it is morally unfair to tax wealth that people wish to pass to their children.

The story of how the estate tax survived is complex, and it is hard to point to any single reason that it endured. But one of the most interesting aspects of this battle is the way that it pitted members of the wealthy class against one another in a clash that revealed starkly divergent notions about wealth and responsibility.

Members of the super-rich families who were trying to kill the estate tax remained publicly silent on the issue, staying far in the back-ground as Republicans spun tall tales about the tax's dire impact on family farms and small businesses. Wealthy opponents of repeal showed no such reticence, and many joined up with Chuck Collins and Responsible Wealth.

Collins had first begun to work on the estate tax in the late 1990s, as the well-coordinated campaign for repeal worked its magic in Congress. "We had no idea what we were up against," he recalled. "Basically, they had had an uncontested run of the game. They had lined up their votes without really any voice on the other side."

After Bush won the White House, and the estate tax battle became more serious, Collins's effort got a big boost when he was contacted in December 2000 by William Gates Sr. (Bill's father), saying that he wished to work against repeal. The message came out of the blue, in the form of an e-mail, and Collins thought it might be a prank. So he wrote back to Gates, saying, "Yeah, and I'm Minnie Mouse." It was no prank. And when they connected by phone, Gates asked, "What can I do?"

Collins had a ready answer: "Draft a public statement, get media coverage, testify before Congress, write letters, op-ed pieces."

Gates replied, "I'm game. Let's do it all."[24]

Given Gates's close association with the largest fortune in the United States, his voice lent immense credibility to the fight to preserve the estate tax. Although his son did not publicly join the fight, it was well known that Bill Gates also wasn't a fan of inherited wealth and, in fact, had pledged to leave only $10 million to each of his children.

Working together, Gates and Collins gathered support from some of America's richest people for a statement opposing repeal of the estate tax. "The more prominent people we got," Collins recalled, "the more it was easy to get prominent people." The statement advocated fixing the estate tax to avoid any pain that it might cause to less affluent households. Agnes Gund, the wealthy New York philanthropist, also joined this effort, explaining to the *New York Times* that she had been raised by her wealthy parents to believe in giving back to the public good.[25] By late February 2001, the effort had yielded 400 signatures, including those of George Soros, David Rockefeller Jr., Steven Rockefeller, Bill Joy, Ben Cohen (of Ben and Jerry's Homemade Ice Cream), Paul Newman, and Ted Turner. A month later, the list had swelled to 750 people. *Newsweek* called the campaign "The Billionaire Backlash," and critics implied that only the super-rich—those with so much money they didn't care about taxes—were signing on to the appeal.[26]

That was incorrect. The list also included scores of "millionaire next door" types, drawing from the ranks of the rich who tended to be more conservative on taxes. "We welcomed all comers. We were interested in small business people, old wealth, and farmers," Collins recalled. "We had farmers who had paid the estate tax and lived to tell the tale. . . . The idea of abolishing the estate tax just smacked a lot of people on the side of the head as being un-American."

Warren Buffett wouldn't sign the petition, saying that it didn't go far enough in its defense of the estate tax. Repealing the estate tax "would be a terrible mistake," Buffett told the *New York Times*, saying it would be akin to "choosing the 2020 Olympic team by picking the eldest sons of the gold-medal winners in the 2000 Olympics." Buffett added, "We have come closer to a true meritocracy than anywhere else around the world. . . . You have mobility so people with talents can be put to the best use. Without the estate tax, you in effect will have an aristocracy of wealth, which means you pass down the ability to command the resources of the nation based on heredity rather than merit."[27] Ironically, the wealthy who supported the estate tax found themselves to the left of the many middle- and working-class Americans who favored abolishing the tax.

Advocates of the estate tax were not able to stop Congress from voting to phase out the tax as part of the Bush tax cuts that extended through 2010, but they did block efforts to permanently repeal the tax, and with the Democratic takeover of Congress in 2006, the drive to repeal the estate tax finally died. At least for the moment.

The upper-class divide over taxes could move liberalism in some new directions. If more rich people are okay about redistributing wealth through fiscal policy, then Democrats may focus on this path to equity, rather than pushing other policies, such as raising the minimum wage, strengthening unions, or capping CEO pay. Messing with business is a sure way to bring thousands of well-paid lobbyists storming onto Capitol Hill. And often they will win, given how U.S. politics tends to advantage narrow and well-organized interest groups—especially those with deep pockets.

Tax hikes on the rich, in contrast, are more diffuse and don't so directly threaten specific interests with lobbying arms in Washington. There is no Association of High Net Worth Individuals inside the Beltway that is committed to fighting across-the-board income tax hikes on the rich. (Not yet, anyway.)

Is it too far-fetched to imagine the Democrats as a business-friendly party that also practices wealth redistribution? Not at all.

That's how Clinton governed: he resliced the fiscal pie with tax hikes on the rich and tax credits for the poor even as he continued Republican deregulatory policies. Democrats gnashed their teeth at Clinton's sellouts, but the late 1990s saw big income gains for Americans at the bottom of the economic ladder. History might have judged this bargain kindly if an era of lax regulation hadn't laid the groundwork for a series of huge corporate frauds such as Enron and, ultimately, the financial crash of 2008.

The challenge for Obama and other Democrats is to find the magic balance: enact enough regulation to curb bad behavior, but don't pull this lever so hard as to alienate those business leaders—such as Netflix CEO Reed Hastings—who will accept higher taxes and explicit redistribution as long as they can still make money.

Bill Gates once commented that he had mixed feelings about both parties because the Republicans were good at encouraging wealth creation but bad at spreading that wealth around, while the Democrats had the opposite problem: they were good at redistribution but threw up roadblocks to wealth creation.

If this is a common view in the upper class, and it seems like it is, it suggests an obvious way to build a Democratic coalition that includes Americans across the income spectrum: spur prosperity but make sure that it is shared.

7

THE BILLIONAIRE BACKLASH

T HE RISE OF THE LIBERAL RICH mainly has its roots in economic
shifts that have changed who gets rich, how, and where. Politics
has played a role, too, however, like the fact that the Republican
Party seems to have lost its mind.

For the GOP, its extremism couldn't have come at a worse time.
George W. Bush emerged as one of the most reckless presidents in
U.S. history during a period when significant new liberal fortunes
came on line and also when a number of extremely rich older liberals
were turning their attention to spending money, rather than making
it. This confluence created one of the biggest surges of liberal funds
into politics and activism ever, fueling not only electoral victories
but a major expansion of the "progressive infrastructure." And the
money kept flowing even after Bush moved back to Texas, leaving
the likes of Sarah Palin and Rush Limbaugh—who both embody all
that is unnerving about the GOP to coastal elites—as leading voices
of the Republican Party.

First, some background. In his 1982 book, *Shifting Involvements*,
the economist Albert O. Hirschman argued that yes, self-interest
tends to be the main motive for human behavior, but that there

often comes a point when private gain and comfort are no longer so compelling to people, and they shift their priorities to the common good. In other words, at some point people tire of piling up yet more money and start to think about giving back or leaving a deeper mark.

Hirschman's book has long stood as a rebuke to economists who dismiss such fuzzy human emotions as altruism and empathy. Looking back to earlier times, Hirschman's thesis helps explain the first great upsurge of philanthropy in the early 1900s, which began at the tail end of the Robber Baron era and was led by men such as Andrew Carnegie and John D. Rockefeller who had burned out on empire building. ("I resolved to stop accumulating and begin the infinitely more serious and difficult task of wise distribution," Carnegie said about his decision to retire from business in 1901.)

But the book also offers insights into the present moment. Many among the mega-rich have been rich for a very long time now. The financier George Soros, the largest liberal donor in recent times, has been on the Forbes 400 list since the mid-1980s. Peter Lewis, another bottomless well of liberal money, has been on the list since 1993. Herb and Marion Sandler, also among the left's biggest funders, started their heavy giving shortly before they officially became billionaires by selling the savings-and-loan that they had run for nearly fifty years.

In addition, the cycle that Hirschman describes has been happening more quickly. Prominent liberal politicians of recent years, such as Jon Corzine and John Edwards, made substantial fortunes relatively early and then threw themselves into public affairs. Activist funders such as the gay rights backers David Bohnett and Tim Gill built successful companies before they were fifty and then cashed out, finding themselves still in the prime of their lives with plenty of time and a mountain of money on their hands. Jeffrey Skoll made a multibillion-dollar fortune at eBay while still in his thirties and then turned to producing liberal films such as *An Inconvenient Truth*. While old-economy wealth is built on hard assets like manufacturing plants or oil refineries that can take many years to build and turn profitable, vast new-economy fortunes can spring up in only a few years.

By the time George W. Bush launched the invasion of Iraq, the amount of wealth in the hands of liberals, young and old, was unprecedented. These fortunes surged further during the boom years before the 2008 crash.

The leftward trend among wealthy campaign contributors didn't start with Bush. It emerged over a decade or more, as did Democratic voting trends in the wealthiest counties. But there is no question that the Bush presidency had a galvanizing effect. Bush radically raised the stakes of politics and forced people to clarify their beliefs. Before Bush, many wealthy Democrats didn't have a strong ideological outlook or see the need for one. They were focused on specific issues, such as the environment or abortion, or they dabbled in politics the way they might root for a sports team or hang out with the "in" crowd. They felt no great sense of urgency during the Clinton years, a period of peace and prosperity, and the world of Democratic fund-raising was largely transactional: write big checks, and you get to attend a dinner with Bill Clinton or Al Gore. Write even bigger checks, and maybe you'll spend a night in the Lincoln Bedroom.

All of that changed with Bush. "People felt like their fundamental philosophical architecture was under attack," said Erica Payne, who had been a top fund-raiser with the Democratic National Committee in the 1990s. Payne dealt with innumerable Democratic donors during the Clinton years but rarely had a conversation with anyone about his or her core beliefs or the larger picture.

Disillusioned with politics, Payne went to get her MBA at the Wharton School and then spent some time in business before returning to the political world in 2002, around the time that the Republicans were steamrolling to a big victory in the midterm elections. Democrats everywhere were panicking. "It was insanity," Payne said. "You're watching conservatives destroy your country." That experience, as Payne saw it, produced a clarification of values for donors who had previously not been very ideological. "Many people's values were lying dormant or unexamined, like being buried under the sand, and when that George Bush wind starts to blow, you can see what's underneath. For the first time, in feeling that jolt to their soul that they hadn't felt before, they started to understand that there is a philosophy beneath their political orientation," and as a result they "started to orient themselves in a values system way."

Beginning in 2003, wealthy donors began to give money to elect Democrats in a way never before seen in U.S. politics. Much of this money was funneled through so-called 527s—nonprofit groups ostensibly set up to advocate for a particular set of issues. In contrast to donors to candidates and congressional committees, it is hard to second-guess the motives of big donors to 527s, who have been the most ideological donors on both sides of the political divide and who include some of America's wealthiest liberals. Between 2004 and 2008, 527s spent nearly $1.5 billion—with most of this money going to support Democratic candidates.

The biggest contributions have come from George Soros, and his evolution says much about the backlash that Bush triggered in some of the loftiest reaches of the upper class.

At this point, Soros has become a familiar and often caricatured figure. Isn't he that zealous left-wing billionaire with the foreign accent whom Bill O'Reilly has called "one of the most feared men in the world"? Didn't Bernard Goldberg put Soros at number 19 on his list of "100 People Who Are Screwing Up America"—just below Al Gore, but above Howard Dean? "George Soros is really the Dr. Evil of the whole world of left-wing foundations," suggested another conservative, the author Phil Kent. "He really hates this country."[1]

Cartoon images aside, what is less known about Soros is that—before Bush—he wasn't very partisan at all. Back in the 1990s, Soros was a widely admired philanthropist, giving away some $400 million a year to support scores of foundations in the former communist bloc and other emerging nations. This giving would lead Richard Holbrooke to call Soros "the most interesting and important philanthropist since Andrew Carnegie."[2] Soros initially gave little money within the United States, and although he supported the cause of drug decriminalization, he was not especially ideological. Soros had studied philosophy in college and spent his career speculating in financial markets. The cornerstone of his worldview was the importance of an "open society," a concept developed by the

Austrian-born philosopher Karl Popper and nearly the opposite of ideological rigidity. In an open society, no one has a monopoly on the truth, and there is plenty of free and fair discussion in which all viewpoints get aired. Creating these conditions worldwide was the goal of Soros's foundation, the Open Society Institute (OSI).

As a Jewish Hungarian immigrant who once lived under Nazi occupation and has a penchant for dense philosophizing, Soros has always seemed a rather exotic figure. But he has certain familiar characteristics of the liberal rich. His father was a lawyer, and Soros grew up in an affluent cosmopolitan setting in Budapest. Later, he spent time at an elite (and liberal) university, the London School of Economics, and then moved to New York City, where he has lived for the last fifty years, to go into finance. Up until the 1980s, Soros was not an especially active Democrat, and his campaign donations were modest. Certainly, he had nothing in principle against Republicans or the Bushes. In 1980, Soros contributed to George H. W. Bush's run for president. Soros also backed Republican senator Jacob Javits.

When Soros finally turned his philanthropy to the United States in the late 1990s, he focused on changing public policies that struck him as irrational. Thus, he not only sought to steer U.S. drug policy toward prevention and treatment, but also gave money to promote needle exchange, which is proven to reduce AIDS, as well as money to advocate alternatives to prison incarceration. Another of his early ventures in the United States was to help naturalize legal immigrants and advocate for their rights, which was undertaken after the 1996 welfare law denied such immigrants access to certain benefits. Soros also put money into death and dying issues and ethics in the professions—hardly left-wing hot buttons. His biggest pledge by far was $125 million for after-school programs in New York City.

In other words, Soros began his U.S. giving as a typical cause-driven donor—albeit embracing edgy causes. The Open Society Institute did form a program that gave grants to think tanks and campaign finance reform groups, run by a former Senate aide, Mark Schmitt, but its budget was tiny in comparison to Soros's other initiatives. At one point, Schmitt commissioned a study on the weak state of liberal think tanks, which, among other things, stressed that liberals lacked the capacity to formulate a political philosophy. Democrats didn't stand for anything, the study suggested, because liberal funders didn't support big-picture thinkers. The report circulated widely within OSI and beyond. Still, OSI resisted entreaties to dramatically ramp up funding for the liberal think-tank world or to more strategically fund the progressive movement. Word percolated out from OSI that Soros—or "George," as everyone called him—was uncomfortable funding groups that were expressly ideological, because it conflicted with his open society approach and, anyway, Soros didn't consider himself a progressive.

All of that changed during the Bush presidency. The administration's doctrine of preemptive war, along with the invasion of Iraq, convinced Soros that "America, under Bush, is a danger to the world," as he told the *Washington Post*. Soros came to feel that every measure should be taken to prevent Bush's reelection. "I don't like being so partisan, but I will advocate for a constructive U.S. role in the world," he said. "Getting rid of Bush is the central focus of my life," Soros said about the presidential race, calling the outcome "a matter of life and death." Soros also became a major funder of the Center for American Progress, the new liberal think tank founded in 2003 with a sharp "we're right, they're wrong" tone that surely would have unsettled him in earlier years.[3]

Soros's conversion to a hyperpartisan drew criticism not only from the Fox News set, but also from longtime associates in the finance world. None of this seemed to faze him. He was entering his midseventies, a period of life when the years ahead are clearly finite and people focus more on their legacy—especially if they're worth billions. He was exactly the kind of enemy the GOP could do without.

Soros played a central role in galvanizing the opposition to Bush. A pivotal moment came in July 2003, when he convened a group of wealthy liberals, labor leaders, and high-level Democratic operatives at El Mirador, his estate in Southampton, New York. The topic was getting rid of George W. Bush, and although the election was still more than a year away, many Democrats were already working at a feverish tempo to elect Bush's opponent—whoever that might be.

Soros had hired two political consultants, Mark Steitz and Tom Novick, to explore the prospects for ousting Bush, and they presented their research at the meeting. Steitz and Novick said the election would be close, but the outcome could be swayed by a big push in swing battleground states. Their findings held that television advertising was unlikely to make a huge difference; the key would be voter mobilization through door-to-door canvassing and other strategies. An operation of this kind would cost $75 million. Also at the meeting was Steven Rosenthal, the political director of the AFL-CIO, and Ellen Malcolm, the president of Emily's List. They had just put together a 527 called Americans Coming Together (ACT). Steitz and Novick recommended that ACT be the vehicle for the mobilization effort. Their message was "We've got to build something," recalled Rob McKay, an heir to the Taco Bell fortune who was present at the meeting. "We've got to build it from the ground up because the party is not capable of doing it."

Soros agreed with the idea and pledged $10 million. Peter Lewis, the billionaire founder of Progressive Insurance, then nearly seventy years old, matched the pledge that day. Others who were present also made big cash commitments, including Lewis Cullman, a financier in his mideighties, and Rob Glaser, the founder of RealNetworks.

The push by ACT would be complemented by other 527s, also funded by Soros and other billionaires. Soros would ultimately spend nearly $24 million on these groups—more than any individual had ever spent on an election in U.S. history, an ironic milestone for a man who had bankrolled the campaign finance reform movement only a few years earlier. Lewis spent nearly the same amount. Herb and Marion Sandler put $13 million into the 527s, as did the super-rich heir Steven Bing. All told, just four wealthy individuals gave nearly $75 million to liberal groups working to elect Kerry in 2004—as much as Kerry received in federal matching funds for the general election. The 527s that backed Kerry and other Democrats raised more than $300 million overall—spending without precedent in U.S. campaign history.

Although 527s seemed to fade from the scene in 2008, they still raised and spent tens of millions of dollars. Soros contributed $5 million this time around, while Bing put in $4.8 million, making these two men effectively the largest financial backers of Barack Obama's campaign. Their combined giving was the equivalent of 49,000 donations at $200 a pop.

One fascinating aspect of the big money operations that Democrats put together in 2004 and 2008 is the degree to which some of America's wealthiest people worked in concert with some of its most progressive labor unions. The AFL-CIO's Steve Rosenthal not only was present at the July 2003 meeting at Soros's house, but also collaborated closely with ACT's rich donors during the election. Andy Stern, who leads the powerful Service Employees International Union (SEIU), was another key player. He attended a major strategy meeting in Aspen in August 2004 that brought together Soros, Lewis, the Sandlers, and another elder billionaire, John Sperling. "I have to admit, I used to think I was doing well when I met millionaires," Stern said afterward. "I'm glad we've got the billionaires with us. But it did feel a bit odd."[4]

Odd, indeed. Financial records of the big liberal 527s, in both 2004 and 2008, showed that these groups received tens of millions of dollars from leading unions, as well as from a range of mega-rich backers beyond Soros and his fellow billionaires—people such as Alida Rockefeller Messinger, the daughter of John D. Rockefeller III, and John Hunting, the office furniture heir.

This alliance between big labor and big money flies in the face of conventional wisdom about wealthy liberals, which is that they'll happily collude with environmentalists or pro-choice activists but have little use for labor unions. It further underscores one of the great ironies of U.S. politics in an age of turbocharged capitalism—which is that some of the biggest beneficiaries of unfettered markets have worked to oust the very same GOP leaders who champion the most laissez-faire policies. The fantastical and unequal riches of the Bush years—a period when only the top 5 percent of households saw signficant income gains—armed the president's opponents with wads of new cash: George Soros's fortune grew by $4 billion during Bush's presidency, while the Sandlers sold their savings-and-loan, Golden West, at the peak of the real estate bubble in 2006 for $2.4 billion.

The reelection of George Bush dealt a stinging defeat to leading liberal funders. The effect, however, was to help catalyze an even bigger push against the right. Even before the grim news of election night, an ambitious effort was under way to mobilize new funds for the progressive movement. One leader of this effort was Rob Stein, a former Clinton official who had developed a PowerPoint presentation that outlined the vast resources going into right-wing groups. The presentation, which Stein began to give in 2003, tallied up annual funding for conservative think tanks such as the Heritage Foundation, right-wing legal advocacy organizations such as the Federalist Society, and conservative journals, media watchdog groups, and leadership-training institutes. All told, Stein estimated that the conservative "message machine" was bankrolled to the tune of $300 million a year from two hundred "anchor donors."[5] Most of the money came from a dozen family fortunes that had been built during the industrial era, mainly manufacturing enterprises in America's heartland. Nearly none was drawn from the new economy.

It wasn't a lot of money in the grand scheme of U.S. politics—not in an era when spending on a single expensive Senate race could easily top $65 million. But the funds were deployed in a strategically brilliant fashion to spread conservative ideas and change the terms of political debate. It was one of the greatest success stories in the history of U.S. philanthropy and helped explain why George W. Bush was in the White House, why both chambers of Congress were ruled by Republicans, and why the judicial branch was increasingly dominated by conservatives. When Andy Rappaport, a Silicon Valley venture capitalist, saw the presentation, he shook his head in wonder: "Man. *That's* all it took to buy the country?" Exactly Stein's point.[6]

Stein's main takeaway—that liberal donors had to radically step up funding for ideas and "infrastructure"—had been offered

many times before, going back to the 1980s when journalist Sidney
Blumenthal had charted the rise of the "conservative counter-
establishment." But it took the presidency of George W. Bush and
the specter of single-party Republican rule for the point to sink in.

Around the same time that Stein was giving his PowerPoint presentation, Simon Rosenberg, a Democratic Party strategist, and Erica
Payne were hatching an effort to better organize liberal donors. Both
were frustrated by the lack of a cohesive progressive movement and
the constant battle among groups on the left for a static pot of funding. They conceived the idea of a venture capital fund that would
put more money into the pot—a lot more—and target that money
strategically. "If we could move the money around more effectively,"
Payne recalled, "then we could drive a set of behaviors in the progressive movement that would allow it to become more effective."
The basic idea was to organize donors to contribute to a new pool of
funds that could be channeled to support key organizations.

After Payne and Rosenberg saw Stein's slide show, the three combined their efforts and became a trio selling the dream of a powerful
progressive movement. Often, they added David Brock to the mix,
the former right-wing journalist who had just published a memoir,
Blinded by the Right. Brock's book had become required reading in
progressive circles, with its chilling inside look at conservative mach-
inations, and Brock was an unlikely celebrity in liberal salons.

An important step forward came when Payne and Rosenberg
arranged for Stein and Brock to talk with Alan Patricof, a veteran
Democratic fund-raiser who was close to the Clintons. Like Soros,
Lewis, and the Sandlers, Patricof was well along in years, entering
his seventies. He had been an early venture capitalist and was still
working, but he had long ago scored his big paydays—like when he
bet heavily on Apple Computer during its start-up phase—and had
grown more keenly interested in his longer-term legacy. In 2001,
Patricof had stepped back from the day-to-day management of his
private equity firm and set out, as he said, to "trifurcate my life"—
splitting time between his venture capital business, helping developing countries, and Democratic politics. After seeing Stein's slide show
and listening to Brock, Patricof asked, "What can I do?"

There was plenty that Patricof could do, it turned out. In the months to come, he would promote the concept of a new progressive funding push to his wide circle of powerful friends—a veritable who's who of Democratic funders in New York City. In December 2003, Patricof helped pull together a session in New York with thirty top progressive funders and operatives, including Soros, Peter Lewis, and former Clinton chief of staff John Podesta. It was a breakthrough moment.

One of Stein's pivotal insights was that "movements are communities of activists, strategists, and donors." Donors are a key glue keeping such communities together, Stein believed, but the progressive wealthy had been largely isolated in different silos. They sat on the board of this environmental group or that human rights organization; they went to a fund-raiser here and bankrolled a candidate there. They were hit up constantly for money by nonprofits and politicians. Yet their participation ended after they opened up their checkbooks. "There was no ongoing contact," Stein said. "There was no place to go. There was no place for them to meet, to get to know one another. You weren't part of anything." Certainly, the liberal rich weren't part of a strategic conversation about how to change America. Stein hoped to remedy that.

An early convert was Robert Johnson, a PhD economist-turned-financier who had been a managing director at Soros's hedge fund. Johnson had left the world of high finance in the 1990s, exhausted by his heavy travel schedule and needing to pay attention to his family and his health. Also, he said, "I had enough money." He began to focus on other pursuits, like building boats and producing music. But all the while, he was becoming more concerned about the country's direction under the Republican Congress and then the Bush White House. He found the 2000 election, decided by the Supreme Court, deeply alarming. An acquaintance from Brazil commented that the whole episode seemed like the way things were done down in South America.

Johnson had grown up in a Republican family in Grosse Pointe, Michigan, and he had been a Republican in his younger days, working on Capitol Hill in the 1980s for the moderate Republican senator Pete Domenici. But Johnson had begun to move left after Newt Gingrich's rise to power in 1995, and that shift accelerated under Bush. It was a familiar story.

In Greenwich, Connecticut, where Johnson lived, he found few kindred spirits. Paul Tudor Jones was someone he came to know and found progressive. But many others in Greenwich's soaring hedge fund world were still largely positive about the Bush administration. "I felt very isolated at that time," Johnson said. He was especially worried about the growing right-wing influence over the media. He had long been familiar with the work of Robert McChesney, the author of books such as *Corporate Media and the Threat to Democracy*. Now Johnson started to read the work of David Brock, including *The Republican Noise Machine*, which was a follow-up to his memoir. Johnson became involved in media reform issues, giving some support to the liberal watchdog group Fairness and Accuracy in Reporting (FAIR). Then he saw Rob Stein's slide show and had tea with Erica Payne. He was immediately captivated by their project and offered to help. "I had found a community," he recalled.

The effort to mobilize new money for liberal groups moved along at a modest pace. In July 2004, a group of top donors and Democratic operatives convened in New York, and Rob Stein was asked to write the first business plan for a new funding organization that would be called the Democracy Alliance (DA). A few months later, when Bush was reelected—despite tens of millions of dollars in spending by 527s along with record voter turnout—the DA took off. The election crystallized the need for long-range investments to rebuild progressive politics and change the terms of public debate. Also, in the wreckage of defeat, there were few inspiring politicians who could play an obvious role in galvanizing the opposition. "Historically, all of these donors had given money to political leaders," Payne said. "In 2004, there weren't any leaders left, so the donors had to step up and be the leaders. . . . There was an empowering aspect to the experience; they were no longer outsourcing the promotion of their value system."

In spring 2005, the DA convened in Arizona for its inaugural meeting. Beyond activist billionaires such as Lewis and Soros, many other lesser-known progressive donors joined the Democracy Alliance during its first year of operation. Most fit the mold of wealth liberalism: They tended to live on the East or the West Coast—with a smattering of members from places like Colorado or Chicago—and had made their fortunes in new-economy industries such as finance, technology, or services, not in the old economy of manufacturing and resource extraction. They included people such as Rutt Bridges, a founder of a geophysical software company; Tim Gill, who had made a fortune in software; Davidi Gilo, a high-tech entrepreneur and the founder of Vyyo, Inc.; Rob Glaser, the founder of RealNetworks in Seattle; Ann S. Bowers, the widow of Intel cofounder Robert Noyce, who invented the integrated circuit; Robert H. Dugger, a managing director of Tudor Investment Corporation (who worked with Paul Tudor Jones); Andy and Deborah Rappaport from Silicon Valley; and Chris Gabrieli, a software entrepreneur and venture capitalist. Other pillars of the progressive wealth establishment—the inherited rich—were also drawn to the Democracy Alliance; they included Rob McKay, whose fortune came from the Taco Bell chain; and Rachel Pritzker Hunter, an heiress to the Hyatt Hotels fortune. There was Hollywood money, too, with Norman Lear and Rob Reiner joining.

By August 2005, the DA had eighty members, all of whom had promised to donate at least $200,000 a year to a pool of funds that the DA would dole out to progressive groups. In 2006, its first full year of operation, the DA moved $50 million out the door. In 2008, after ironing out its organizational challenges, the DA served as a pass-through for more than $80 million—money that went to thirty-five different groups. Nearly half of the groups that the DA funded hadn't existed only a few years earlier.

A cynic can always dismiss electoral donations as being motivated by a desire for political access. But the DA was an explicit effort to build up progressive power and move U.S. politics to the left. (A right-wing watchdog group dubbed the DA "billionaires for big government.") A central tenet behind the group's founding was that the Democratic Party needed a stronger ideological backbone. Nearly all of the alliance's grants went to organizations that were firmly on the left; no money went to centrist groups such as the Brookings Institution or the New America Foundation.

Even as each member of the DA pledged to contribute $200,000 a year, many gave much more that. And nobody spent more on building up the left's infrastructure than the three biggest backers of the alliance: Soros, Lewis, and Herb and Marion Sandler. Together, for instance, they bankrolled the Center for American Progress (CAP), the most important new organization in the progressive universe.

Modeled on the hard-hitting Heritage Foundation and run by John Podesta, CAP began operations in 2003 with a budget of more than $9 million, nearly all of which was reportedly provided by Soros, Lewis, and the Sandlers. By 2008, its budget had grown to more than $25 million a year, as the core funders sustained or increased their giving. The Sandlers alone put $20 million into CAP during its first five years. The DA pledged $4.5 million a year to CAP, while Podesta pulled in money from other super-wealthy liberals, such as Steve Bing.

A decade earlier, CAP would never have achieved this size. There simply were not enough wealthy donors who were ready to back liberal ideology writ large. Although some single-issue liberal groups that focused on environmentalism or human rights became as big as the Heritage Foundation (which had an annual budget of around $50 million in 2008), no liberal think tanks had even come close. CAP was the first.

Both Peter Lewis and the Sandlers were relative newcomers to progressive politics, and their money made a huge difference. The arrival of the Sandlers on the scene was especially important. When the couple sold Golden West, they promptly put half of that money into the Sandler Foundation. The Sandlers are different from many younger, wealthy progressives who grew up in places like New York and the Bay Area to professional parents and who made money fast. Herb Sandler had been born on the Lower East Side to a family of modest means. Marion grew up in Maine, where her family ran a hardware store. They had made their money the old-fashioned way: slowly, over decades. And although they had long given funds to groups such as Human Rights Watch, philanthropy became the central focus of their days after they cashed out of their business. It's a common trajectory for the super-rich, going back to Andrew Carnegie, who sold his steel business at the age of sixty-six and in his late second career tried to change the world. Or, in the Sandlers' case, tried to save America from conservatives.

In their first year after selling Golden West, the Sandlers gave away $75 million. Beyond their large stake in CAP, the Sandlers single-handedly created or scaled up two new major organizations. One was the Center for Responsible Lending, which had been a struggling group that worked against predatory lending in North Carolina before the Sandlers adopted it. By 2008, the center had a $16 million annual budget and was among the leading critics of corporate lending practices. The Sandlers also threw big money at an investigative news project they started in 2007 called ProPublica. They committed $30 million over three years to the group, whose mission was to produce "journalism that shines a light on exploitation of the weak by the strong and on the failures of those with power to vindicate the trust placed in them."

For years, various liberal journalists had tried to start something similar to ProPublica, only to find that funding was elusive. Wealthy donors simply weren't interested in funding modern-day Upton Sinclairs and the kind of muckraking that had advanced reforms in previous eras. For instance, Russ Baker, a veteran investigative reporter, hit a brick wall with funders when he tried to start something called the Real News Project. Yet after less than a year—thanks to one checkbook—ProPublica emerged from scratch to have bustling headquarters in New York's financial district and a staff of more than twenty editors and investigative reporters.

Media Matters for America is another notable liberal outfit that sprang out of nowhere. Media Matters was started in 2004 by David Brock, with the mission of "monitoring, analyzing, and correcting conservative misinformation in the U.S. media." The group polices a range of media outlets for perceived right-wing bias and puts out daily corrections and reprimands. Bill O'Reilly, Rush Limbaugh, and Sean Hannity are some of its main targets, but the mainstream networks and national newspapers also come in for regular scolding.

Mounting an operation like Media Matters has been a longtime fantasy of activists on the left. Starting in 1986, the liberal group Fairness and Accuracy in Reporting (FAIR) tried to undertake this task, only to find that it was impossible to raise enough money. FAIR barely scraped through the 1990s, and by the early Bush years, its annual budget was only a few hundred thousand dollars. In contrast, the conservative counterparts to FAIR—the Media Research Center and Accuracy in Media—had a combined annual budget of nearly $15 million in 2005. FAIR failed to thrive because it didn't fit into the neat program guidelines of liberal foundations, while most wealthy donors on the left limited their giving to narrow causes, like saving the rain forests. Right-wing philanthropists understood that influencing media coverage—or "working the referees," as pundit Eric Alterman put it—had to be part of any ideological movement's plan for success. Left-wing donors hadn't grasped this point, in large part because they didn't see themselves as funding a movement in the first place.

That changed during the Bush years, and Media Matters was able to raise big bucks right out of the gate. Brock was close to John Podesta and had been part of the original Democracy Alliance meetings. These ties helped him raise $2 million in seed funding from donors such as Leo Hindery Jr., who had made a fortune in cable television; Susie Tompkins Buell, the cofounder of the fashion company Esprit; James C. Hormel, who came from inherited wealth in San Francisco (and had been America's first openly gay ambassador under Clinton); and Gail Furman, a New York psychologist who was married to a wealthy real estate developer.[7] In 2005, the DA pledged $7 million to the group over two years, while additional money would come in from the Tides Foundation, the Arca Foundation, and other sources. Peter Lewis and Rachel Pritzker Hunter also contributed (Pritzker joined the board of Media Matters, as did Lewis's son, Jonathan). In 2007, after only a few years of operation, Media Matters pulled in $8.5 million in donations.

Andy Rappaport had been right to express surprise at just how little money it cost to sway U.S. politics through think tanks and the media. For about the same investment that, say, Johnson and Johnson made to advertise Tylenol every year (some $250 million), conservative donors had moved the nation to the right. When progressive donors finally copied this strategy—tapping the vast new riches of the second Gilded Age—their spending helped push the ideological needle in the opposite direction.

Something else woke up the social conscience of the rich in the early 2000s—which was related to, yet distinct from, an extremist GOP—and this was the many problems piling up in the United States and the world. The stock market collapse in 2000 and the attacks of September 11 brought an end to one of the most peaceful and prosperous decades in U.S. history. The national mood turned sober against a backdrop of fear and war. The global outlook seemed grimmer, too: climate change was happening faster than anticipated; the AIDS epidemic was accelerating, killing two million people a year; and rapid globalization had barely made a dent in entrenched global poverty.

In these darker times, it became harder for the upper class to lead insulated lives. It also became harder for anyone to believe that the free market could solve the worst problems facing the United States and humanity.

Market fundamentalism had few upper-class critics in the 1990s, when a rising tide was lifting all boats (more or less) and most of the affluent were still focused on building their fortunes. Things changed during the Bush years. Around the same time that more wealthy people stepped back from business—both the young who'd scored quick paydays and the old who'd had enough—the problems of capitalism were becoming more apparent. Income gains in the United States under Bush went overwhelmingly to the top 5 percent, and inequality was soaring. Best-selling books such as *Wealth and Democracy* by Kevin Phillips and *Perfectly Legal* by David Cay Johnston argued that a plutocracy was emerging in the United States, while the scandals at Enron and WorldCom exposed a culture of corruption in business. Crushing poverty was the norm in many parts of the world, despite the extraordinary rise of India and China.

Well before the crash, even wealthy beneficiaries of laissez-faire could see that something was terribly askew and that self-interest had gone too far. In 2007, Lloyd Blankfein—who stood at the epicenter of Wall Street greed as the CEO of Goldman Sachs—commented to the *Times* of London that rising inequality was "poisoning democracy" and that people were right to have concerns. Blankfein didn't offer to cut his own gigantic pay package, which would come to nearly $100 million in 2007 or, say, promise better wages to the janitors who worked at Goldman, but he did say that he would be voting for a Democrat in 2008.[8]

A more sincere skeptic of capitalist excess was the biggest philanthropist in history: Bill Gates. During the 1990s, Gates very much fit the profile of the modern robber baron. Like Standard Oil a century earlier, Microsoft was renowned for its monopolistic drive and the unfair tactics it used to achieve total dominance of the software industry. There was little to indicate that the Gates who found himself in the crosshairs of the Justice Department's antitrust division was anything other than an ardent supporter of unfettered markets. Or that he cared much about anything other than Microsoft. Before he turned to philanthropy, expanding the H1-B visa program to bring more skilled immigrants to his company seemed to be the only public policy issue about which Gates was passionate. For years, long after he had become a billionaire many times over, Gates was criticized for his low level of giving, and there was some surprise when he told an audience in Seattle in 1996 that "philanthropy is one of the greatest pleasures I have."[9]

Gates's early ventures into large-scale charity followed the model established by John D. Rockefeller—namely, to avoid politics and throw vast resources into solving big problems. Gates and his wife, Melinda, even chose the same two issues that were the focus of much of Rockefeller's early giving: public health in developing countries and education in the United States. Rockefeller had been entranced by the idea that his money could mitigate dreaded diseases, and Gates developed a similar fixation. Rockefeller had concentrated on hookworm and yellow fever; Gates chose malaria. One of his larger early gifts was a $50 million grant in 1999 to develop a new vaccine to prevent malaria, a disease that took the lives of nearly two million people a year. In the next decade, Gates would spend $1.2 billion fighting malaria.

Like many politically moderate business leaders, Gates didn't see social problems through an ideological lens. His approach was much more pragmatic; he assumed that the human condition could be improved through the application of new knowledge, talent, and resources. Gates said little, if anything, about the need for systemic reforms that would change the basic power arrangements of society. And he offered few criticisms of a free market system in which vast inequities are the norm. Some people who knew Gates considered him to be a liberal—certainly, people knew that his father, William Gates Sr., was a liberal, given his involvement with Planned Parenthood in Seattle and other causes. But if Bill was a liberal during the 1990s, he was a closet liberal with a multinational corporation to run. He tended to split his political giving between both parties, and in 2004 he had contributed $25,000 to a Republican committee working for Bush's reelection.

But as Gates stepped back from the day-to-day management of Microsoft—announcing his intention to retire by 2008—and as he became less of a corporate leader and more of a philanthropist, he started to think more critically. For instance, during its first years, the Gates Foundation had discussed its education work in narrow terms, as an effort to raise performance and expand opportunities for low-income students. In 2006, though, this work was enfolded in a new U.S. Program that explicitly acknowledged deep inequalities in the United States. "America is supposed to be the land of opportunity, but it simply isn't for everyone," stated the 2006 annual report. "Inequities divide the country. Some people have to beat overwhelming odds just to have the same opportunities many of us take for granted." The U.S. Program included a special initiatives fund directed by Hilary Pennington, a longtime liberal advocate who came to the Gates Foundation fresh from a stint as a fellow at the Center for American Progress. The foundation was clear that the U.S. Program's mission included advocacy: "Calling attention to the problems in the United States that we focus on and motivating others to help solve them."

It took decades for the Ford and Rockefeller fortunes to be put at the disposal of liberal think tanks and civil rights groups that openly criticized U.S. capitalism and the inequities it produced. The Gates Foundation embarked on such giving before Bill Gates had even retired from Microsoft. In 2007 and 2008, the foundation gave money to a litany of liberal groups: $12 million to the Center for Budget and Policy Priorities; $2 million to CAP; $900,000 to PolicyLink; $1 million to the NAACP; $375,000 to the Mexican-American Legal Defense Fund; $370,000 to the Pride Foundation; and $400,000 to the Center for Law and Social Policy. (In 2008, the Gates Foundation also made a $600,000 grant to Demos, the liberal think tank where I work.) During this same period, the foundation made only two grants to conservative policy organizations: $400,000 each to the American Enterprise Institute and the Hudson Institute.

The Gates Foundation also started to put money into advocacy work aimed at swaying U.S. policy overseas. It helped bring to scale a new policy center in Washington, the Center for U.S. Global Engagement, that had been founded in response to the Bush administration's unilateralist—and heavily militarized—approach to the world.

All of these investments reflected a growing appreciation by Bill and Melinda Gates that they would succeed in their work only to the extent that they mobilized the vast resources of government behind their causes. Markets couldn't solve problems by themselves, and neither could charity. The Gates Foundation may be the largest philanthropic enterprise in history—with annual spending greater than $3 billion in 2009—but these resources are small compared to government's. New York City alone spends $22 billion a year on its public schools. "We're a tiny, tiny little organization," Gates said at one point.[10] As other foundations had long ago discovered, all of the demonstration projects in the world are for naught if government won't pony up the money to bring new ideas to scale. That's where advocacy and politics come in, so it's no surprise that Gates has not only begun to fund elements of the progressive infrastructure, but has also veered toward the Democratic Party. Gates made a $10,000 contribution to the Democratic Congressional Committee in 2008, and he and Melinda each contributed the maximum of $50,000 to Barack Obama's inauguration fund.

Gates also began to openly criticize capitalism. By 2008, he had come to believe that free markets had fundamentally failed to meet the basic needs of people at the bottom of the global income ladder. To raise up the lives of the poor and truly conquer dread diseases, he believed that a new kind of capitalism would be needed.

Gates put forth this thesis during a keynote address at the 2008 meeting of the World Economic Forum, long a venue for celebrating the market's virtues. Gates told the assembled crowd of luminaries that capitalism was a great system—except for poor people who don't have any money. The market had plenty of incentives to address problems that rich people worried about—for instance, finding a cure to baldness—but there were no incentives to tackle the problems that plagued the poor, such as finding a vaccine for malaria. "So, the bottom billion misses the benefits of the global economy," Gates observed. Thus, a seminal challenge facing humanity was "to find a way to make the aspects of capitalism that serve wealthier people serve poorer people as well."

In effect, Gates proposed designing a new kind of system to create incentives, which would include profit and recognition, that would make it desirable to do more for the poor. He called it "creative capitalism." Ultimately, the profit incentive by itself would never go far enough; it needed to be unified with the desire among both individuals and companies to do good and be recognized for doing good.

The creative capitalism speech was yet more evidence that Gates was evolving into a systemic thinker—one who was willing to reject the cornerstone premise of conservative ideology, namely, that the free market could solve all of the problems of the world if meddling bureaucrats just got out of its way.

Does this make Gates a liberal? Not quite. Or, rather, not yet. If history is any guide, however, Gates is already well along a familiar trajectory in which philanthropy that starts with a pragmatic bent migrates steadily leftward over time. The reason for such migration is not, as conservatives often suggest, that liberal "philanthrocrats" seize control and subvert the intent of the founders. (Although, to be sure, there is some of that.) Rather, it's because tackling deep social ills requires bigger reforms than donors initially understood.

The billionaire backlash of the early 2000s helped transform politics in the United States. It was a chief reason that Democrats and liberals were finally able to compete with the conservative movement in terms of campaign cash and money for policy groups. Obama's election, a Democratic Congress, and a new progressive infrastructure are among the fruits of this shift.

Just to be clear: the liberalism of the newly activist rich goes only so far. Most want to reform the free market moderately, not radically. The elite desire for nip and tuck reforms is a familiar one. Again and again, during the last century, concerned members of the upper class have seen liberal reforms as a way to save capitalism from itself— either because of too much instability or corruption in markets or because of too much inequality that threatened to unravel America's social fabric. Andrew Carnegie famously wrote that the "problem of our age is the proper administration of wealth, so that the ties of brotherhood may still bind together the rich and poor in harmonious relationship."[11] The liberal businessman Edward Filene argued much the same thing in the early decades of the twentieth century. American capitalism, he said, was great at creating wealth but not so good at spreading the wealth around. A century later, amid a Gilded Age redux, concerns about capitalism were again common in parts of the upper class.

In his 1972 book *Fats Cats and Democrats*, an early look at the role of big money in the Democratic Party, the leftist academic William Domhoff wrote that politics is in the "hand of the grasping rich, whether of a halfway humane or a reactionary hue."[12] Like C. Wright Mills before him, Domhoff didn't see much difference between Democrats and Republicans, lumping them all into the "Property Party."

This critique is basically right: there is no real debate in the upper class about capitalism versus something else, and most of the liberal rich described in this book would probably be on the right in Europe. But if the differences among the wealthy might seem trivial to a Marxist, the battle between reactionaries and the "halfway humane" is actually a big deal in the U.S. context.

And there is no question that at the very top of the income ladder, the reactionaries have been losing ground.

8

LEFT-COAST MONEY

B ARACK OBAMA'S ELECTION VICTORY on November 4, 2008, did not mean that his formidable fund-raising operation closed up shop. Obama had barely sealed his victory when his fund-raisers turned to another project: collecting money for his inaugural festivities. The effort went splendidly. A week before Obama laid his left hand on Abraham Lincoln's decaying, oversized Bible, team Obama announced that it had achieved its fund-raising goal and pulled in more than $40 million. That total included donations of less than $200 apiece from tens of thousands of people, but the bulk of the money came from big-ticket donors who contributed up to $50,000 each.

This torrent of cash flowed in from across the country, but the largest share of contributions—by far—came from one state: California. Fewer than four hundred deep-pocketed Californians pumped $6.4 million into Obama's inauguration fund, a third more than the amount that wealthy New Yorkers contributed. The list of top California donors was a showcase of the new liberal wealth coalition. It included a large Hollywood contingent, such as the actors Halle Berry, Tom Hanks, and Sharon Stone, as well as billionaire producers such as Steven Spielberg and George Lucas.

(The combined haul from DreamWorks alone was $275,000.) In addition, sizable checks arrived from technology entrepreneurs: top executives at Google, including Larry Page and Eric Schmidt, gave a total of $175,000, while other technologists, for example, Lotus 1-2-3 designer Mitch Kapor and GeoCities founder David Bohnett, also contributed the maximum. California financiers gave generously as well, even as some absorbed staggering losses thanks to the meltdown on Wall Street. Those who gave the maximum $50,000 included mutual fund executive David Fisher, billionaire money manager Howard Marks, and venture capitalist Ellen Pao. Other major inaugural donors were super-successful lawyers, surgeons, and real estate developers. Finally, money came from the inherited rich, who were spread across California, enjoying the state's sunshine and easy lifestyle.

It is no surprise that the Obama inaugural committee struck gold in California. After all, Californians had already given Obama's campaign $76 million by election day. This total dwarfed the $31 million that the state had given to John Kerry four years earlier. Obama's fund-raising in California far exceeded what he raised in other states, to the point that Obama raised as much money in California as he raised from New York, Connecticut, and Massachusetts combined. The bulk of this money came from Los Angeles and the Bay Area, two of the richest, most liberal metro areas in the United States.

Such numbers say much about the rise of the liberal money class. The story of the upper class's shifting ideological allegiances is, in no small measure, the story of how big money has migrated west. Here, the knowledge economy has minted some of the largest fortunes ever seen in the United States. Here, on the so-called left coast, the creative and tolerant ethos inherent to that economy has fused with countercultural currents that still flow strongly in California and the Pacific Northwest. Some of the most activist members of the liberal money class are the products of this synthesis.

We have seen this movie before, but in reverse. The early postwar era of California prosperity yielded a notably conservative culture and two iconic Republican leaders, Richard Nixon and Ronald Reagan. Many business leaders in the new West leaned libertarian, combining the fierce individualism of that region with a bias against social-engineering elites and tax-and-spend government. Fueled by a booming defense sector, Southern California was the most suburbanized area of the United States, and its politics reflected the conservatism that once was synonymous with suburban living. Orange County, just south of Los Angeles and filled with L.A. transplants seeking lower taxes and fewer minorities, was among the most well-known Republican bastions in all of the United States. (Nixon was born in the county and had his "Western White House" in San Clemente.) Wealthy California businessmen played a key role in moving U.S. politics to the right, most notably the small group of millionaires, including the auto dealer Holmes Tuttle and the financier Charles Wick, who backed Ronald Reagan's political rise. The GOP won California in seven straight presidential elections between 1960 and 1988.

All of this is now ancient history. California hasn't given its electoral votes to a Republican in more than twenty years, and the state's residents and businesses have grown both richer and more liberal at the same time. Vast new fortunes began to emerge in the Bay Area during the 1980s, as the technology industry boomed, while the entertainment industry in Southern California grew by leaps and bounds. (The aerospace industry, by contrast, has withered.) Orange County still includes some of the wealthiest communities in the nation—and an estimated 115,000 millionaires—but barely a majority of county residents are now registered Republicans, down from 74 percent in 1984. Meanwhile, north of California, significant new wealth sprang up in the Pacific Northwest, and that region—at least, along the coast—has grown markedly more liberal.

Exactly how much richer has the West become in recent decades? Well, consider that up through the 1960s, New York had by far the largest number of millionaires of any state in the nation. Yet by 1982, California had far surpassed New York in this regard, with the Census Bureau estimating that 64,000 millionaires lived in the Golden State, compared to 30,000 in New York.[1] By 2004, the

Census estimated that the number of Californians with a net worth of at least \$1.5 million had soared to 428,000—growing sixfold in some twenty years. California had more millionaires, in fact, than the second two top states—New York and Florida—combined. In the Pacific Northwest, the number of millionaires grew fivefold in Washington and sevenfold in Oregon. Another study in 2008, by the private research firm TNS, analyzed the top ten U.S. counties with the highest number of millionaires. Five out of ten of these counties were in California, one was in Washington, and only two were in New York. Los Angeles led the way by a sizable margin, with an estimated 261,000 millionaires. Santa Clara County, where Silicon Valley is located, has more millionaires than Manhattan—or any county in New York or Connecticut.[2] (Of course, all of these numbers are lower after the crash.) The West Coast counties with large numbers of millionaires vote Democrat by a more substantial margin than comparable East Coast counties do.

The Forbes 400 list also shows the tectonic westward shift in wealth. When the list first appeared in 1982, it included 77 New Yorkers and

2008 Election Results: Top Wealthiest U.S. Counties, by Millionaire Households

County	Millionaire Households	Obama	McCain
Los Angeles County, CA	261,081	69%	29%
Cook County, IL	168,422	76%	23%
Maricopa County, AZ	126,394	44%	55%
Orange County, CA	115,396	47%	51%
Harris County, TX	107,513	50%	49%
San Diego County, CA	100,727	54%	44%
King County, WA	75,616	70%	28%
Santa Clara County, CA	72,932	70%	29%
Nassau County, NY	71,869	53%	46%
Suffolk County, NY	71,343	52%	47%

Source: TNS Global and "Election Results 2008" on www.nytimes.com.

44 Californians. Starting in 1991, however, California took the lead, and by 2006, the Forbes 400 featured 89 Californians and 56 New Yorkers. The new wealth in the Pacific Northwest was even more striking. Just one Washington resident made the Forbes 400 in 1982: timber baron William Reed. By 2006, the list included 9 billionaires. Of the top twenty richest people in the United States in 2008, only two lived in New York and six lived in California or Washington.

These trends have had profound ramifications for U.S. politics. The West Coast has grown exponentially richer at the same time that its politics have turned from red to blue. The result: Democratic politicians and liberal activists have been able to tap a vast new reservoir of West Coast money to finally compete on an equal footing with conservatives. Just as important, these donors have pushed the Democratic Party to the left and funded harder-hitting think tanks and advocacy groups. The liberal upsurge of recent years has been attributed to many factors, such as the polarizing Bush presidency or the liberalism of the Millennials or the harnessing of new technologies toward political organizing. Perhaps as important as any of these, though, is the influx of new West Coast money into progressive politics.

Certainly, Barack Obama's rise to the White House would not have been possible if some of the wealthiest liberals on the West Coast had not lined up behind his candidacy early on.

If there was any one moment when Obama first emerged as a serious rival to Hillary Clinton, it was the night of February 20, 2007, when Obama proved that he could hold his own in the all-important "money primary." The occasion was a star-studded fund-raiser in Beverly Hills, thrown by the three founders of DreamWorks: David Geffen, Jeffrey Katzenberg, and Steven Spielberg. Obama was barely halfway through his first term as a junior U.S. senator, and it had been less than two weeks since he had formally joined the presidential race. Still, the fund-raiser was the hottest ticket in town. Originally planned for a restaurant that could hold four hundred people, the event was moved to the ballroom of the Beverly Hilton. A who's who of Hollywood bought tickets to the event, including

Tom Hanks, Jennifer Aniston, Ben Stiller, Morgan Freeman, Ron Howard, Eddie Murphy, and Denzel Washington—as well as the heads of Universal Studios, Walt Disney Studios, and Paramount Pictures. Lucky bundlers who sold at least twenty tickets, at $2,300 a pop, were promised a private dinner reception with Obama at Geffen's mansion in Beverly Hills—the 13,600-square-foot former home of Jack Warner that Geffen bought for $47.5 million and spent another $45 million renovating.

The event was the first large Hollywood fund-raiser of the 2008 presidential contest—this in a town that had once seemed like a lock for Hillary Clinton. It raised $1.3 million, a remarkable amount of money so early in a primary. A haul of this size showed that Obama could match the Clinton fund-raising machine and, by extension, that he could match her campaign operation in the field and thus have a serious shot at the nomination.

Hollywood's left-wing politics date back to the early days of the film industry. During the 1930s and 1940s, a great many movie stars and screenwriters had strong leftist politics, and some belonged to the Communist Party. McCarthyism and blacklisting put a damper on leftist politics in Hollywood. But the 1960s saw the emergence of a new kind of liberal activism in Hollywood. Marlon Brando was perhaps the most outspoken of the new activists, backing nearly every cause of the 1960s with his name, time, and money. He was among a number of celebrities—which included Burt Lancaster, Harry Belafonte, Charlton Heston, and James Garner—who attended the 1963 civil rights march on Washington. Along with Paul Newman, Brando also participated in the Freedom Rides that aimed at desegregating bus facilities in the Deep South. A few years later, stars like Newman would be galvanized by Eugene McCarthy's antiwar candidacy and then, in 1972, McGovern's doomed liberal campaign. Hollywood got its first political action committee in 1984, when a dozen or so wealthy liberal women—including Barbra Streisand, Jane Fonda, and Marilyn Bergman—got together to form the Hollywood Women's Political Committee (HWPC). The group became the premier liberal operation in town, mobilizing millions of dollars for candidates and any number of activist causes. It became the must-see group for every politician and activist on the left, bolstering Hollywood's clout on the national scene.

This new big money was super-liberal from the start, and one reason is that it comes from a world far removed from Washington and the East Coast corridor, places dominated by neckties cinched tight and more pragmatic reflexes. "There is a culture of thinking outside the box about what should be, not what is possible in Washington," said Marge Tabankin, who ran HWPC through the mid-1990s after spending more than twenty years working inside the D.C. Beltway as an advocate and a government official. Tabankin had come to feel morally and spiritually beaten down by Washington, with its relentless focus on the art of compromise. "I felt a deadening of my energy and belief system." But all of that heaviness lifted in the perpetual sunshine of Los Angeles, where she worked with some of the most idealistic rich liberals in the United States.

Wealthy donors in Hollywood tend to be busy people who are deeply engaged in their work of making movies, running studios, or writing TV shows. They don't know a great deal about the inside politics of Washington, and they aren't thinking about how a bill might fare in this or that congressional committee. "They are focused on what they think is right for the world," said Tabankin. While this might seem naive, it is also very powerful, and Hollywood is the preeminent home of liberal "ideology donors." Of course, this has long been true. So, what is new about Hollywood money today?

The scale. Los Angeles has grown fantastically wealthier, and one reason is globalization. Nearly two-thirds of box office receipts now come from overseas, with worldwide receipts totaling $27 billion in 2007—up from $17 billion in 2001. The fast-growing global reach of American movies helps explain why fifteen out of twenty of the top-grossing films of all time have been released since 1999. Another reason is technology. Sales of DVDs, which barely existed in the 1990s, have emerged as an all-important cash machine. Domestic rentals and sales of DVDs now generate more than double the revenue of domestic box office receipts, or about $23 billion in 2007.[3] Meanwhile, the adult movie industry—largely centered in the

San Fernando Valley—has turned into a huge moneymaker, thanks in no small measure to the Internet. According to one analysis, porn generated $13.3 billion in revenues in 2006, with nearly 20 percent of that money being spent on the Internet.[4]

The cable television revolution has been huge, too. In 1975, fewer than 10 million U.S. homes had cable television, and revenues for the industry were less than $1 billion. In 2008, 65 million households had cable—most with premium channels—and the industry raked in $81 billion. Content producers in Hollywood, including those who create original shows for channels such as HBO and Showtime, take a nice slice of this revenue.[5]

Then, of course, there is the video game industry and the music industry, both of which are also heavily based in Los Angeles. Sales of video games, which are much more sophisticated now, thanks to advances in computer chips and graphics, amount to about $10 billion a year—more than triple the 1996 total.[6] The recording industry may be famously troubled, but Americans still spend more than $10 billion a year on CDs and digital music.[7]

One upshot of all of the new money flowing into Los Angeles is that the city's creative talents—typically, the most liberal elements of the entertainment industry—are infinitely richer than they were in earlier times. Left-wing movie stars such as Marlon Brando and Warren Beatty made good money for their time, but it wasn't the kind of money that allowed them to be heavyweight political donors, and it is nothing compared to what movie stars make today. For instance, according to *Forbes*, Harrison Ford earned $65 million in 2008, while Will Smith pulled in $45 million and Eddie Murphy made $40 million.[8] It was easy for Tom Hanks to write a $50,000 check to Barack Obama's inaugural committee when Hanks was paid a reported $50 million to star in *Angels and Demons*, a prequel to *The Da Vinci Code*. Even a washed-up star like Sharon Stone could easily spare the $50,000 she donated to the Inaugural Committee, given that she banked $13.6 million for *Basic Instinct II* in 2006.

Top Ten Actor Political Contributors, 1978–2008

Name	Total	Democrat	GOP	Special Interest
Barbra Streisand	$656,776	90%	0%	10%
Rob Reiner	$629,083	94%	0%	6%
Michael Douglas	$598,950	97%	0%	3%
Marlo Thomas	$409,400	77%	0%	23%
Paul Newman	$286,000	81%	1%	18%
Heather Thomas	$260,314	93%	0%	7%
Chevy Chase	$223,675	93%	0%	7%
Joanne Woodward	$218,250	79%	1%	20%
Jane Fonda	$203,796	64%	0%	36%
Kate Capshaw	$194,875	92%	0%	8%

Source: www.newsmeat.com.

Creative figures in the entertainment industry are now more generous political donors than the top CEO contributors from corporate America. The difference is that Hollywood money goes nearly exclusively to Democrats.

Of course, when it comes to donating to politicians and causes, movie stars are cheap—at least, compared to moguls, who have an ownership stake in everything they do and who pull in the real money in Hollywood.

For decades, the most generous Democratic donor in Hollywood was Lew Wasserman—who was also the most powerful man in the movie business for quite a while. Wasserman gave $1.5 million to Democrats between 1978 and 2002 and considerable sums in previous years, going back to the 1960s. Wasserman, though, had a modest fortune by today's standards. He was never worth more than half a billion dollars. Other moguls of an earlier era were worth much less—such as Jack Warner, who left an estate of only $15 million when he died in 1978.[9]

Compare these figures to the moguls of today. David Geffen was worth an estimated $5 billion in 2010. Steven Spielberg and George Lucas were both worth $3 billion. Jeffrey Katzenberg had a net worth of about $900 million. All three men have given money almost exclusively to the Democratic Party. Together, Geffen, Spielberg, and Katzenberg have donated upward of $4 million to the Democratic Party since 1992 and have raised many times that much.

Meanwhile, Steven Bing—a real estate heir turned writer/director/producer—makes these donors look like tightwads. Although he is little known, Bing has introduced a level of liberal political giving never before seen in Hollywood. Bing has donated some $10 million to the Democratic Party since 1999. He also contributed $18.6 million to liberal 527 groups during the 2004 and 2008 presidential elections. Beyond this giving, Bing has spent millions on ballot initiative battles in California. In 2006, he shelled out a stunning $49.6 million to back Proposition 87, which would have taxed oil companies to fund the development of alternative fuels. (The initiative attracted a who's who of liberal supporters, including Al Gore, but was rejected by voters.) Bing has also poured money into the Center for American Progress and Bill Clinton's foundation.

Haim Saban is another deep-pocketed donor who is not well known outside of Los Angeles. A television producer and media mogul worth $3.3 billion in 2010 who made a fortune on the *Mighty Morphin Power Rangers*, Saban has given $13 million to the Democrats since 2000.

Finally, no account of big progressive money in Hollywood would be complete without mention of Norman Lear, who is worth hundreds of millions of dollars, thanks to his hit sitcoms of the 1970s, such as *All in the Family* and *Sanford and Son*. Lear is no ordinary Hollywood political donor. Although he has given nearly as much money to the Democrats as Geffen or Spielberg has, he made his biggest mark by founding People for the American Way in 1981. The group was formed to push back against the evangelical right, and it emerged as the leading opponent of Reagan's judicial appointments—for example, Robert Bork's nomination to the Supreme Court. Lear has also given money to a variety of progressive organizations, such as the Natural Resources Defense Council.

The liberal leanings of some of the entertainment industry's most successful leaders help explain why Democrats are awash in Hollywood money (and why they rarely criticize the trashy, violent, and just plain dumb cultural products coming out of that town). In 1992, Democrats raised $9.8 million from people in movies, TV, and music. In 2008, Democrats raised $37.5 million from Hollywood. Other industries contribute more money to Democrats—for example, lawyers, who gave Democrats $235 million in the 2008 election cycle—but Hollywood and Los Angeles, broadly, play a more crucial role in the money primary. Gary Hart was able to mount a viable campaign against Walter Mondale in 1984 in part because he did exceptionally well raising money in Hollywood, drawing on contacts with Warren Beatty and other celebrities he had cultivated as McGovern's campaign manager in 1972. Michael Dukakis emerged as the Democratic nominee in 1988 in part because he built a "money machine" in Los Angeles "that has shattered all Democratic presidential fund-raising records in California," according to a report at the time by the *Los Angeles Times*.[10]

Four years later, Hollywood money would give Bill Clinton an important edge. Clinton was strongly helped by his close ties with Linda Bloodworth Thomason and her husband, Harry Thomason, producers of CBS-TV's hit shows *Designing Women* and *Evening Shade*.[11] Among other things, the Thomasons persuaded their Hollywood friends to think less about Clinton's iffy centrist past—including his founding membership in the Democratic Leadership Council—and more about his history of antiwar activism, his friendliness toward gay rights, and his other liberal credentials.

To be sure, Hollywood has always had its share of Republicans. During the 1980s, Reagan and then Bush received backing from celebrities such as Bob Hope, Tom Selleck, Sylvester Stallone, and Arnold Schwarzenegger. In October 2008, John McCain raised $4.7 million at a Beverly Hills fund-raiser. Stars in attendance that night included Stephen Baldwin, Robert Duvall, Gary Sinise, and Jon

Voight. Still, Republicans in Hollywood are generally a minority and tend to be secretive about their conservatism, for fear of professional retaliation.

Why is it that creative leaders in the entertainment industry tend to be liberal? For that matter, why is that creative leaders in other fields—theater, literature, the fine arts—also trend heavily left?

One answer would seem to lie in the very nature of creative work. Those involved in culture and art rely on their imagination, rather than on their competence in practical affairs, to succeed. Often, they are nonconformists whose originality comes from taking a critical or untraditional look at the world and pushing the boundaries of acceptable expression. As Richard Florida wrote in *The Rise of the Creative Class*, "the new lifestyle favors individuality, self-statement, acceptance of difference, and the desire for rich multidimensional experiences."[12] The lifestyle of cultural workers also tends to reinforce a bohemian outlook, given that the pay can be low and sporadic, and the working hours can be erratic. It is a rare filmmaker, screenwriter, novelist, or artist—if they are at all successful, anyway—who dresses up every day and reports to an office. The informal Hollywood aesthetic, where casual attire rules—although not for the studio "suits"—and where many creative leaders work out of their homes, epitomizes a mainstream bohemianism found around the cultural sector.

Hollywood is also filled, more than ever, with many of the same super-educated types that you'll find elsewhere in the knowledge economy. For instance, Hollywood has become such a common destination for Harvard graduates that there is now an organization called Harvardwood dedicated to helping these alums make it in town. "When I first came out here, you could count the Harvard people on two hands," director Jonathan Mostow has said. "Moving to Hollywood was like running off to join the circus."[13] Not anymore. Now the town is filled with Harvard grads and other elite college grads who are bringing with them a liberal cultural background and value set.

Another factor that may push Hollywood's biggest winners to trend liberal is the sheer amount of luck that it takes to reach the top and the crazily lopsided rewards given to winners. Everyone who has made it big in Hollywood knows other talented people—more talented, in some cases—who didn't make it. Life in the entertainment industry can feel more like the lottery than a meritocracy. The serendipity and randomness of success make it hard for the town's wealthy to tell themselves an Ayn Randian story about their individual triumphs. Instead, they "understand their privilege," said Marge Tabankin, and they "want to reach out and help others."

The story of Hollywood and the Democrats is yet more evidence that rich donors don't always move the party to the right. Hollywood's rising clout has had the opposite effect. Its priorities since the 1960s have included civil rights, Vietnam, the nuclear freeze, Central America, gun control, reproductive rights, civil liberties, Darfur, and—above all, in recent times—the environment.

The passions of liberal Hollywood help explain the shifting focus of the Democratic Party, starting in the 1960s. It became a party less focused on the economic plight of working-class voters and more focused on postmaterialist concerns. This shift was probably inevitable, and left-wing parties in Europe have also lost working-class support. Still, Democrats didn't help their situation by coming to rely heavily on money from the most socially left segment of the upper class. In particular, the tight alliance with Hollywood has hobbled Democrats in the fight over moral values since the 1980s. Even as a bipartisan majority of Americans grew deeply concerned about the negative messages coming from popular culture, Democrats have rarely criticized the entertainment industry.

Unlike on Wall Street, the wealthy donors of Hollywood are not known for being socially liberal while economically moderate. They tend to be liberal across the board, even if their passions have mainly been focused on things such as Tibet or the melting polar ice caps. If the Democratic Party tacks further left on economic issues, there is no reason to think that it risks losing its donors in Bel Air and Brentwood.

The big money in California's Bay Area is harder to read. Wealthy technologists have only tentatively embraced progressive politics, and their pet causes—and pet peeves—are only starting to come into focus.

The vast wealth of Silicon Valley—as well as in the Seattle area— has become such a fixture in America's collective conscious that it is easy to forget how new these fortunes are. Although Silicon Valley has long been a high-tech center, going back to World War II and earlier, it wasn't until Apple Computer's successful initial public offering (IPO) in 1980 that the valley became synonymous with great wealth. By the late 1980s, the tech industry had still produced only a handful of world-class fortunes, and it wasn't until the Internet boom of the 1990s that the technology rich had emerged as one of the central pillars of the far upper class. By the early 2000s, Silicon Valley was home to many more millionaires than Manhattan was.

The popular image of rich geeks is that they lean libertarian— that is, when they think about politics at all. If the tech world had a political icon, it was the hacker—the antiauthoritarian genius who could stick a finger in the eye of powerful institutions. In *Cyberselfish*, Pauline Borsook's chastising book about the libertarian tech world, Borsook says that Ayn Rand is so revered in this world that techies name their start-ups and even their children after characters or institutions in Rand's novels. Borsook argues that "libertarianism is the techie equivalent to the Judeo-Christian heritage of the West." It influences everyone in this world, even subconsciously.

Borsook's book was published in 2001, and much of its research was about the 1990s. Since then, the high-tech rich have remained a political work in progress. Like much of California, Silicon Valley has been trending Democratic for years, and a Republican presidential candidate hasn't won Santa Clara County—which covers much of the valley—since 1984. Obama won 70 percent of the votes in the county in 2008, while Kerry won 64 percent. These margins are as high as nearly anywhere in the country.

And big tech money is flowing to Democrats, too. For most of the 1990s, Democratic politicians didn't bother much with Silicon Valley, which donated only modestly at election time. For example, the tech industry gave only $5.2 million in campaign contributions in 1992— nearly a third less than the amount Hollywood gave. Bill Clinton raised a paltry $83,000 from the entire software and computer industry when he ran for president that year. Political contributions from rich techies grew during the 1990s, but the money tended to be split evenly between the two parties. Clinton may have pledged to build "a bridge to the future" during his 1996 campaign, and his vice president may have been a technophile who had backed early funding for the Internet, but the tech industry still gave more money, by a slight edge, to World War II veteran Bob Dole.

Tech money finally became a potent force in politics during the dot-com boom, and it has remained so ever since. In 2008, for instance, residents of Atherton, California—the most affluent town in Silicon Valley and home to many high-tech executives—donated four times as much money to politics as they did in 1996. Three-quarters of this money went to Democrats. Overall, the tech industry gave twice as much money to Democrats as to Republicans in 2008, a sharp departure from previous trends.

Microsoft has been foremost among tech companies in its new political giving. Back in 1992, Microsoft employees contributed a mere $60,000 in political donations. In 1998, as the company's stock approached an all-time high, these employees gave nearly $1.5 million, and in 2008, they contributed $3 million. Serious Microsoft money went to Republicans when the Clinton Justice Department slapped the company with an antitrust suit. But links to the GOP ebbed rapidly during the Bush years, and the biggest individual donors at Microsoft gave almost exclusively to Democrats during that period. In 2008, 71 percent of Microsoft's political donations went to Democrats.

The tech sector's new heft in political fund-raising—and particularly its growing role in the Democratic money primary—was driven home when all three of the top Democratic candidates visited the Googleplex in Mountain View well before the first primary was held in January 2008. They came not only because Google's headquarters had become something of a shrine of the Information Age, a required pilgrimage for any public figure who wanted to seem hip to high tech. They also came because Google had emerged as one of the richest and most liberal top companies in the United States. In only a few years, Googlers had gone from giving almost no money to politics to being the second-biggest donors in the tech industry in 2008, just behind Microsoft.

Google's IPO in August 2004 may be a milestone remembered for any number of reasons; certainly, it should be remembered by Democratic fund-raisers. An estimated one thousand millionaires were minted at the newly public Google, as well as a few billionaires, the vast majority of whom were Democrats. In 2004, only the tiniest sliver—just 1 percent—of political donations by Googlers went to Republicans, an ideological purity unmatched at any of the top technology companies. Barack Obama was smart enough to make a point of visiting Google in 2004, and he was definitely wise to visit Google again in November 2007. During the following year, Googlers became the fourth-largest bloc of donors to Obama's campaign, giving nearly as much as employees of Goldman Sachs. Eric Schmidt even hit the campaign trail for Obama, one of the few high-profile CEOs to do so.

Wealthy technologists on the West Coast haven't only begun to bankroll Democratic politicians at an entirely new level, they have also thrown their money and skills into building the progressive

Top Ten West Coast Tech Companies by Employee Political Contributions, 2008 Election Cycle

Company	Total	Democrat	GOP
Microsoft	$2,976,322	71%	28%
Google	$1,582,447	83%	17%
Cisco Systems	$1,226,604	67%	33%
Oracle Corp.	$ 812,983	71%	29%
Hewlett-Packard	$ 644,469	67%	33%
Yahoo!	$ 464,983	89%	10%
eBay	$ 450,710	56%	44%
Symantec	$ 384,376	84%	15%

Source: Center for Responsive Politics.

infrastructure. MoveOn.org is the best example of this. It was created in 1998 by two Bay Area software entrepreneurs, Wes Boyd and Joan Blade, and emerged during the Bush years as perhaps the single most important group on the left.

Boyd is a familiar figure in wealthy liberal circles. He is the son of a political science professor who spent his childhood years in Ann Arbor, Michigan, before moving to Berkeley, where his father taught at the University of California. Boyd was a campus brat and something of a prodigy. He started writing computer programs at the age of fourteen and continued programming as a student at UC–Berkeley. He dropped out of school to work full-time on software and later, with his wife, founded a company called Berkeley Systems. The company created the computer trivia game "You Don't Know Jack" and the Flying Toasters screensaver. Sales of the software soared, and profits started to roll in.

By 1997, Boyd and Blade were ready for other challenges and sold their company for a modest fortune. They were rich. But they were also young, still in their thirties, and soon they were at work on starting something new, in the area of education software, which they saw as a big growth field of the future.

Around the time that Boyd and Blade began their new venture, a troubling background noise had arisen in their lives: a drumbeat of news stories about Clinton's affair with Monica Lewinsky. Special prosecutor Ken Starr seemed to be on the news constantly. "It was oppressive," Boyd said.

Boyd's politics were predictable for someone of his background: he was progressive, but like many in the tech sector, he wasn't very engaged. At Berkeley Systems, politics were rarely discussed, except in the most cynical terms. Being totally unengaged in and dismissive of politics "was almost like a badge of honor," said Boyd.

When the Clinton scandal snowballed into impeachment proceedings, Boyd and Blade felt compelled to take action. They circulated an online petition arguing that the Congress should censure Clinton, not impeach him, and then the country should "move on." "You had to know there were better things for our nation to be focused on," Boyd said. "And there were."

The petition spread virally over the Internet in a way that neither Boyd nor Blade ever imagined. MoveOn.org emerged as a player in the impeachment fight, and the organization took over their lives, pushing aside work on the education software company. "We were waylaid by politics," Boyd said.

After the impeachment fight, MoveOn.org had an e-mail list of three hundred thousand and a new model of civic engagement—one that reflected the distinctive mind-set of West Coast technologists. Boyd and Blade decided to stick with the project, at least through the 2000 election. They wanted to go after the Republicans who had managed the impeachment effort in the House, and they raised $2.5 million for this effort through the first-ever online PAC.

They also wanted to further develop their model. "What we saw when we looked at politics was an immense vacuum," Boyd said. "There was a participation problem. The heart of America stopped playing." That was because the traditional model of politics did little to bring ordinary people in. It was top down, revolving around money and celebrity endorsements, and focused on periodic elections with zero-sum outcomes in which one side either won or lost. There weren't a lot of ways for people to engage in a more ongoing fashion. The professionalization of politics, dominated by consultants and pollsters, "was just wrong and it was a dead end." Boyd and Blade wanted to change all of that. "We were naive enough to believe that technology and communications could play a role in binding people to politics," Boyd said.

Gore's defeat in 2000, sealed by a 5–4 Supreme Court verdict, added a new urgency to MoveOn's work. Boyd and Blade realized they were in for the long haul and wouldn't be going back to their business ventures any time soon. During the next four years, MoveOn. org would become the foremost vehicle for mobilizing opposition to the Bush administration. "There was a real crisis," Boyd said. "The right really began a blitzkrieg. A lot of people woke up and felt it was really dangerous. And they stepped forward." Through its many initiatives and campaigns, MoveOn soon compiled the biggest e-mail political outreach list since the dawn of the Internet.

It was not only ordinary people who got involved; wealthy people also began to back the organization, and MoveOn came to epitomize a partnership that has been at the core of recent progressive successes: citizen activists and big liberal money. In 2004, MoveOn raised millions of dollars in substantial contributions from billionaires such as George Soros and Peter Lewis. Its efforts continued into 2006 and 2008. All told, mobilizing both large and small donors, MoveOn has raised $100 million for Democratic candidates and ad campaigns. It transformed political organizing and served as a model for the Internet fund-raising machines built by Howard Dean and Barack Obama.

Wealthy technologists were behind other progressive ventures, too, such as Air America Radio, which received heavy backing from Rob Glaser, the CEO and chairman of the Seattle-based RealNetworks. Glaser is the perfect embodiment of modern wealth liberalism, only he is both richer and more leftist than most people in this world. Born in the early 1960s to activist Jewish parents, he grew up in suburban Yonkers outside of New York City. His mother was a social worker who worked with inner-city kids, while his father ran a print shop. As a kid, Glaser went to protests with them and handed out leaflets to support the United Farm Workers' grape boycott. He went to one of the most liberal private schools in New York, the Ethical Culture Fieldstone School in Riverdale. There he learned how to program on the school's mainframe computer and, at one point, also set up a pirate radio station that broadcast to the cafeteria.

Glaser went on to Yale University, where he wrote a political column for the *Yale Daily News*, "What's Left," and directed a student peace organization that fought the new draft registration law enacted by Jimmy Carter in 1980. (A law that Glaser himself refused to comply with.) He majored in economics and computer science and worked so hard that he also got a master's in economics during his four years at Yale. After graduating, he considered taking a job with the Farm Workers Union, but instead signed on with a small software company in Seattle called Microsoft. Before he headed West, he told friends that he hoped that the left could master technology and use these skills to change society.

Glaser was a star at Microsoft, working on programs like Word and becoming its youngest vice president at one point. Stock options made him a multimillionaire by the time he was thirty, and Glaser left in 1993 to start a new venture with an activist vision. He wanted to create an Internet company that would disseminate content with liberal messages and bypass corporate-controlled media. Glaser and his cofounder, David Halperin, called the company Progressive Networks and imagined it as a cross between PBS and MTV. "It's fair to say that our original objective was social revolution," Halperin told *Wired* in 1997.[14] Things didn't turn out as planned. The political vision never materialized, but with the spread of music file sharing, the technology they developed became wildly popular. RealAudio, their first product, allowed listeners to stream radio over the Internet, and it was a major hit. The company changed its name to RealNetworks and emerged as one of the big success stories of the dot-com boom, turning Glaser into a billionaire before the company's stock plummeted back to earth with the NASDAQ crash, where it has since lingered.

Glaser never lost his interest in reshaping media, and like so many liberals, he spent the 1990s deeply disturbed by the right's message machine, particularly talk radio, where hosts such as Rush Limbaugh were a dominant presence. So, when a chance came along to help level the airwaves, through a new venture called Air America Radio, Glaser was ready to open his checkbook. He became one of the largest investors in Air America, pouring at least $10 million into the network and eventually owning 36 percent of the company.

Air America—and the idea of a liberal radio network—had generated excited buzz since its first official fund-raiser at Arianna Huffington's home in Brentwood in 2002, which attracted a number of celebrities. It was the brainchild of two Chicago entrepreneurs, who set about raising money and, just as important, recruiting Al Franken to be an anchor host when the network went live in the spring of 2004. Later that year, Glaser signed on to be chairman of Air America's board. It would be a rocky ride, as the network was beset by continual problems and burned through its start-up funding. In 2006, Air America tumbled into bankruptcy, only to be quickly resurrected by the liberal New York real estate baron Stephen Green and his brother Mark (the politician and author). Glaser has yet to recoup his investment, but that doesn't seem to bother him much. By 2009, before it again went bankrupt and closed down. Air America had 1.5 million weekly listeners.

Glaser also emerged as one of the biggest campaign contributors from the tech world. He was part of a group of top progressive funders who converged on George Soros's estate in Southampton in 2003 to map out a big-money strategy for ousting Bush from office. Soros pledged $10 million at the session to the 527 called Americans Coming Together. Peter Lewis matched that pledge, and Glaser promised to kick in $2 million. He would spend a bit more than that.

Two years later, Glaser became a founding member of the Democracy Alliance and also gave a lot of money through his foundation. Among his investments has been $1.4 million to fund the Progressive Studies Program at the Center for American Progress (CAP), which aims "to increase public understanding of what it means to be a progressive given our nation's history and the challenges we face today."

There is a long list of other important tech donors on the left. Steve Kirsch, who invented the optical mouse and founded the Web portal InfoSeek, has been among the largest contributors to the Democratic Party over the past decade. "People in Silicon Valley have been able to make a difference in the Democratic Party," Kirsch said in describing the new alignment of tech money behind Democrats. Mitch Kapor, who made his fortune from the software program Lotus 1-2-3, has been funding a range of liberal groups for years. David Bohnett and Tim Gill, as mentioned earlier, have used their tech money to help create the modern gay rights movement.

Andy Rappaport, a Silicon Valley venture capitalist and electrical engineer by training, has been a major donor to CAP and other groups such as People for the American Way, as well as to many smaller organizations working to boost voter turnout. Rappaport made hundreds of millions of dollars betting on the right technology start-up companies and only became an active donor in 2004. Along with his wife, Deborah, he soon made up for lost time. Beyond giving their own money to liberal groups—and more than $4 million to fund various 527s in the 2004 election—the Rappaports created the New Progressive Coalition, to link up wealthy donors with progressive causes.

The flow of tech money to Democrats and progressive groups in recent years may only be a warm-up for things to come. Google has changed how people use the Internet; it may also, in time, help change the political landscape. The company's founders, Sergey Brin and Larry Page, have barely touched fortunes that rank among the most sizable in the world. When they do get around to large-scale philanthropy, there is little doubt that the two men will support progressive causes. One sign of where Brin and Page stand politically came when they gave a combined total of $140,000 to defeat Proposition 8, the 2008 California ballot initiative to ban gay marriage.

Google's CEO and chairman, Eric Schmidt, has emerged as an active player not only in politics, but also in policy. He has given more than $1 million to the New America Foundation, a think tank that positions itself as centrist but supports a range of progressive thinkers and projects. Schmidt also chairs the board of New America. Like many of Silicon Valley's rich, Schmidt has barely scratched the surface of his potential philanthropy. After Google went public, he began to transfer tens of millions of dollars into the Schmidt Family Foundation and ramp up his giving. But these funds represent a small fraction of his net worth, which stood at $6.3 billion in 2010.

Slowing climate change and developing clean energy are among the top priorities of Google.org, the company's foundation, reflecting a strong passion among all three of Google's top leaders. This environmental streak came through strongly during the 2006 fight over Proposition 87, a California ballot initiative that would have taxed oil companies to fund clean energy technologies. Google's cofounders made their largest political contributions ever when they each gave $1 million to help sway Californians to vote for the initiative. Schmidt's wife, Wendy, also put $1 million into the campaign. Other Silicon Valley heavyweights kicked in as well, including Terry Semel, then the CEO of Yahoo; the venture capitalist John Doerr; the billionaire and Sun Microsystems cofounder Vinod Khosla; Jeff Skoll, the cofounder of eBay; and Irwin Jacobs, the chairman of Qualcomm.

Proposition 87 didn't fly with voters, but serious Silicon Valley money has continued to flow into environmental causes. Eric and Wendy Schmidt have sunk millions of dollars into groups such as the Natural Resources Defense Council and the Energy Foundation, while Intel cofounder Gordon Moore—as already discussed—is emerging as one of the biggest environmental philanthropists of all time. Many wealthy technologists also make personal use of green technology. Both Brin and Page own Priuses, and hybrid vehicles are everywhere in Silicon Valley. In fact, the region now boasts 15 percent of all newly registered hybrid cars in California and 10 percent of all electric cars.[15]

It is no surprise that climate change has so galvanized the tech crowd. Scientists like hard problems, and few get tougher than this. Reducing greenhouse gases is a vast and complex challenge, and meeting it will require major new technological breakthroughs in clean energy. For many in Silicon Valley, climate change has become not only an activist cause, but also a major focus of investment, with venture capitalists such as John Doerr deciding that green technology is the next big thing. If a "green-industrial complex" emerges in coming years, expect to find Silicon Valley near its center.

Education is another cause that excites the valley's wealthy, and many have pushed for putting more money into public schools. In 2000, Doerr was the largest funder of a campaign to pass Proposition 39, which aimed to make it easier for localities to pass school bonds and raise property taxes—in effect, watering down Proposition 13, the granddaddy of right-wing antitax initiatives, which was passed in 1978 and which limits property taxes. Doerr sank $6 million into the campaign. Other supporters included Netflix CEO Reed Hastings, who contributed $1 million.[16] Numerous technology companies endorsed the measure, such as Adobe Systems, Advanced Micro Devices, Broadcom, Hewlett-Packard, Intel, and Novell. All told, the tech industry put more than $20 million into supporting Proposition 39, which passed. "It's an amazing phenomenon that you've got a pro-education, pro–public schools initiative that's substantially funded by business," said Hastings. "Normally, pro–public education initiatives are funded by the education establishment—the unions, the school boards."[17]

The same year that Silicon Valley mobilized behind Proposition 39, it rose in opposition to another education ballot initiative, Proposition 38, which would have funded private vouchers. A tech venture capitalist, Tim Draper, was behind this initiative, but few of his industry peers supported the idea—and many contributed funds to block the initiative, which was rejected by voters.

Will the technology wealthy continue to migrate leftward? There are good reasons to think so. Like Hollywood, Silicon Valley is a place that runs on creativity. Many techies are scientists who lean heavily on their imaginations to generate new ideas and products. They are not bohemian, exactly, although many are nonconformists who sit comfortably outside the mainstream. They are known for their odd hours, casual style, and offbeat behavior—like when Larry Page and Sergey Brin rolled onstage on inline skates at the G1 mobile phone launch. Apple Computer captured this spirit in its famous 1997 ad as part of its "Think Different" campaign. The ad, narrated by the liberal actor Richard Dreyfuss, said, "Here's to the crazy ones, the misfits, the rebels, the troublemakers, the round pegs in a square hole, the ones who see things different. They're not fond of rules and they have no respect for the status quo." The ad went on, flashing footage of Albert Einstein, Martin Luther King Jr., John Lennon and Oko Yono, Gandhi, and others. It was the first ad campaign approved by Steve Jobs after his return to Apple.

Beyond their noncomformity, techies tend to be highly educated, a trait that correlates closely with liberal politics. Google's leadership is a case in point. Brin's background is as geeky as it gets. Both of his parents are Russian Jewish mathematicians, and Brin—who emigrated to the United States at age six—was partly home-schooled by his father, a professor at the University of Maryland. Brin started to take college classes when most kids his age were still in junior high, and he earned his degree when he was nineteen. After that, he started graduate studies in computer science at Stanford. Brin's cofounder, Larry Page, is also the child of academic parents. His father taught computer science and researched artificial intelligence at Michigan State University; his mother taught computer programming, also at Michigan State University. Before cofounding Google, Page spent his entire adult life in an academic environment, first at the University of Michigan and then as a graduate student at Stanford. Eric Schmidt also came out of academia, spending years getting his PhD in the left-wing environs of Berkeley before heading to Silicon Valley.

Logging time on a university campus doesn't guarantee a liberal political affiliation, but it does correlate with such views. A 2007 Harvard study, "The Social and Political Views of American Professors," found that although academics were nowhere near as radical as conservatives often charge, they were quite liberal. Three-quarters of professors voted for Kerry in 2004. Computer scientists aren't as liberal as other academics, such as social scientists or English professors, are. Still, only 33 percent of computer scientists supported Bush in 2004. And out of all campuses, the PhD-granting elite universities—the kinds of places where future billionaires get their training—tend to have some of the most liberal professors.[18] None of these findings should be all that surprising, because political ideology often correlates closely with education. Exit polls showed that in 2008, Obama won some of his biggest margins among voters with postgraduate educations, just as Kerry did in 2004 and Gore in 2000.

The universities of the Bay Area were deeply influenced by the counterculture and political movements of the 1960s. The University of California at Berkeley was a hotbed of activism and the hippie lifestyle. Stanford University, with close ties to Silicon Valley, was a haven for alternative thinkers and drug experimentation (Ken Kesey had gotten his start there), and the computer research labs were part of this scene. Fred Moore, a young technologist, emerged from this climate to become an innovator of personal computers. He was also a political activist and a crusader for social justice, and he saw these two parts of his life as closely linked. He and many other PC visionaries saw the personal computer as a way to break the grip of authoritarian institutions and empower ordinary citizens. "Computers are mostly used against people instead of for people; used to control people instead of to free them," stated the first newsletter of a Silicon Valley organization called the People's Computer Company that Moore helped found in the early 1970s. "Time to change all that."

In his book *What the Doormouse Said: How the 60s Counterculture Shaped the Personal Computer Industry*, John Markoff argues that it was inevitable that the PC would emerge on the West Coast. "The East Coast computing industry didn't get it," Markoff wrote. "The old computing world was hierarchical and conservative." Markoff documents how computer engineers in the Bay Area—such as Douglas Engelbart, who would invent the computer mouse—experimented with LSD, believing that the drug could spur their creativity. Others pathbreaking technologists, such as Larry Tesler—who worked with early versions of the PC at Xerox's Palo Alto research lab—were committed political radicals.[19]

Steve Jobs exemplified the link between the PC revolution and the counterculture. In the mid-1970s, Jobs dropped out of Reed, an alternative college in Oregon, and backpacked through India. He returned to the United States as a Buddhist with a shaved head and dressed in traditional Indian garb. He used LSD and other psychedelic drugs, later saying that these experiences were among the most important of his life. Jobs is a devoted Beatles fan who once dated Joan Baez, and he is also a vegetarian. He rarely shows up in public wearing anything other than jeans, a black turtleneck, and New Balance running shoes.

It's hard to imagine that a man with this profile would be anything other than a Democrat, and, sure enough, Jobs's political giving over the last fifteen years has gone exclusively to the Democratic Party—including a $100,000 donation to the DNC in 1996. Jobs's wife, Laurene Powell Jobs, is the far more active political donor in the family, making numerous gifts every year to Democratic politicians around the United States.

Jobs is not especially known for his ideological leanings. Certainly he's not known for his philanthropy, which has been virtually nonexistent—to the point that there is a spoof floating around on the Internet, *The Complete Book of Steve Jobs' Philanthropy*, which is a PDF document consisting of fifty blank pages. But the man does have $5 billion, and one day—when he's no longer obsessed with "i" this or "i" that—Jobs will turn inevitably to philanthropy. Chances are, that philanthropy will reflect his countercultural roots and Democratic sympathies.

The great technology fortunes of the United States remain very new, and many are in the hands of relatively young people. Steve Jobs was born in 1955. Bill Gates is the same age, as is Eric Schmidt, the "grown-up" in Google's high command. Jeff Bezos of Amazon was born in 1964. The eBay billionaires Jeff Skoll and Pierre Omidyar were born in 1965 and 1967, respectively. Sergey Brin and Larry Page were both born in 1973. Marc Andreessen made a fortune on Netscape in the 1990s and would seem to be a senior statesman in Silicon Valley; he was born in 1971. Facebook's Mark Zuckerberg, who could well emerge as one of the richest technologists of the twenty-first century, was born in 1984.

Political scientists have long noted that civic participation rises with age. Young people have the lowest rates of voting and volunteerism; the retired have the highest. Young adults are often too caught up in early life challenges to think much about influencing the broader world, while people at the height of very busy careers may not have time to do much beyond vote.

It makes sense that the wealthy—like most of us—tend to turn to public concerns over time. By this logic, we are probably just at the start of Silicon Valley's era of political and philanthropic engagement, and even some of the most "cyberselfish" of the late 1990s may end up leaving a very different legacy. Bill Gates didn't turn to large-scale giving until he had been at Microsoft for nearly twenty years. (In the 1990s, he was more famous for having a huge gadget-filled mansion, Xanadu 2.0, than for having a big foundation.) Gordon Moore founded Intel in 1968; it wasn't until 2000 that he and his wife established a family foundation and began to channel serious money into environmental causes. The bulk of William Hewlett's fortune, amassed through the Hewlett-Packard computer giant, wasn't made available for philanthropy until after Hewlett's death in 2001. The William Flora Hewlett Foundation is now among the top five foundations in the United States and supports a wide array of progressive organizations.

Steve Jobs isn't alone in his lack of philanthropy. Amazon's Jeff Bezos hasn't gotten around to giving away large chunks of his wealth, either. Nor has Larry Ellison of Oracle, the third-richest man in the United States, or Microsoft's Steve Ballmer, who was worth $14.5 billion in 2010. Inevitably, though, these and other giant tech fortunes will one day be harnessed to some kind of public purpose, as they are too big to be disposed of privately. Only then will we have a full picture of how the technology sector's vast new wealth is likely to affect the United States and the world.

9

PATRICIAN POLITICIANS

PHILANTHROPY AND POLITICAL GIVING are the most typical ways for the wealthy to influence how the country is run. But these avenues aren't always satisfying, whether in terms of impact or of ego, and more wealthy people are going into politics. A large majority of them are Democrats, and some have emerged as among the most liberal elected leaders in the United States.

The wealthy statesman has been a familiar figure in U.S. politics since the founding of the republic. George Washington, for example, was not only the nation's first president, but also its richest to date, with a fortune that might have exceeded $1 billion in inflation-adjusted terms. Many of his fellow founders, including Thomas Jefferson, were also extremely affluent. A century later, the Gilded Age saw a huge influx of the wealthy into politics, so much so that the Senate was often referred to as a "millionaire's club," given the many prosperous men in that body.

The second Gilded Age has produced a similar phenomenon. What's different now is that a much larger number of upper-class people are angling for office, and, in contrast to the last Gilded Age, many who choose public life see their mission not to uphold their class interests, narrowly defined, but rather to advance liberal ideals. To that end, some are willing to spend millions or even tens of millions of dollars of their own money.

This trend may be good for public policy—at least, if you care about things like progressive taxation, slowing climate change, and strengthening the social safety net. But the rising tide of the super-rich trying to buy their way into elected office can't possibly be good for democracy.

Jared Polis, who was elected to Congress as part of the 2008 Democratic sweep, exemplifies the new breed of rich progressive politicians, as well as the ironic contradictions inherent in this role. Polis was born to artsy liberal parents in the progressive enclave of Boulder, Colorado. Both his mother and his father had been members of Students for a Democratic Society and active in the antiwar movement and other causes. Polis's grandparents—a postal worker and a social worker who lived in New York City—were also well to the left and politically active.

Polis was drawn to technology as a teenager and started his first Internet business while still in college at Princeton. After selling that business, he teamed up with his parents to create an online greeting card business, Bluemountainarts.com, which they sold to Excite@ Home at the apex of the dot-com bubble for $780 million. (A few years later, after the bust, the business would be resold for only $35 million.) Polis then went on to start ProFlowers.com, an online florist that he sold for $400 million. Estimates of his net worth range from $160 million to $200 million.

Polis is not exactly a latecomer to politics. At age thirteen, he volunteered for the Dukakis campaign, and at fifteen, he volunteered on a Senate campaign. He remained politically active during his years in business and ramped up these involvements after making his fortune. He ran for the Colorado State Board of Education in 2000, spending more than $1 million of his own money and winning the seat by 90 votes. This kind of spending was unheard of in Board of Education races, dashing any kind of level playing field and securing Polis's narrow victory over an opponent who spent only $11,000.

Polis used his position on the board to push for reform and played a key role in stopping cuts to the state education budget. Meanwhile, he created the Jared Polis Foundation, which focuses on education and access to technology, and he founded two new schools, one for homeless youths and one for the children of migrants. Polis brought tremendous creativity and drive to education, quickly distinguishing himself as an out-of-the-box thinker who could get results. He was the kind of social entrepreneur that the U.S. education sector so desperately needs: someone deeply committed to equity, but who was willing to shake up the system to get change. Democrats and Republicans alike had good things to say about him. "He's not just another rich guy who wants power," a GOP strategist told the *Wall Street Journal*. "He's actually done some really good, concrete things with education."[1]

Polis also branched out beyond education, working to change the politics of Colorado writ large. In 2004, he teamed up with three other wealthy liberal Coloradans to pour large sums of money into statewide electoral races. This effort helped deal a crushing defeat to conservative forces in Colorado and allowed Democrats to win control of the state legislature for the first time in forty years. Among other things, this shift led to a partial rollback of the Taxpayer Bill of Rights, a law that limited taxes and crippled the state government.

If Polis were a right-winger, his outsize political spending—and its clear impact—would have triggered fear and outrage in the state's liberal circles. As it was, people didn't quite know what to make of a twenty-something multimillionaire who bought his way into political office and threw around his fortune in order to do good things. The fact that Polis was openly gay only complicated the picture.

The irony of Polis's personal spending on behalf of the public interest was driven home by his efforts to influence ethics legislation in Colorado. Polis spent heavily to help win approval of a ballot measure in 2006 that sharply curtailed the gifts that Colorado legislators could receive from lobbyists—even a free cup of coffee was forbidden—and then spent more of his own money to ensure that the new law was properly enforced. Polis helped pay for lobbyists and consultants who worked to shape the details of enforcement. In other words, Polis poured gobs of money into the political system in order to prevent the influence of money in politics—which didn't exactly seem consistent to some critics, especially to Republicans. "Jared Polis is a rich kid who thinks he can buy the state of Colorado," House Republican minority leader Mike May said. "He thinks only Jared Polis should have influence in the legislature. He can spend whatever he wants, but not others."[2]

Liberal groups were generally silent about Polis's spending, perhaps because they agreed with the end result: tougher rules that prevented private power from subverting the public will. The fact that Polis himself epitomized the kind of clout that money could buy in a medium-size state like Colorado may have elicited grumbling but little open criticism.

The mixed emotions about Polis resurfaced when he upped the ante and engaged in record spending to win the Boulder congressional seat that Mark Udall vacated when he ran for the Senate. The seat was safely Democratic, but Polis faced two primary opponents, the most formidable of which was Joan Fitz-Gerald, a state senator who had won the endorsement of Emily's List. Fitz-Gerald had more than paid her dues as a public servant, becoming the first woman ever elected as county clerk in Jefferson County, serving three terms in the state legislature, becoming the first woman Senate majority leader in Colorado history, and working tirelessly to elect more Democrats to high office in the state as chair of the Democratic Legislative Campaign Committee. She seemed ideally qualified to fill Udall's vacant seat, and in another time and place, her years of service would have been rewarded by a chance to move upward on the political ladder.

Fitz-Gerald had the misfortune, however, to find herself running against Polis, who tapped his large fortune to finance his campaign. In fact, Polis had begun to use his money against Fitz-Gerald long before the primary battle, when he paid for radio ads to push the new state ethics law and singled out Fitz-Gerald for criticism—a ploy that many saw as nakedly political and unfair. Now, with infinitely deep pockets for the primary race, Polis could afford to spend heavily on television ads, radio ads, mailings, and a professional campaign staff. Polis even spent money to fly himself over to Iraq for a fact-finding mission that helped burnish his foreign policy credentials.

Fitz-Gerald was badly outspent from the beginning. Ultimately, Polis poured $5.7 million of his own money into his campaign and spent three times more than Fitz-Gerald did. The contest was the third most expensive House race in the nation and shattered all previous spending records for the district. Polis's millions proved decisive in his victory over Fitz-Gerald by only 4 points.

Polis defended his spending with the familiar argument that he would not be beholden to any special interest groups or PACs when he got to Congress. Certainly, there is something to the notion that Polis will have fewer favors to repay. In some ways, Polis represents the best face of a new progressive politics: he is willing to embrace ideas—such as charter schools—that may make traditional Democratic constituencies uneasy but is guided by a set of core progressive principles and is among the most left members of Congress. As a candidate, Polis backed a single-payer universal health-care system, raising mileage standards on cars to 50 miles per gallon by 2020, cutting the defense budget by 15 percent, and an immediate end to the war in Iraq.

When Congress passed the McCain-Feingold bill in 2002, restricting campaign contributions, it included the so-called Millionaire's Amendment—a modest effort to limit the advantage of self-financed candidates. The law allowed candidates facing a self-financed opponent to receive contributions above the legal limit from individual funders, as well as unlimited party support. But the Millionaire's Amendment was struck down by the Supreme Court in June 2008, and in many races it didn't make much difference anyway. When asked about the Millionaire's Amendment after Polis's primary victory, a campaign spokeswoman said, "Jared does support the Millionaire's Amendment. . . . Jared believes we need to level the playing field in all respects for candidates in elections. He was supportive of it all along."

Wealthy candidates spent a total of $37 million of their own money on congressional races in the 2008 election cycle, according to the Center for Responsive Politics. Polis spent more than any of these candidates but far less than the personal fortunes that others such as Jon Corzine have spent running for office.

The ability of the rich to buy political power for themselves—or at least try to—is one very big way in which they are different. It is another example of what the scholar Paul Schervish has called "hyperagency." Of course, such hyperagency is not a new thing. It has been true of the rich—more true, even—in earlier periods, and this sense of personal empowerment has often led the wealthy to go into politics, an arena where people really do have a chance to make history. At the height of the Gilded Age, up to a third of the U.S. Senate was composed of millionaires, and the figure is even higher today. Moreover, for every wealthy candidate who has gotten elected in recent years, there are many who have tried and failed to win office.

The great boom of the last quarter century has produced a sharply upward trend of wealthy people going into politics. In 1984, only 3 congressional candidates self-financed to the tune of $1 million or more, according to political scientist Jennifer Steen. In 2006, some 30 candidates spent their own money at this scale. All told, 180 candidates for the Senate and the U.S. House of Representatives spent their own money running for office during this period.[3]

Steen's figures include only candidates for Congress; many other candidates have drawn on their own fortunes in state or local races. Well-known self-financers include Michael Bloomberg, who spent $73 million on his campaign to become mayor of New York (and even more on his two reelection bids), while more obscure self-financiers include people such as Tony Sanchez, who spent $63 million running for governor of Texas, or Blair Hull, who spent $28 million on her Illinois Senate race.

According to Steen's research, the Democratic rich have been far more likely to try to buy their way into politics than Republicans have. And Democrats have outnumbered Republicans by three to one among what Steen calls "extreme self-financers": those candidates who have spent $4 million or more of their own money.

It makes sense that wealthy Democrats would be more likely to spend heavily to win public office. It is liberals, after all, who believe in government.

Liberal self-financiers have included Maria Cantwell, who made millions off stock options during a brief stint at RealNetworks in Seattle and then spent $10 million to finance a successful bid for the Senate. Cantwell, who had been in politics before going to RealNetworks, has been consistently rated as one of the most liberal members of the U.S. Senate.

John Edwards launched his political career by drawing on a fortune he amassed as a personal injury lawyer. He made tens of millions of dollars suing corporations before running for the U.S. Senate in North Carolina and using his money to beat several more experienced—and, some might say, deserving—politicians in the Democratic primary. Later, Edwards drew on an extensive network of wealthy trial lawyers to finance his presidential race and emerged as one of the most progressive voices in U.S. politics.

Eliot Spitzer also used his personal wealth to buy his way into politics. Spitzer received as much as $9 million from his father to finance his two bids for state attorney general during the 1990s. An archetypal Manhattan rich kid, educated at Horace Mann, Princeton, and Harvard, Spitzer went on to become a nemesis of some of the most powerful members of his own class when he sought to punish wrongdoing on Wall Street following the business scandals that exploded in 2001 and 2002.

Michael Bloomberg certainly should be on any list of liberals who have bought their way into government. Bloomberg was a self-described liberal Democrat before changing parties to run for mayor. Among his signature accomplishments has been raising property taxes in New York by nearly 20 percent, a record hike that hit the rich hardest.

Other wealthy progressives have not fared so well in their bids for elected office. Ned Lamont poured $17 million of his own money into a losing effort to oust Joseph Lieberman from his Connecticut Senate seat in 2006. Lamont typified a strain of old-money liberalism that is common in New England, and, like many on the left, he was furious at Lieberman for his support of the Iraq war and other Bush policies. Lamont's candidacy crystallized the Democratic Party's left turn in 2006, and he commanded the enthusiasm of the antiwar "netroots," as well as big-name endorsements, after he beat Lieberman in the Democratic primary. But it would not be enough when Lieberman ran successfully as an Independent.

Other losers include Chris Gabrieli, the Massachusetts software entrepreneur and founding chair of the policy group MassInc., who spent more than $10 million running unsuccessfully for governor in 2006, and Rutt Bridges, a geophysicist who made a fortune on oil exploration software before founding a progressive think tank in Colorado, the Bighorn Center, and then running without success for the U.S. Senate in 2004 and the governorship in 2006.

The Senate seems to have a magnetic appeal to the rich and ambitious, and that chamber includes any number of multimillionaires. (John Kerry is the wealthiest senator, followed by Herb Kohl. Ted Kennedy had been the third richest senator before his death in 2009.) Many of the Senate's most affluent members are also very liberal, and that has long been the case. In 2005, *National Journal* tallied the lifetime voting records of all members of the U.S. Senate. Five of the ten members on the most liberal list were also among the richest senators. At the top of the list was a little-known senator named Mark Dayton.

How did Dayton get into the Senate? By spending $12 million of his own money.

Dayton is part of a generation of wealthy heirs who were radicalized by the events of the 1960s. His grandfather was George Dayton, who started Dayton's department store in downtown Minneapolis. Mark Dayton grew up in a wealthy neighborhood, amid privileged insularity, and attended Blake School, a private day school in Hopkins, Minnesota. His best friend was Charles Pillsbury, an heir to the Pillsbury flour fortune. Dayton went to Yale, where he was a goalie for the hockey team and studied pre-med.

Before 1967, he had never been very political. His father, who ran Dayton's, was a Republican, and there wasn't any talk of politics around the family dinner table. For Mark's first two years of college, he didn't think about much else beyond blocking pucks and becoming a doctor.

Things started to change in his junior year, which spanned 1967 to 1968, one of the most turbulent periods in U.S. history. The Johnson administration was escalating the Vietnam War, and riots convulsed U.S. cities such as Newark and Detroit. "I was increasingly becoming aware of the social upheaval in the country and the social activism and in particular the Vietnam War. And I felt, from my beginning of understanding of that, that it was wrong."

Dayton's first political hero was Robert Kennedy, and he avidly followed Kennedy's presidential run in 1968. Late one night in June of that year, sitting in the basement of his parents' home, Dayton watched with satisfaction as Kennedy won the California primary. "My parents had gone to bed because they didn't even like the Kennedys. So I was down watching by myself." After Kennedy's acceptance speech, Dayton was leaning forward to turn off the television when Kennedy was shot.

"There was something about watching my first political hero die for the causes that he believed in that was just like a spark, like a catalyst within me. I could never be comfortable just being comfortable in my parents' comfortable home again. So that rally started my social activism."

Meanwhile, Dayton had become rich. His father had expanded the family department store company, taking it public in 1967. He set up a trust for Mark, who came into the first part of his inheritance at the age of twenty-one, in January 1968. It was less than a million dollars but still a substantial amount of money for the time. And the fund would grow rapidly in the years ahead, as the company's stock rose with the success of its discount chain, Target. In time, Mark Dayton would be worth tens of millions of dollars.

When Dayton graduated from Yale, he took a job teaching ninth-grade science at a tough high school on the Lower East Side.

As part of a new program, Dayton lived with an African American welfare family during his first summer in New York City. There were six people in the family, all crammed into a two-room apartment: a mother with three daughters, a ten-year-old son, and two granddaughters. Dayton slept in a sleeping bag on the floor.

The experience had a profound impact on him. It seemed outrageous to him that the children in that family, "who by no choice or fault of their own, were born into such drastically different circumstances in the same country. I just felt it was very unjust, very unfair, and very wrong. And something that I wanted to try to change."

In the mid-1970s, Dayton went to work in Walter Mondale's Senate office in Washington and later on the 1976 presidential campaign in Georgia. He was consumed by the action, and after that, his life was all about politics. Dayton also traveled deeper into the world of wealth liberalism in 1978 when he married Alida Rockefeller, the daughter of John D. Rockefeller III, whom he had met through a growing network of wealthy young heirs who were committed to social change. Rockefeller, then thirty, was among the richest heiresses in the United States, and her brother, Jay Rockefeller, was the governor of West Virginia. (The marriage ultimately didn't last. In recent years, Alida has been among the largest donors to Democratic causes.)

Dayton returned to Minnesota to begin his political career and turned to his growing fortune to help. He made his first bid for public office in 1982, spending $7 million on a Senate race. His main primary opponent was the former antiwar senator Eugene McCarthy. Dayton used his superior funds to beat McCarthy but lost the general election to David Durenberger. Dayton spent part of the 1980s working in state government and then ran again, this time for state auditor, in 1990. He lost that race, too, as well as a race for governor in 1998, where he spent more than $1 million. In 2000, he ran again for the Senate, this time spending $12 million, and finally won.

As a senator, Dayton embraced the populist progressivism long associated with the upper Midwest. He voted against all of Bush's tax cuts and against the war in Iraq. He championed the cause of low-income seniors, donating his Senate salary to a group that took busloads of Minnesotan seniors to Canada to buy cheaper prescription drugs. He consistently ranked among the most liberal members of the Senate. In 2005, *National Journal* put him at the top of its list of senators with the most liberal lifetime voting records.

Dayton left the Senate in 2007, after one term, and soon set his sights on running for governor. He is partly financing this race with his own money. "I've been blessed with not having to do the one thing I hate to most in politics, which is asking people for money," he said about his self-financing. "It allowed me to be more independent. It allowed me to be true to my own values and principles, which are progressive."

The reformist tradition of patrician public service is often dated back to Theodore Roosevelt, whose rise in politics was enabled by his inherited wealth, but who used the presidency to try to dismantle an emerging U.S. oligarchy. Roosevelt came from old money, with few ties to the new rich of the Gilded Age. His wealth made possible an early focus on writing, adventure, and politics—a pattern that would be seen later in the lives of other wealthy politicians with progressive leanings, such as John F. Kennedy.

In 1902–1903, as Roosevelt began his presidency, at least twenty-two members—or nearly a third—of the Senate were millionaires. Almost all were Republicans, and they had made their fortunes in the top industries of the time, such as railroads, mining, coal, and banking. Key to the rule of big business during this era was its control of state legislatures, which in turn allowed business interests to determine the composition of the U.S. Senate. (It was not until 1913 that the Constitution was amended to allow the popular election of senators.) Some of the senators picked by business interests to go to Washington were political hacks, but many others were themselves wealthy businessmen. The wealthy dominated not only the Senate, but by extension the federal judiciary, because the Senate approved all judicial choices.

Robber baron politicians used their power in reactionary ways. They beat back the rising tide of populism in the late nineteenth century, kept organized labor at bay for years, and blocked a host of progressive reforms, while enacting policies that furthered the interests of the rich. Big money poured into Washington as never before, and great mansions sprang up in the District of Columbia—places such as Anderson House, a 50-room, 40,000-square-foot home completed on Massachusetts Avenue in 1905.

Roosevelt moved steadily to the left after assuming the presidency, pushed in part by the ever-growing power of the industrial trusts and public fear of this power. Although he would never be called a class traitor, as his cousin Franklin was, he spoke harshly about the wealthy class in ways unheard of for a patrician politician, using terms like the *criminal rich* and the *malefactors of great wealth*. And he sharply attacked the way that government had been turned into a tool of the wealthy.

To radical critics, the progressive leanings of affluent politicians have never been more than strategic concessions to ensure popular support for capitalism. And, to be sure, these leaders have often made this point explicitly, arguing to their prosperous peers that reform was preferable to revolution. It was a strategy that worked, too. As E. Digby Baltzell observed in his book *The Protestant Establishment*, "the patrician reformers who led the Progressive movement eventually took the steam out of the populist revolt."[4]

Yet if the split between conservative and progressive wealth elites has been minor, as seen through the eyes, say, of a European, it has nonetheless been fierce in the U.S. context. And in this battle, Theodore Roosevelt's side would gradually become stronger during the twentieth century, as a growing number of wealthy politicians embraced progressive ideas. The most famous, of course, would be Franklin Delano Roosevelt.

By the 1960s, wealthy liberal politicians were no longer such a novelty. The immensely rich Averell Harriman—heir to a vast railroad fortune—parlayed diplomatic service under FDR into a political career, becoming a stalwart of the Democratic Party's liberal wing. He served as governor of New York for one term, where he raised taxes, and he competed twice during the 1950s for the Democratic presidential nomination. He was beaten both times by the more moderate Adlai Stevenson.

Herbert Claiborne Pell, an heir to the Lorillard tobacco fortune, was another prominent patrician liberal of the mid-twentieth century. Raised in wealth in Tuxedo Park, New York, and Newport, Rhode Island, Pell became a progressive politician and, in the words of his biographer, a "Brahmin in revolt." His son, Claiborne Pell, would continue the family tradition as a six-term liberal senator from Rhode Island who was responsible for, among other things, creating a new federal financial aid system to help low-income students go to college ("Pell grants"), and for helping to create the National Endowment for the Arts and the National Endowment for the Humanities. Pell consistently ranked among the most liberal members of the U.S. Senate; he was also one of its more affluent members, because his own inherited wealth was bolstered by his marriage to Nuala O'Donnell, who was part of the Hartford family and an heir to the Great Atlantic and Pacific Tea Company fortune.

Pell arrived in Washington in 1961, the same year that the eighth-richest president in U.S. history took office. John F. Kennedy embraced a moderate liberalism that stressed greater investments in education, new initiatives to combat poverty, and a cautious support for civil rights. His brothers Robert and Edward moved considerably further to the left and established the Kennedy family as the embodiment of patrician liberalism. The political trajectory of the Kennedy brothers was an increasingly common one in American life. Their father, Joseph Kennedy, had been obsessed with making a fortune—so obsessed that his tactics included bootlegging and insider trading. Such was his success that Kennedy would later boast, "None of my children has the slightest interest in making money. Not the slightest."[5] Joseph Kennedy's fortune not only bankrolled the political careers of two generations of progeny; it also subsidized a liberalism that the hard-nosed Kennedy might have found hard to take.

Reformers such as the Roosevelts, the Kennedys, and the Pells operated in the tradition of noblesse oblige as heirs who never had to earn a living and were free to focus on public service starting early on. Some of today's wealthy progressive politicians, like Mark Dayton, would fit into that tradition. Others, such as Jared Polis, tend to have been born into middle-class families and made great fortunes on their own. These self-made multimillionaires are skipping the multigenerational journey into public service, whereby some flinty businessman makes a pile of money and then his liberal heirs use it to bankroll political careers. Now the cycle happens more quickly, as liberal business leaders cash out of the private sector as soon as they are rich and plunge into the public sector. And while some of these leaders have come from predictably liberal places like Boulder, San Francisco, and Seattle, others have emerged from Wall Street.

A case in point is Jon Corzine, whose evolution from Wall Street banker to arguably the most liberal governor in the United States, before his defeat in 2009, says much about the new ways in which money and politics now intersect. Corzine has an unusual background for a mega-rich liberal, which is to say that he wasn't raised by professional parents in a progressive metro area and didn't go to an elite university. Quite the opposite. He was raised on a family farm in Illinois and was the quarterback of his high school football team, as well as the captain of the basketball team. He went to college at a state school in Illinois, enlisted in the U.S. Marine Corps Reserve, and married his high school sweetheart. After getting an MBA, he started his business career at Midwestern regional banks, before moving to New York to work as a bond trader for Goldman Sachs. Eventually, he rose in the company to become chairman and CEO, and later, when the company went public, Corzine converted his ownership stake into a fortune estimated at $300 million.

Like many rich people who run for office, Corzine started his involvement with politics as an active campaign contributor. He and his wife gave generously to Democratic candidates during the 1990s, spreading their money far and wide in more than a dozen contributions per year, as well as making large gifts to the Democratic National Committee. Campaign giving at this level is a way for the super-rich to express their political views; it is also a way to create a profile in party circles, as well as build up chits among party leaders that can be called in at a later time. This is yet another advantage enjoyed by wealthy supercitizens.

Corzine entered politics in 2000 to run for the U.S. Senate seat in New Jersey being vacated by retiring senator Frank Lautenberg. His first order of business was to win the Democratic primary by knocking off his opponent, former governor Jim Florio. By any measure, Florio deserved the nomination far more than Corzine did. Florio was a smart and courageous politician who had been New Jersey's governor in the early 1990s but lost his bid for reelection after raising taxes to close a gap in the state's budget. He had been waiting for years for a chance at a political comeback, only to find himself buried by Corzine's millions when that chance finally arrived. Corzine spent $33 million in his primary race against Florio—a sum that dwarfed any previous spending to win office in New Jersey. Corzine then went on to swamp his general election opponent, Congressman Bob Franks, with another $30 million.

Corzine's election to the Senate represented the worst kind of subversion of democracy by big money. It was neither fair nor right that a man with so little experience in public life could beat out two opponents who had committed most of their careers to public service. As *New York* magazine later observed, "Corzine was saved only by his money and his willingness to promiscuously spend it to get elected."[6]

Yet, as things turned out, Corzine was no vanity candidate looking for a fancy title. He quickly distinguished himself as an unusually hardworking U.S. senator ready to challenge the conservative order that held sway in Washington (not to mention being the only senator with a beard, just as he had been the only top Wall Street executive with one). He was present for nearly 90 percent of the votes held on the Senate floor and cosponsored more than a thousand bills. He was also extremely liberal—so liberal that Americans for Democratic Action gave Corzine a perfect 100 percent liberal rating for three out of the five years he served in the Senate. *National Journal*, in compiling its analysis of lifetime voting records among U.S. senators in 2005, ranked Corzine the fourth most liberal senator.

Corzine showed more willingness to clash with Wall Street and corporations than many of his colleagues did, defying the stereotype that wealthy Democrats tend to be liberal on social issues but centrist on economic concerns. Indeed, analyses of voting records by

National Journal, which breaks votes down by issue area, find that there is little ideological variation across areas—those who are liberal on social or foreign policy issues also tend to be liberal on economic issues, and vice versa. Liberals in Congress, it would seem, aren't so different from liberals in the general public: a majority of self-described liberals, polls find, are liberal on both economic and social issues.[7] Corzine sided with the most progressive lawmakers in Congress when it came to increasing oversight of Wall Street, raising the minimum wage, strengthening the right to form unions, pushing for universal health care, and so on.

Corzine tapped his fortune again in 2005 when he ran successfully for governor of New Jersey against Republican Douglas Forrester, this time spending nearly $40 million of his own money. That investment came on top of the millions that Corzine gave to local politicians and state organizations starting in 2000, helping to buy political allies. All told, Corzine spent more than $100 million—or nearly a third of his entire fortune—on his political career in only six years.

Corzine pursued a strongly progressive agenda during his one term as governor. In fact, New Jersey—which Republicans won in the presidential elections of 1980, 1984, and 1988—now ranks as among the most progressive states in the country, and Corzine has been partly responsible for this distinction. Among other moves, New Jersey became the second state to enact a paid family-leave law in 2008 and was the first state in recent decades to abolish the death penalty. It has also been one of the few states to recognize gay civil unions. In addition, the state sharply raised taxes on the wealthy in 2008 to help close its budget gap, showcasing a preferred progressive solution to fiscal hard times.

But if Corzine has been a leader in pushing New Jersey to the left, he has also been something of a follower. Twenty years ago, a politician with Corzine's views might well have gotten nowhere in New Jersey. Since then, the state has been a case study in many of the demographic trends that are moving the United States to the left. These include rapid growth of the state's educated professional class, who tend to be more liberal, and the increasing ethnic diversity of the state as more immigrants have poured in during recent years. Since the 1970s, New Jersey has gone from red to purple to deep blue. Corzine's defeat for reelection in 2009, by a Republican challenger, reflected more a reaction to corruption scandals in the state than any major shift in voter ideology.

New Jersey's political metamorphosis offers another insight into the calculus of wealthy and progressive would-be politicians. It is not only that politics may seem like an exciting next act for those who have made millions; it's also that public support for conservative policies has been draining away in recent years, creating more opportunities to get something done—to truly "make history." As in past eras, the most successful wealthy public servants are those who both respond to shifts in public opinion and find ways to channel those shifts into real change.

THE CORPORATE LIBERAL

IN 1982, WHEN *FORBES* PUBLISHED its first list of the four hundred wealthiest Americans, many on the list were heirs. Back then, before the long boom, the ranks of the rich were far smaller, and old money loomed much larger in the upper class. To crack the moral code of the ultra-affluent required understanding the business elite, to be sure, but even more, it required a sociological dissection of the WASP aristocracy. In the early 1980s, Dingby Baltzell's classic book *The Protestant Establishment* still reigned as one of the preeminent studies of America's wealthy. Other scholars of the upper class, such as William Domhoff, the author of *Who Rules America*, devoted elaborate energy to proving that the rich weren't a bunch of blueblood swells lolling around Newport and Palm Beach but, rather, were drawn primarily from the ranks of business.

Nobody would dispute this claim today. Images of the well-to-do are now indelibly linked to the overflow of wealth in the business world, and the newly rich have supplanted old money as the dominant focus of public attention. Heirs occupy a far less prominent role in society these days, and the very idea of aristocratic wealth seems out of step with our times. There are still plenty of inherited fortunes—more all the time—but these sorts of rich people make up a smaller percentage of the upper class as a whole. In 1982, a full fifth of the combined fortunes of people on the Forbes 400 list was still in the hands of a few old-money families, such as the Rockefellers, the DuPonts, and the Hearsts. By 2008, that percentage had fallen to less than 2 percent.[1]

Something else has changed since the 1980s, which is that the business rich are no longer reliable pillars of the Republican coalition. That's not only true of West Coast techies or hedge fund eggheads. It's also true of mainstream corporate America, where prevailing norms are increasingly at odds with right-wing orthodoxies. Key ideals of the 1960s are penetrating deeply into one of the last strongholds of conservatism in the United States: the executive suite.

This might sound surprising if you hang out on the left and read magazines such as *Mother Jones* and books like *Fast Food Nation*. In his edited anthology *The I Hate Corporate America Reader*, Clint Willis organized a mountain of new writing on business sins under such chapter headings as "They Lie to Us," "They Steal from Us," "They Poison Our Culture," and so on. Willis had plenty of material—and readers.

Of course, you don't actually need to be on the left to see truth in these claims. You simply need to read the *Wall Street Journal* every morning, with its unending reports of scandal. Ruthless bottom-line thinking and unchecked greed, as well as outright criminality, have raged out of control in the business world. More executives have been sent to prison in recent years than at any time in U.S. history.

A good portion of corporate America also remains deeply conservative—just look at all of the corporate money going to right-wing think tanks or how executives from large defense, agribusiness, and energy firms fill GOP coffers at election time. And whatever the ideology of CEOs, corporate power remains a reactionary force, as witnessed in the first year of the Obama administration, when business interests sought to stop every progressive reform taken up by Congress, including a climate bill, tougher banking rules, a credit card bill of rights, the "card check" labor organizing bill, a public health-care option, and more. An army of almost fifteen thousand lobbyists, mostly hired by business, laid siege to the government during 2009, and spending on lobbying neared a record $4 billion.

Yet to see corporate America solely as a predatory force and a right-wing ally is to miss a fundamental shift that is under way. More executives are reordering their strategies and workplace environments to honor values such as sustainability, feminism, and multiculturalism. More are supporting greater public investments in education, infrastructure, and scientific research, all of which are key foundations of prosperity in a knowledge economy. And globalization has made the U.S. business elite more internationalist and less xenophobic.

The MBA set remains largely Republican, but it has less and less in common with the likes of Rush Limbaugh and Sarah Palin. Today's business leaders have been left without a natural political home, as the GOP has become more provincial, intolerant, and nationalistic. Meanwhile, a growing number of authentically liberal executives and entrepreneurs are working to recapture business culture from the right. Some are talking about a "triple bottom line," in which the drive for profits is complemented by a focus on environmental and social responsibility. Others are backing the Democratic Party and liberal causes with record amounts of cash. Many companies have embraced a Bobo (Bourgeois Bohemian) ethos in their corporate culture, dispensing with dress codes and overly rigid hierarchies. Google, one of the most influential companies in the United States today, personifies these trends. Its top executives contribute almost exclusively to Democrats and have made the company carbon-neutral. "Don't be evil" is Google's informal corporate slogan.

In his famous 1971 memo charging that the free enterprise system was "under broad attack," Lewis Powell called on business leaders to push back against liberalism. Many heeded this call, helping bankroll the rise of the conservative "counter-establishment" and a new age of

Republican power. Now the political dynamic is changing again as some business leaders tack left.

What happened?

A good place to pick up the story is in 1962, when the economist Milton Friedman published *Capitalism and Freedom*, in which he addressed, among other issues, the role of corporations in society. Friedman argued that business executives had one job and one job only: to increase profits. Any other objective was not only wrong-headed but downright dangerous. "Few trends," Friedman wrote, "could so thoroughly undermine the very foundations of our free society as the acceptance by corporate officials of a social responsibility other than to make as much money for their stockholders as possible. This is a fundamentally subversive doctrine." Friedman was going against the current when he made this argument. The early 1960s were the heyday of "welfare capitalism," an era of benign big business when many executives felt an obligation to a wide range of stakeholders, including workers and the communities in which they operated.

Friedman would have none of it. He kept up his attack during the 1960s, as some businesses moved in an even more liberal direction, heeding calls by President Lyndon B. Johnson to join the war on poverty with voluntary actions to lift up the poor and minorities. It would not be until the early 1970s that a real opening emerged for Friedman's arguments. This period saw rising foreign competition, a falling U.S. stock market, and new regulations around the environment and consumer product safety. The 1970s also saw growing demands for corporate affirmative action for women and minorities.

Thus it was that Friedman hit a nerve when he reprised key points of *Capitalism and Freedom* in a 1970 article in the *New York Times Magazine* titled "The Social Responsibility of Business Is to Increase Its Profits." The article, which was widely read and discussed, took aim at the executives who claimed that "business is not concerned 'merely' with profit but also with promoting desirable 'social' ends; that business has a 'social conscience' and takes seriously its responsibilities for providing employment, eliminating discrimination, avoiding pollution and whatever else may be the catchwords of the contemporary crop of reformers." Friedman wrote that such ideas amounted to "unadulterated socialism. Businessmen who talk this way are unwitting puppets of the intellectual forces that have been undermining the basis of a free society these past decades."[2]

The neoconservative leader Irving Kristol also played a role in stiffening the resolve of business to fight liberalism. Like Powell before him, Kristol argued that business needed a concerted strategy to stop the left's growing assault on free enterprise. Kristol worked to forge an alliance between corporate America and the conservative movement starting in the late 1970s. That alliance mounted a push to roll back taxes and shrink government. Many companies also adopted a more ruthless approach to labor unions, using illegal tactics to thwart organizing efforts. And the compensation of CEOs and other executives began its skyward climb.

The next chapter of the story is well known. Corporate values shifted sharply in the 1980s, the "greed is good" era in which vast pay inequities and frequent downsizing became normalized. Conspicuous consumption by corporate chieftains and Wall Street big shots—frowned on in the early postwar decades—returned on a grand and gaudy scale. The new business stars of the moment were brash figures unembarrassed by their mean streaks, such as Donald Trump and Carl Icahn.

Milton Friedman's argument—that profit was the overriding goal of corporate leaders—was taken to its logical extreme in a wave of leveraged buyouts in which entire companies were dismantled and communities devastated for the sake of short-term shareholder gains. The notion that business had a wider set of responsibilities was increasingly seen as quaint, if not grounds for a hostile takeover by raiders purporting to act on behalf of shareholders. Events in Washington reinforced and facilitated the leaner, meaner ethos as Republicans moved to dismantle the federal regulatory state.

Other trends were also at work. Pressures mounted on business as foreign competition increased and as growing ranks of stock investors became more insistent that companies boost earnings every single quarter. For the corporate leaders of the 1980s, all incentives— economic, political, cultural—pointed to an embrace of Milton Friedman's narrow dictates about profit.

Yet even as this new orthodoxy rose to dominance, yanking the business world sharply to the right, a parallel trend was emerging— which in time would pull executives and wealthy entrepreneurs leftward: an emerging corporate social responsibility movement.

Arnold Hiatt was among those who pioneered the new liberal business ethos as the CEO of Stride Rite, the successful children's shoe company. Hiatt never imagined going into business as he came of age near Boston. He embraced liberal politics and looked down on business, majoring in history and planning to teach. But after he got engaged at the age of twenty-one, he realized that he would need to make more money to support a family. He decided that he didn't want to go to law school, so he enrolled in an executive training program. Not long after finishing the program, Hiatt was hired by a bank to turn around a small company that made shoes in Lawrence, Massachusetts. Later, that firm was bought out by Stride Rite, and Hiatt soon became president of the company in 1968. At the time, he said that he would stay for only seven years, he recalled, "because I didn't want to spend my life in the world of business. I thought there were more important things to do." Hiatt would end up staying for nearly twenty-five years.

Early on, Hiatt decided that Stride Rite would go beyond the usual business approach to charity. "We didn't want to just write checks," he said. The company had its headquarters in Roxbury, an impoverished African American section of Boston. Hiatt wanted to do something for the neighborhood, so the company started a child-care center in its headquarters for neighborhood kids. The children of employees were also soon included. The center offered more than simply child care: it provided hot meals and medical and dental care for the children. With this step, Stride Rite became the first company in the United States to offer on-site child care.

Hiatt also wanted to help the local schools, so he started a program whereby Stride Rite employees could go into the schools and mentor low-income students on company time. "The reason I focused on early intervention is that it could have much more impact on the life of someone than trying to do remedial stuff later on," he recalled.

Corporate involvement in public schools has since become common, but it was still rare when Hiatt started the mentoring program. Even more cutting edge was the family leave policy that Hiatt introduced. That move came near the end of Hiatt's tenure at the company, during the presidency of George H. W. Bush. The Bush administration was then opposing even the most paltry unpaid leave allowances, and Hiatt took pride in thrusting the company into this debate with one of the most generous paid family leave policies in all of corporate America.

Another of Hiatt's innovations was to channel a small portion of Stride Rite's profits into a company foundation. The amount was initially 1 percent, but Hiatt convinced the board to agree to 5 percent over time. It was an unheard-of level of corporate philanthropy at the time.

Hiatt's steps to turn Stride Rite into a pioneer of social responsibility were not popular with his board of directors. "But they were dependent on me," he recalled. Also, Hiatt led the company to spectacular growth and returns. During the late 1970s, Stride Rite expanded by buying Keds and Sperry Top-Sider, and those brands soared during the 1980s. Stride Rite's high and steady earnings made it one of the top-rated stocks on Wall Street.

Hiatt's combination of stellar returns and social conscience sparked interest from other companies, which began to contact Stride Rite for information about its policies and invite Hiatt to give speeches. Hiatt didn't pretend to have any magic formula that linked social responsibility to performance, but he did argue that there was a correlation. He explained that "people wanted to work at Stride Rite. The turnover was very negligible. . . . If you don't have turnover, you save an awful lot of money." He also said that "our productivity levels were higher and quality was higher."

The attention to Hiatt's methods reflected a broader shift under way in corporate America and among investors and activists, one that gathered steam from the 1960s onward. During the Vietnam War, a tactic of antiwar activists was to pressure and shame defense contractors—most notably, Dow Chemical, which made napalm. Socially responsible investing, which had a long history beginning with the Quakers, grew in prominence during this period. The Pax World Fund was started in 1971 as the first socially responsible mutual fund, avoiding any investments in the defense industry. The Calvert Social Investment Fund was launched in 1982, with a broader vision of socially responsible investing. Among other strategies, these new funds sought to improve corporate behavior by introducing shareholder resolutions at annual meetings. Also starting in the 1970s, nonprofit advocacy organizations began to develop new tactics for pressuring corporations. The successful boycott of table grapes, which resulted in concessions to unions in 1970, encouraged other similar efforts—most notably, the famous Nestle boycott launched in 1977 to protest the company's marketing of unhealthy baby milk substitutes.

The biggest victory for the early CSR movement came with efforts to force companies to disinvest in South Africa, in hopes of weakening the apartheid government there. By the early 1980s, a number of major U.S. companies had responded to this pressure by pulling out of South Africa, often losing money in the process. These included Mobil, Nabisco, Johnson and Johnson, and Goodyear. In a book on CSR, Jeffrey Hollender, the founder of Seventh Generation, wrote about the disinvestment push that "for the first time in history, iconic American companies had been punished where it hurt most—in their balance sheet and in their shareholders' brokerage firm statements."[3]

The losses from South African disinvestment, along with the damage to Nestle, signaled the rise of a new business reality: executives who weren't attuned to the moral claims of activists could put their companies at financial risk. David Vogel has called this form of oversight "civil regulation" and has argued that citizen pressure on corporations has risen in response to cutbacks in government regulation.

But what's been happening is more than grudging reforms, as activists have gotten better at torching corporate brands. Simultaneously, a growing cadre of progressive business leaders has worked from within the business world to change its values.

Josh Mailman has been near the center of these efforts for more than two decades. Mailman, the heir to a fortune his father made in various ventures, got involved in alternative models of business when he was just out of Middlebury College and living in Vermont. "I was interested in how business could be a vehicle for social change," Mailman said. He was an early investor in Stonyfield Farm, an organic yogurt maker that started as an organic farm school in New Hampshire and went on to become the second-largest yogurt company in the United States. Mailman also forged a close friendship with Wayne Silby, the founder of the Calvert Social Investment Fund. And he came to know a number of other businesspeople in the 1980s who had been involved in social movements and who saw for-profit ventures as a way to advance their liberal values. "They wanted to create nontraditional companies and change how business operated," Mailman said.

In 1987, Mailman brought together seventy-two individuals at a retreat in Colorado to found the Social Venture Network (SVN), an organization dedicated to the idea that business could and should be a vehicle for creating a more "just and sustainable world." SVN grew quickly, attracting progressive business leaders and entrepreneurs who valued its meetings as a place where they could discuss how to make a profit while also trying to make the world a better place.

Along the way, CSR began to evolve from a few general ideals to a well-developed set of strategies. Wayne Silby has said about the early days of SVN that "we were inventing a language, a way of thinking and talking about these issues that has become so widely accepted today that it's easy to forget how original it was, how wild and strange and threatening to the status quo it once seemed."[4]

Mailman and SVN helped incubate a number of spin-offs, including Business for Social Responsibility (BSR). Arnold Hiatt was among the founders of BSR and became its first board chair. The new group emerged as liberal companies such as Stride Rite and Levi

Strauss found themselves fielding a rising number of queries about their practices. This led to the insight, Hiatt said, that if they could share such information more widely and provide hands-on help for executives with a social conscience, "we could influence the conduct of companies."

Hiatt and other liberal executives were especially anxious to counter zero-sum thinking that saw good social and environmental policies as undermining the bottom line—"as opposed to the view that they could complement each other." And they were intent on loosening the right's grip on business organizations. "We were sick and tired of having the Chamber of Commerce being the voice for business," said Laury Hammel, who owned a chain of health clubs in the Boston area and played a key role in conceptualizing BSR.[5]

Business for Social Responsibility opened its doors in Washington, D.C., in 1992, the year that Hiatt retired as CEO of Stride Rite and began to run the Stride Rite Foundation that he had built up over the years, giving to various charities and liberal causes. (Hiatt also emerged as one of the Democratic Party's larger donors in the 1990s.) But it was in helping build BSR where he made his greater impact.

Initially, the group was something of a fringe operation, attracting smaller, privately held companies. Founding members included the Body Shop, Aveda, Lotus Development, Ben and Jerry's Homemade Ice Cream, Working Assets, and the clothing company Esprit. Many of the leaders of these companies had emerged out of the counterculture —people such as Doug and Susie Tompkins of Esprit and Ben Cohen, a frizzy-haired Grateful Dead fan turned ice cream maker.

Smaller companies remained the main members of BSR during much of the 1990s. These firms were "run by young people who were more principled," recalled Hiatt. "They didn't buy into the corporate culture." And their leaders "were looking for more meaning in their lives and their businesses."

One reason for the upsurge of socially minded business leaders in the 1980s and 1990s, suggested Mailman, was that politics and the public sector were dominated by conservatives. Government was either unsupportive of or hostile toward ideas such as clean energy and organic farming. "The kind of people who might have gone into government started to look at how they might do things in the business world," he said.

Efforts to recruit larger companies to BSR were unsuccessful, at least at first. "We could never reach the CEO of a company," said Hiatt. "It was usually someone on the vice presidential level." Big companies didn't join because it was "alien to their culture."

That started to change in the late 1990s, as more consumers began to align their shopping habits with their social values. Tapping into this new awareness were better organized activists who demonstrated new power to hurt the bottom line of major corporations. Nike's searing experience in the 1990s, in which it saw its brand badly tarnished by revelations that it used sweatshop labor, was a pivotal moment. The public flaying of "sweatshop queen" Kathie Lee Gifford around the same time further underscored the dangers of being deaf to social concerns.

"People were sending Phil Knight hate mail," remembered Hiatt of Nike's CEO. Knight called BSR looking for help, and the group helped Nike design an international code of conduct. Nike's executive vice president then joined BSR's board.

Things really took off for BSR during the Bush years as major companies started to join the group. Within a decade of its founding, BSR had hundreds of corporate members, and an annual budget of $8 million, and it played a central role in training private-sector leaders in the principles of corporate responsibility. By 2005, more than two thousand companies were issuing annual CSR reports and more than a thousand had CSR codes of conduct.

Business for Social Responsibility unequivocally hit the mainstream in 2007, when its annual conference attracted 1,350 participants to the Hyatt Regency in San Francisco. A veritable who's who of top companies in the United States were there, including Chevron, ExxonMobil, Ford, and Home Depot.

By the early 2000s, the CSR movement hadn't merely spawned new organizations and a set of alternative ideas about "sustainable business," it also had its own posse of iconic leaders and heroes. These include Howard Schultz, the CEO of Starbucks—a company that defied the typical chain store model of retail by giving health insurance to every employee who worked more than twenty hours a week; Yvon Chouinard, the founder of Patagonia; Gary Hirshberg and Samuel Kaymen, the founders of Stonyfield Farm; and John McKay, the cofounder of Whole Foods Market.

By showing that it was possible to build profitable companies and be socially responsible, these leaders stood as a gilded rebuke to Milton Friedman's argument that the two goals were necessarily separate. Indeed, in a 2005 debate in *Reason* magazine with Friedman, John McKay castigated the economist for his narrow, "crabby" notion that the only goal of corporations was to increase shareholder wealth. "Like medicine, law, and education, business has noble purposes," McKay wrote, "to provide goods and services that improve its customers' lives, to provide jobs and meaningful work for employees, to create wealth and prosperity for its investors, and to be a responsible and caring citizen."

At Whole Foods, McKay said, the company measured its success by how much value it created for a half-dozen different stakeholders, ranging from investors to the environment. "The ideas I'm articulating result in a more robust business model than the profit-maximization model that it competes against, because they encourage and tap into more powerful motivations than self-interest alone. These ideas will triumph over time, not by persuading intellectuals and economists through argument but by winning the competitive test of the marketplace. Someday businesses like Whole Foods, which adhere to a stakeholder model of deeper business purpose, will dominate the economic landscape. Wait and see."

Some early players in BSR believe the group has sold out to corporate America because it does not advocate for liberal policies in Washington—as a direct counter to the U.S. Chamber of Commerce and other business groups—and because it accepts members that have terrible social and environmental records. "We were willing to be a big tent for saints and sinners," Hiatt acknowledged. But he pointed out that this was a conscious decision, so that BSR could have more impact by trying to influence companies from within. Many critics question this approach, arguing that such CSR policies often merely provide cover for companies as they continue their negative practices.

There is much to this critique, and CSR is no substitute for strong policies to protect workers, consumers, and the environment. Civil regulation will never have the muscle of government regulation. As it turns out, though, this is not an either/or choice; both strategies are important.

What's remarkable is how far civil regulation has gotten at a time when capital is more powerful than ever and, until recently, laissez-faire Republicans ran the federal government. Given the raw power of big business—with its armies of Washington lobbyists, capacity to move offshore, and dismally weak labor opponents—you'd think that wealthy executives would have simply thumbed their noses at the Arnold Hiatts and the Ben Cohens of the world, with their liberal dreams of a corporate conscience.

The exact opposite has happened. The reason is not people like Hiatt or Cohen, but rather that ordinary consumers have become ever more socially focused since the first sweatshop scandals in the 1990s.

One of the worst fears of CEOs is that they will miss the next big thing and see their companies outflanked by competitors. And what has happened in corporate America during the last few years is that more executives have come to believe the prediction of John McKay and others that socially responsible business will rule the future. Driven by a long-term fear of being left behind and a near-term terror of being zapped by activists, executives are jumping on the CSR bandwagon.

Such fears are not irrational. In her book *Value Shift*, Harvard Business School professor Lynn Sharp Paine argues that global shifts in public opinion have raised the bar for corporate behavior. "Today's leading companies are expected not only to create wealth and produce superior goods and services but also to conduct themselves as 'moral actors'—as responsible agents that carry out their business within a moral framework. . . . Contrary to theorists who for centuries have declared the corporation to be an entirely amoral creature and thus incapable of such behavior, society today has endowed the corporation with a moral personality."[6]

Paine bases this claim on polls taken in the United States and abroad. She points out that even back in 1999, before CSR became so trendy, the public was already holding companies to a high standard. A worldwide poll taken that year found that a fifth of respondents had avoided products of certain companies because of disapproval of their actions. Sixty percent of people said that they judged companies based on their track records on issues such as the environment, labor standards, or ethics. Ninety percent said they expected companies to focus on more than profitability. Among U.S. respondents, three-quarters expected companies to avoid child labor, not discriminate, protect the environment, and respect workers' rights and safety.[7]

Another poll, taken of Americans in 2007, found that these views had become more widespread. Nearly half of the respondents in this survey said that they hadn't bought a company's product because of its lack of social responsibility. The poll found that about half of the U.S. public considered a company's social reputation when they shopped for a car, chose a bank, or picked an insurer. A majority also said that their concern about CSR had increased in the last few years.[8] Other polls found that more Americans were choosing where to work based on a company's environmental or social reputation. This was particularly true of the Millennial generation, which tends to be more liberal than Gen Xers or baby boomers.

Thus, even as the conservative movement reached a high-water mark under Bush, with control of both branches of the federal government, the public was fast turning against a key idea of market fundamentalism, namely, Milton Friedman's narrow view of corporate obligation. This change has left executives with little choice but to evolve in their own outlook—or risk punishment in the marketplace. And that is exactly what many have done.

Surveys of business leaders show a large-scale shift in attitudes about corporate responsibility in recent years. A 2005 McKinsey

Global Survey of more than four thousand executives worldwide, for example, found that 84 percent said that large corporations should seek to balance higher returns to investors with contributions to the broader society. "Unquestionably, the global business community has embraced the idea that it plays a wider role in society," the survey said. "Only one in six agrees with the thesis, famously advanced by Nobel laureate Milton Friedman, that high returns should be a corporation's sole focus."[9]

A smaller 2006 poll, taken of executives in Fortune 500 companies, found that an overwhelming majority believed that CSR was important and had become more so since the Enron scandal. But this belief didn't mean that these executives had experienced any kind of deep change in values themselves. The press release on the poll stated, "67 percent of business leaders say the number one reason they would implement a social responsibility policy would be to maintain their brand image. This is followed closely by enhancing employee morale and reducing legal liability." The McKinsey poll found something similar: "Only eight percent think that large corporations champion social or environmental causes out of 'genuine concern.' Almost nine in ten agree that they are motivated by public relations or profitability, or by both concern and business benefits in equal measure."[10]

Findings like this might confirm the cynical view that CSR is a sham. On the other hand, evidence is everywhere of real change. Fifty years ago, top U.S. companies were pillars of an all-male, all-white power structure; today, many Fortune 500 companies embrace women's and civil rights, at least in their official policies. Even as Republicans bashed affirmative action during the 1980s and the 1990s, corporate America moved in the opposite direction, and diversity emerged as a key goal in boardrooms.

Something similar has been happening with gay rights during the last decade. Even as conservatives sounded the alarm about a growing acceptance of the "gay lifestyle," most Fortune 500 companies moved to bar workplace discrimination based on sexual orientation. Even as opposition to gay marriage became a central GOP plank during the Bush years, one major corporation after another has enacted domestic partnership benefits for their employees. By 2009, a majority of Fortune 500 companies offered such benefits, which granted gay partners one of the most important advantages of marriage. Even conservative companies such as Walmart and FedEx have officially changed their definition of "family" to include a same-sex partnership that is recognized under state law.

Every year, Human Rights Campaign, the largest gay advocacy group in the United States, publishes a "Corporate Equality Index" that rates companies on a range of issues affecting gay and lesbian employees, which includes providing insurance coverage for sex-change operations. In 2002, only 13 corporations received a 100 percent rating; by 2008, that number had risen to 195 companies. The average rating for a Fortune 500 company was 81 percent. Banking and financial services had the highest ratings of any industry; energy companies were among the lowest.[11]

Many corporations go even further, by contributing to gay rights organizations. Corporate donors to Human Rights Campaign include American Airlines, Bank of America, BP, Citi, Chase, Dell, Deloitte Touche, Google, IBM, Merrill Lynch, Prudential, and Shell. In 2008, Google's cofounders, Sergey Brin and Larry Page, gave $100,000 and $40,000, respectively, to block Proposition 8, a ballot initiative that would have repealed gay marriage rights in California. Apple and other tech companies also contributed to the campaign. Brin wrote on the official Google blog, "While we respect the strongly-held beliefs that people have on both sides of this argument, we see this fundamentally as an issue of equality. . . . We should not eliminate anyone's fundamental rights, whatever their sexuality, to marry the person they love."[12]

It's no surprise that companies such as Apple and Google put money behind efforts to stop Proposition 8. Tech companies have been on the vanguard of the CSR movement, and the rise of the knowledge economy helps explain the values shift that is under way in business. As more corporations have emerged that are powered by the creative class, corporate policies have changed to reflect the values of this class, which include not only tolerance and multiculturalism but also environmentalism. Tech firms are routinely ranked as among the most socially responsible companies in the United States. An example is the list of "100 best corporate citizens" that is published annually by *Corporate Responsibility Officer* magazine. The list weighs corporate behavior in more than half a dozen categories, including the environment, human rights, philanthropy, employee relations, and governance. Nearly every major high-tech company in the United States made the 2009 list, and six were among the top twenty.[13]

Quite apart from this values shift related to the knowledge economy, corporations take a tolerant stance toward gays for the same reasons that they embrace diversity more generally. They don't want to fall out of step with an American public that increasingly accepts homosexuality as normal—an acceptance that is especially widespread among Millennials, who are fast emerging as the biggest generation of consumers in history. Corporations also understand that a gay-friendly stance can improve their market share with gay consumers. According to one 2002 study, nearly half of all gay consumers stated that they preferred "to purchase products from companies that provide financial and/or in-kind support to nonprofit organizations serving the gay and lesbian community over competing products from companies that do not."[14] As well, corporations don't want to scare away talented employees who might be gay or who expect to work in a gay-friendly environment.

Although the leftward drift among corporate leaders has many sources, it is fast taking on its own momentum, thanks to consulting firms and business schools.

McKinsey and Company has long been known for inculcating executives with harsh management techniques—bucking them up, for instance, to fire the bottom 10 percent of workers every year—but recently the firm has also taken up the cause of CSR. "Business leaders must become involved in sociopolitical debate not only because their companies have so much to add but also because they have a strategic interest in doing so," stated a McKinsey analysis in 2006. "Social and political forces, after all, can alter an industry's strategic landscape fundamentally; they can torpedo the reputations of businesses that have been caught unawares and are seen as being culpable; and they can create valuable market opportunities by highlighting unmet social needs and new consumer preferences."

The McKinsey analysts pointed out that the expectations of companies were changing fast, and that new "frontier" expectations were emerging that executives ignored at their peril. For example, the obesity crisis shifted from being an issue of personal responsibility to one of corporate responsibility, as critics called on food makers to change both their products and their advertising approach. The same thing happened years earlier with tobacco. Only by taking CSR seriously could companies hope to stay ahead of the curve as activists rewrote the rules of responsible business.

McKinsey has gone so far as to create a special initiative on climate change, aimed at leading executives through the thicket of CSR challenges around this issue. McKinsey consultants now stand ready to help executives answer questions such as, "What is the likely value associated with 'going green'? Should we carve out leadership in this field or just stay with the pack?" or to help them understand "climate change and supply side management."

Of course, such insights could be redundant to younger business leaders fresh out of MBA programs that have an increasingly liberal tint. According to research by the Aspen Institute, business schools are rapidly integrating CSR training into their curriculum. In 2001, only 34 percent of top MBA programs required students to take a course examining business and society issues; by 2007, 63 percent of schools had this requirement. Between 2005 and 2007 alone, the number of courses at top business schools with some environmental and social content increased by nearly 50 percent. By 2008, thirty-five business schools offered special concentrations that allowed students to focus on CSR.

At some schools, the faculty can't keep up with student demand for such offerings. A quarter of MBA students at Stanford earned a special certificate in CSR-related issues in 2006, and the business school there now offers more than thirty elective courses on topics such as environmental sustainability. Other business schools are adding or expanding new centers that explore how to blend the pursuit of profit and the social good, such as Yale's Program on Social Enterprise and Cornell's Center for Sustainable Global Enterprise.

This activity may seem just a passing fad, but it partly reflects a long-term effort by liberal activists to reshape the business school experience. An organization called Net Impact has been at the forefront of this work since the early 1990s. Net Impact had its origin when Josh Mailman asked a Harvard Business School professor, Mark Albion, how to bring socially responsible values to business schools. That conversation led Albion to found Students for Responsible Business, later renamed Net Impact. The group now has more than 10,000 members and 200 campus chapters, including in many of the top business schools in the world, and hosts an annual conference that, in 2009, drew 2,500 students, business professors, and others. Albion has become a tireless crusader for teaching social values to MBA students, writing books such as *More Than Money* and speaking at hundreds of business schools. *Business Week* has called him the "the savior of B-school souls."

A decade ago, it was hard to find much guidance on how to be a moral business leader in an MBA program; now such advice is hard to avoid.

To critics on the right, the CSR movement has spun out of control. They see a vast liberal campaign to attack corporate America and co-opt even the most stalwart defenders of free enterprise. So it was that in 2007 the Capital Research Group, a right-wing watchdog organization, published a report titled "Wal-Mart Goes Left." The report stated that "Wal-Mart, the family-friendly, patriotic company founded by the late Sam Walton, has transformed itself into a reliable ally of the political left in order to boost revenues by pacifying its growing chorus of critics. The company now funds radical groups and intimidates its suppliers into adopting its liberal, Big Government agenda."

Well, not quite. Walmart remains a conservative company. But a decade ago, it would have been unimaginable to hear such things being said about Walmart. That was before the CSR movement hit critical mass, and Walmart took sweeping actions to change its image—and yes, even its behavior in some areas. If CSR values can gain a toehold at Walmart, anything is possible. Which is exactly what worries the acolytes of Milton Friedman.

Critics on the left see a very different picture, including those who know the corporate world firsthand, such as Leo Hindery. Hindery is a longtime businessman who helps lead the private equity firm InterMedia Partners. He has been the CEO of five companies and is also a major player in Democratic politics, having served as an economic adviser to John Edwards and later to Barack Obama during the 2008 election. Hindery has given Democrats nearly $1 million during the last decade.

In 2005, not long after the scandals at Enron and WorldCom, Hindery published a scathing indictment of corporate America, *It Takes a CEO*, that blasted everything from greedy CEOs to outsourcing to deregulation to union-busting, and more. Hindery doesn't think much has changed, even after the financial collapse. He points to the massive campaigns to sink health-care reform and climate change legislation during Obama's first year in office, as well as ongoing excesses in compensation. "I can find you CEOs that are doing the right thing, but the power balance is still out of kilter," Hindery said. "I don't think there has been a great shift in values."

Hindery has a point. Executives may be embracing CSR in droves, but don't confuse these people with the CEOs of the 1950s and the 1960s. Back then, social responsibility meant—first and foremost— sharing profits with workers in an equitable fashion, not to mention paying hefty corporate income taxes.

So far, today's CSR craze has done little to revive such largesse in the executive suite. Between 2000 and 2007, corporate profits as a share of GDP rose to their highest level in forty years, while wages fell to their lowest share *on record*. Translation: the people who own and run corporations are getting richer, and the people who work for these companies are getting stiffed. Corporate income tax receipts also fell to a historically low level during this period, as corporations have shifted money offshore and made aggressive use of tax shelters.[15]

Whatever the noble words—and deeds—professed by companies when it comes to sustainability or diversity, most remain ruthlessly dedicated to the bottom line in those areas that have the greatest impact on profits, such as where goods are produced and what workers get paid. Even Stride Rite long ago shipped its production facilities overseas. In this sense, the outlook of many progressive-minded executives seems typical of the watered-down liberalism that abounds in the upper class—namely, a genuine commitment to social rights and a cleaner environment but little concern for economic equity.

Of course, entrenched corporate greed also says something about the recent priorities of liberal activists. Corporations often do change if they are pressured, and that hasn't happened much on issues like wages and outsourcing. Diversity and environmentalism have been at the center of progressive politics since the 1980s, and corporations have felt scorching heat from activists working these beats. But aside from sweatshop labor, they've largely gotten a free pass on the upward flow of profits and stagnant wages for workers. Organized labor, which used to force owners to share the wealth, has been in steep decline, now representing less than 8 percent of all private-sector workers, while the general public hasn't gotten too worked up about inequality.

All of the hype around CSR has made it easier for executives to keep the spotlight off deep structural inequities. The dramas of good and evil in business have played out on other, less important stages, and by showing an open mind on social and environmental issues, many corporations have come out with burnished reputations. Big business didn't invent CSR and has often fought the idea, but ultimately it granted the wealthy a powerful way to steer the debate over business and society away from the perilous shoals of profit redistribution. This fits a Marxist picture of how putative liberal elites will offer up reforms to capitalism that are strictly cosmetic, all the while defending the most unjust features of the system.

Such criticisms of CSR, though, don't change an exciting truth about what has happened in recent years, which is that some of the wealthiest and most powerful business leaders in the world have responded to shifting public values and activist pressures by changing course in certain areas—all without government regulators lifting a finger.

These same leaders can be pressured to change on a wider range of issues, such as profit sharing and worker rights. "It's very early in the movement," said Josh Mailman about CSR. "We are starting to see more businesses that are looking at their labor practices. Not enough, but it's growing."

If you think that a unified wealthy business class will fight such ideas to its last breath, think again. Clearly, this group has never been the monolithic bloc of capitalist purists that critics imagine. Rather, executives throughout history have, at different points, gone along with public opinion and caved to concerted pressure campaigns, even when this decision cut into their own pay. They have shared the wealth before and may well do so again if income inequality emerges as a major issue in American life. That hasn't happened yet, but stay tuned. If the middle class remains prostrate after the Great Recession even as corporate bonuses recover—which seems to be the emerging pattern—pressures for change will grow.

A (Very) Liberal Education

WILL THE UPPER CLASS keep getting more liberal? One way to glimpse the future is to look at elite private schools, the institutions that are educating America's wealthiest kids.

Watch an episode of *Gossip Girl* or the reality TV show *NYC Prep*, and you may think you have a fix on the posh world of private schools. These places are dominated by spoiled rich white kids who ride around in limos and shop at Prada with daddy's credit card. Right?

Yes and no. Although there is a lot of mindless privilege at prep schools, many have also emerged as bastions of liberal values. Take Sidwell Friends, as an example. The Washington, D.C., private school is famous as the place where the Obama girls go, and before that, it was famous because Chelsea Clinton went there. Richard Nixon's daughters also attended Sidwell Friends, as did Al Gore's kids. Founded by Quakers, Sidwell Friends is known as one of the most liberal private schools in Washington, which is one reason that the Obamas chose it for their daughters.

But the children of public servants have never made up more than a sliver of students at Sidwell Friends. Mainly, the school caters to the wealthy of the Washington metro area, whose ranks have grown rapidly in recent years. The three richest counties in the United States, as measured by median income, are located in the suburbs of Washington. Much of this wealth is relatively new. Some has been created by the tech corridor in Northern Virginia, where many software and Internet companies are based, including AOL. But most of the new wealth can be traced to one of the fastest-growing sectors of the knowledge economy in the D.C. area—lobbying and government contracting, a world filled with elite educated lawyers.

If you live in Bethesda and you pull down $1.2 million a year at a Washington law firm, you probably don't send your kids to public schools. You support public schools in principle, of course, but you don't want to compromise your kids' education for that principle. So you shell out $30,000 a year, per kid, to send them someplace with a sprawling campus, multiple athletic fields, state-of-the-art science labs, a theater that would suffice on Broadway, a thriving Mandarin Chinese language program, and so on. Maybe you send them to Georgetown Day School, or to Maret School, or perhaps to St. Albans School. Or you send them to Sidwell Friends. And although you may be a liberal, chances are that you're nowhere near as liberal as the school is.

For starters, there is Sidwell Friends' focus on diversity. Although the school is located in Northwest D.C., one of the whitest parts of Washington's highly segregated metro area, 39 percent of Sidwell Friends' students are kids of color. A quarter of the faculty is also nonwhite. The school has four full-time diversity coordinators, who keep busy with various diversity programs for students, faculty, and parents. The school affirms various ethnic groups with special events to commemorate Black History Month, Hispanic Heritage Month, and the Chinese New Year. Then there are school clubs such as the Diversity Club, the Black Student Union, the Jewish Cultural Club, the Asian Student Alliance, and the GLSBT (Gay, Lesbian, Straight, Bisexual, Transgender) Alliance. There are also separate parent committees for Latino and black students.

None of this is accidental. Sidwell Friends has made a huge push on diversity and has put substantial resources into the effort. Beyond paying for its team of diversity coordinators, it spends $5 million a year on financial aid, and 22 percent of its students receive awards that cover most of the tuition. Sidwell Friends also works closely with local private scholarship funds, such as the Latino Student Fund and the Black Student Fund.

In 2005, Sidwell Friends School won the Leading Edge Award for Equity and Justice from the National Association of Independent Schools (NAIS). With fourteen hundred members and a $15 million budget, NAIS has focused on diversity for years. It started the People of Color Conference in 1986 and the Student Leadership Diversity Conference in 1993. NAIS also sponsors an annual Summer Diversity Institute, which is a weeklong immersion in diversity issues for private school staff and faculty. This offering is so popular that NAIS routinely runs out of space and has to close registration for the event. For years, NAIS has offered up various diversity curricula to help private schools institutionalize their efforts. Sidwell Friends has been an eager consumer of such ideas.[1]

Private schools may still have a reputation as being elitist and WASPy, but that stereotype doesn't fit today. This world isn't run by blueblood prigs as much as by open-minded baby boomers, quite a few of whom were drawn to education as a place to further social change. It is a world that strongly embraces a number of core liberal ideas and works hard to put those ideas into practice, shaping the values of the young and wealthy. (Campaign records also show that faculty members at top prep schools donate overwhelmingly to Democrats.)

Sidwell Friends may have a national reputation as being liberal, but it is hardly an outlier in its values. In fact, it is squarely in the mainstream of the elite private school world—certainly, in its diversity policies.

A century ago, America's most elite private schools were committed to defending the cultural hegemony of Anglo-Saxon Protestants. That outlook ebbed rapidly in the 1960s amid the civil rights movement. In 1965, for example, the headmaster of the Groton School—whose alumni include FDR, Dean Acheson, and McGeorge Bundy—brought seventy-five students to Boston to march with

Martin Luther King Jr. in a civil rights demonstration. Groton had accepted its first African American students a few years earlier. Georgetown Day School, one of the other schools that the Obamas considered for their daughters, was founded in 1945 as the first racially integrated private school in Washington and ranks as among the most prestigious schools in the D.C. area. Kids of color now comprise a fifth of all private school students nationwide—a ratio far higher than that of most affluent suburban school districts.[2]

The new conventional wisdom in private school circles is that future leaders, operating in a diverse United States and a global economy, must be skilled at dealing with many kinds of people to succeed. These schools believe that teaching such "cultural competence" is nearly as important as anything else. Private school leaders have also embraced the empirical research that shows that diverse school environments have many positive effects on students, such as higher academic achievement, greater self-esteem, and a stronger capacity for critical thinking.

So it is that a place like St. Paul's School in New Hampshire, once an archetype of Protestant white privilege—J. P. Morgan went there—has as one of its top strategic priorities to incorporate "diversity and a global perspective across the entire curriculum and within the entire community." St. Paul's has made a big push to create a very diverse student body; 35 percent are kids of color. The school, which has an endowment of more than $400 million and only 533 students, has managed this through active recruiting and generous financial aid, the same strategy pursued by Sidwell Friends. Like the Groton School, St. Paul had started its push for diversity in the decades after World War II. In 1960, the school's rector wrote to the alumni, "We reach out to the world of which we are a microcosm. . . . Every segment of American society is here. Nearly a fourth of the student body is on formal scholarship in varying amounts."[3]

Sidwell Friends is hardly unique with nearly four out of ten students of color. The oldest and most elite private schools are among the most diverse of all—for example: Milton Academy (40 percent students of color), Choate Rosemary Hall (38 percent), Phillips Exeter Academy (36 percent), the Hun School of Princeton (34 percent), and

Deerfield Academy (26 percent). International students comprise some of the kids of color at these schools, but typically not a majority.[4] It's no coincidence that these institutions are among the most well-endowed private schools in the United States. Like St. Paul's, they have tapped their huge endowments to fund the scholarships, the outreach, and the staffing needed to execute ambitious diversity strategies.

Supporting gay and lesbian students is a more recent twist on diversity in private schools. Most of America's top prep schools now have Gay-Straight Alliance (GSA) chapters, often supported with school funds. In fact, the second Gay-Straight Alliance club in the United States was started in 1988 at Phillips Andover Academy, where George W. Bush and his father went. It was modeled after the first GSA, which was established at nearby Concord Academy. Surveys find that antigay harassment is pervasive in private schools, but that the climate in these schools is less hostile to LGBT students than in public schools. For example, a 2005 survey by the Gay, Lesbian, and Straight Education Network (GLSEN) found that although 64 percent of all LGBT students felt unsafe at their schools, the figure was 49 percent for such students at private schools. More broadly, GLSEN's research has found that anti-LGBT harassment correlates closely with a school's economic characteristics, with students less likely to be harassed about sexual orientation at schools that have wealthier student populations.[5] One reason for this is that wealthier schools are more likely to have the resources to intervene and deal with harassment. Another, of course, is that today's educated and wealthy class is less homophobic than many other parts of society.

Every year, *Gay Parent* publishes a list of scores of private schools that are gay friendly. The list gets longer every year. In New York City, some private schools, such as the Greenwich Village Academy, even send delegations to march in the city's Gay Pride Parade under the school's banner.

Surely, another attraction of Sidwell Friends for Barack and Michelle Obama was the school's stellar environmental record.

The new Sidwell middle school may be the greenest school building in the United States, earning a platinum rating from the U.S. Green Building Council, the highest possible rating, when it was finished in 2007. It uses solar panels and passive solar design to dramatically cut energy costs, as well as a "constructed wetland" and water-efficient landscaping to sharply reduce water usage. Other buildings at Sidwell use geothermal pumps, recycled materials, and super-efficient lighting systems and windows. The school's cleaning and food services are also eco-friendly. Nothing but Green Seal Certified cleaning products are used at Sidwell, and all paper products, such as toilet paper and paper towels, are made of recycled materials. Fair trade coffee is served in the faculty lounge. Much unused food ends up in a composter purchased by a student environmental group, which uses the compost for organic fertilizer.

Sidwell Friends is hardly unique in its conservation efforts. Punahou School, the progressive prep school in Honolulu that Obama attended, also has one of the greenest middle school buildings in the United States—paid for by alum Steve Case, the founder of AOL. In addition, other elite schools are building green as environment sustainability sweeps the prep world. Here again, the National Association of Independent Schools has been working to push its members in a progressive direction. Expectations are rising, NAIS said, that independent schools demonstrate "their commitment to social responsibility and environmental sustainability." Not only that, but schools are a prime venue to "educate students about ecology and how to live as environmentally responsible citizens." To Patrick Bassette, NAIS's president, it is a golden opportunity. "If it's true that the 'hand that rocks the cradle rules the world,'" he said, "we should take heart: independent schools have a disproportionate access to the future generation of leadership in the cradle we call school."[6]

In 2003, NAIS hired a "sustainability consultant" named Wynn Calder. The timing couldn't have been better, as numerous private schools hustled to become greener, propelled by the combination of liberal faculty and eco-minded students. Calder put together a summer institute on sustainability for NAIS, which quickly became a popular event. The premise of the institute, NAIS explained, is that "a viable future for humanity depends on overcoming extraordinary environmental, social, and economic challenges; and that independent schools have a significant leadership role to play in creating positive change."

Calder's gig with NAIS generated so much activity that he created his own consulting outfit, Sustainable Schools, which works with private schools around the country to go green. He is a very busy man. Unlike public schools, which are hostage to government budgets and regulations, private schools have the resources to move fast in turning values into action. Here again, the wealthiest, most elite schools are in the vanguard. For instance, Hotchkiss—with a $430 million endowment and fewer than six hundred students—hired a full-time "Director of Environmental Initiatives," Josh Hahn, in early 2009. What does this guy do all day? A lot of things, such as work to achieve Hotchkiss's goal of becoming carbon-neutral, oversee the school's organic farming initiative, coordinate environmental service projects for students, and infuse sustainability themes across the curriculum.

Hotchkiss—where Henry Ford sent his sons—was already well along in becoming an environmentally friendly school before Hahn arrived. The school has overhauled its lighting systems to make them more energy efficient, and every major construction project at the school is designed to qualify for Leadership in Energy and Environmental Design certification. The school gets nearly a quarter of its electricity from wind power. Hotchkiss's dining service is a model of sustainable food practices. It buys as much food as it can from local sources, recycles cooking oil for biodiesel, serves fair trade organic coffee in the snack bar, composts waste, and so on. Hotchkiss's food service contractor, Sodexo, partners with the Food Alliance, a nonprofit organization dedicated to sustainable agriculture.

The story is much the same at other top private schools. Phillips Andover Academy hired a sustainability coordinator in 2006 and is pushing forward with its own goal of becoming carbon-neutral. The school has been a top contender in the annual "Green Cup" competition, in which private schools compete to reduce energy consumption during a one-month period. (The competition was started by the Phillips Exeter Academy.) Other top prep schools, such as Deerfield Academy and the Lawrenceville School, also have full-time sustainability coordinators and big plans to shrink their carbon footprint. In 2007, dozens of private schools came together to form the Green Schools Alliance, with members signing a pledge to reduce carbon emissions by 30 percent in five years and achieve carbon-neutrality by 2020. Within two years, 180 schools had taken the pledge, Sidwell Friends among them.

Beyond diversity and sustainability, private schools have embraced another key progressive idea: *global citizenship*. The term alone is enough to make the Sarah Palin demographic shudder and imagine black helicopters; it is less likely to faze a wealthy business class keenly attuned to globalization.

Exposing students to the larger world has long been a focus of private schools and helps explain why the Establishment leaders of the mid-twentieth century, educated at places like Exeter, were so internationalist. Later, the Vietnam War infused many private schools with a critical stance on U.S. foreign policy and a strong liberal bent on global affairs. Faculty and students alike at many schools were active in the antiwar movement. NAIS president Patrick Bassett recalled that as a young English teacher at Woodbury Forest School in Virginia, he drove a van full of students to the huge antiwar March on Washington in 1971. "It was a very risky thing to do," Bassett said—not because he would get in trouble with his school, but because it was impossible to keep tabs on the students in the vast crowd.

That kind of teacher-facilitated activism wasn't unusual for private schools, either during the Vietnam War or around causes such as the nuclear freeze or the antiapartheid movement. When the disinvestment push sprang up in the 1980s, both students and faculty were involved in pressuring private schools to sell stocks in companies that did business with South Africa. In New York City and elsewhere, top administrators huddled with colleagues from other elite schools to figure out a collective response. In 1985, the NAIS sent a letter to all one thousand member schools, urging "trustees, heads, faculties, and students in member schools to declare their opposition to apartheid as part of their educational responsibility."[7]

These days, the big thing is promoting a "one world" ethos among students. At the forefront of this effort is the Global Youth Leadership Institute. That venture was sparked by the events of September 11, 2001, and was begun by the Independent School Association of the Central States (ISACS), based in Chicago. John Braman, then the president of that association, drove the venture. "I saw that there is a giant misunderstanding about Islam, and I was very worried that it would add to the burden that people of color are carrying in our schools," Braman recalled later. "There was a need for stronger medicine to be applied to the challenges of multiculturalism."

To better expose students to other cultures, Braman forged a number of partnerships, such as with the Pluralism Project of Harvard University, the Earth University in Costa Rica, and the Lama Foundation, a spiritual community in New Mexico. After several pilot projects, the Global Youth Leadership Institute was established in 2005. Its mission is to "nurture collaborative leadership for global communities and to assist schools in their missions to inspire socially responsible young people."

A cornerstone event for the institute is an annual summer student leadership conference in Costa Rica, jointly sponsored with the NAIS. The idea is to bring small teams of student leaders from about twenty private schools in the United States and twenty from other countries, accompanied by faculty advisers, to spend a week talking about global issues. In 2008, the focus of the conference was human rights, and 120 participants spent their time chewing over the Universal Declaration of Human Rights and then drafting a statement to world leaders. Among other things, the students urged world leaders to cancel foreign debt, adopt fair trade, and guarantee health care for every person on the planet. They also urged a campaign against racial oppression, citing the Jena Six incident in Louisiana, among other events, as evidence of ongoing "racist crimes." The 2009 conference focused on global water issues.

During the last few years, NAIS has been working to institution-
alize global education in its member schools, arguing that the goal
of a private school education shouldn't be to set kids on the "road to
college," but rather to set them on the "road to global citizenship."[8]
Among other things, the NAIS has made a big push to expand
Mandarin Chinese language offerings at private schools. Learning
the most commonly spoken language in the world, the logic goes, is a
key way to prepare prep students "to be global citizens and successful
global leaders."

Service is another theme that looms large in the private school
universe, and it is a rare preppie nowadays who isn't asked to give
back in some way. At Sidwell Friends, the youngest students in
the school begin every year with an assembly about hunger and
homelessness. The event is led by representatives of Martha's Table,
a local social service organization that Sidwell Friends partners
with to expose its students to the needs of the less fortunate. Then,
during the year, the students each bring a vegetable to school every
Wednesday to help make soup for the homeless. The students—and
their families—take turns helping out at Martha's Table on every
third Saturday.

Spring break in St. Bart's or Aspen may be one kind of field
trip for rich kids; another involves traveling to some of the poorest
places in the United States—and the world—to lend a hand. Phillips
Exeter Academy sent sixty-five students and staff members down
to New Orleans in 2006 to help rebuild a flood-ravaged neighborhood. (Students from many other private schools, such as Horace
Mann, also went to New Orleans.) Hotchkiss students have traveled
to Botswana to join the antipoverty service work of the Maru-a-Pula
school. Greenwich Village Academy students have volunteered with
Habitat for Humanity to refurbish homes in the slums of Bridgeport.
And students from the Groton School have gone to Peru to work on
projects at an impoverished rural school. (The list is nearly endless.)

This kind of thing is often dismissed as résumé-polishing for
rich kids, and it's also tempting to see voluntarism as a conservative idea that elevates cosmetic fixes over systemic change. There is
some truth in both charges. If you take a closer look at many service

initiatives, however, you see something else: that the spirit of VISTA (Volunteers in Service to America) and the Peace Corps is alive and well in some of the poshest corners of U.S. education.

This is more than a coincidence, because the current wave of service programs is largely an invention of baby boomers who came of age in the 1960s and have hoped to reignite the idealism of that decade in young Americans. In turn, these boomers have drawn on a progressive tradition dating back nearly a century. John Dewey was an early proponent of service-based learning, and in 1906, the philosopher William James first introduced the idea of nonmilitary service in his essay "The Moral Equivalent of War." Service was a major part of the New Deal through the Civilian Conservation Corps, and it emerged as a central pillar of the Great Society when Lyndon Johnson built on the Peace Corps model to create not only VISTA, but also the National Teacher Corps, the Job Corps, and University Year of Action. The sixties also saw the creation of the Senior Volunteer Corps, the Urban Corps, and the Youth Conservation Corps, which engaged young people in addressing environmental problems. The term *service learning* was first used in conjunction with a project in Tennessee that involved university students and faculty in fighting Appalachian poverty. Twenty-five years later, President Bill Clinton invoked the ideals of the 1960s to create AmeriCorps, as well as a sister program, Learn and Serve America.

By the late 1990s, most private schools in the United States had some kind of service program, many of which are quite good. A 2001 study by the NAIS evaluated hundreds of private school service programs against a set of quality indicators and found that most rated well. "Independent school programs seem strong in meeting a real need in the community, in that working in homeless shelters, tutoring in public schools and visiting elders are the most common projects," the study found.[9] One chronic problem with service programs, the study said, was a shortage of resources—particularly transportation to and from service activities. This is less likely to be an issue at richer schools. At Sidwell Friends, the school provides transportation for all community service. It also has a full-time director of its community service program.

Thus yet another irony: the richest kids at the wealthiest schools may get the best opportunities to tackle social problems. Money is no object in exposing these kids to hardship in even the most distant corners of the world. For instance, a dozen students and three teachers from the Lakeside School in Seattle—Bill Gates's alma mater—have traveled to a rural village in China three years in a row to teach English at the local elementary school. Other Lakeside students have traveled to places such as Senegal, India, and Morocco to fulfill the school's requirement of eighty hours of service. "Our goal is to inspire and empower students to be agents of change both in their local communities and in the international arena," Lakeside says about its well-funded Global Service Learning Program.

And many students are empowered by these experiences. The big investment in service programs by private schools is another factor aiding the rise of a new class of wealthy "supercitizens" whose members are adept at engaging with the broader world.

Elite universities reinforce the liberal values of private schools. Students who move from top prep schools to top colleges are likely to hear an unbroken gospel about diversity, sustainability, and community service. There might once have been a time when these messages were little more than background noise at elite universities, easily brushed off en route to Wall Street jobs or law schools. Now they are impossible to ignore.

Although the liberalism on college campuses is hardly news, a funny thing has happened in recent years, which is that the ferocious fights over "PC" policies in higher education have ebbed, even as the reach of such policies has expanded, with environmentalism moving front and center. Any regular visitor to college campuses—I've visited scores lately—can't help but notice that there isn't a lot of conflict going on, as if some great war has finally ended. By and large, the PC agenda has triumphed, and there is not much left to debate. Partly, this is about generational change: the Millennials are a more liberal crop of students than the Gen Xers were, and they tend to take for granted that a college should stress diversity and embrace sustainability. Partly, it is that progressive university policies have come to seem normal after years of being institutionalized.

This doesn't mean that elite universities have become more effective incubators of opportunity or equality. They haven't. In his 2005 study *Equity and Excellence in American Higher Education*, William Bowen found that only 10 percent of students in nineteen elite colleges and universities came from low-income families, and that this percentage has been falling, not rising, in recent decades.[10] (The share of minority students has been rising, but many are from well-off households.) Other research shows that household wealth is one of the biggest predictors of educational success and that, these days, dumb rich kids are more likely to go to college than are smart poor kids. Moreover, America's best-endowed universities didn't get that way by accident; they built their wealth by giving preference to alumni kids, many of whom come from money, and to so-called development cases—the children of wealthy donors or potential donors. In *The Price of Admission*, reporter Daniel Golden documents a systematic bias on the part of elite universities to admit rich kids. In that sense, these universities may do more to entrench today's inequality than to challenge such patterns.

That said, the progressive values now being inculcated at elite universities matter. Universities have a long track record of turning rich kids into critics of the existing order. Any number of radical efforts have emerged from exclusive universities—including, of course, Students for a Democratic Society and its extremist spin-off, the Weather Underground. In his 1971 memo that rallied business leaders to oppose attacks on the free enterprise system, Lewis Powell identified universities as the "single most dynamic source" of that attack. Today's upper-class students at places such as Columbia and Brown may no longer be imbibing Herbert Marcuse, and don't expect them to be assembling pipe bombs any time soon. But the climate in which today's college students are being educated is actually more institutionally liberal than at any time in U.S. history, including the 1960s—an era in which student radicalism was commonplace, yet university leadership and policies remained quite conservative.

Although it's true that older, more liberal faculty members have begun to retire, the professoriate remains reliably on the left. The 2007 Harvard study "The Social and Political Views of American Professors," mentioned in an earlier chapter, found that 62 percent of faculty members identified themselves as either liberal or very liberal, while only 19 percent confessed to any sort of conservative leanings. Comparing their findings to a similar 1972 study, the authors found that the ranks of conservative faculty members have dwindled over the last three decades. In 2004, 77 percent of the faculty surveyed voted for John Kerry; only 20 percent voted for President Bush. Even professors of economics and business went overwhelmingly for Kerry. The study also found that faculty at liberal arts colleges and elite universities—the places where the wealthy tend to be educated—are much more liberal than are professors at state schools and community colleges.[11]

Another ideological gauge of professors and administrators can be found by looking at campaign finance data. In 2008, Barack Obama raised more money from employees of the University of California than he did from Goldman Sachs, Microsoft, or Google. Harvard and Stanford were also among the top ten sources of Obama's campaign cash, where Obama outraised McCain by overwhelming margins. (A mere 12 percent of campaign donations from Harvard went to McCain.) Democrats also outraised Republicans at every other elite university by wide margins, for example, Columbia (91 percent contributions for Democrats to 9 percent for Republicans), the University of Chicago (94 percent to 6 percent), Yale (90 percent to 10 percent), Georgetown (89 percent to 11 percent), Penn (87 percent to 13 percent), Princeton (84 percent to 16 percent), MIT (92 percent to 8 percent), the University of Michigan (90 percent to 10 percent), and Duke (84 percent to 14 percent). Democrats even outraised Republicans by a margin of 10 to 1 at Southern Methodist University, a school that has long educated wealthy Texans and that George W. Bush chose as the site of his presidential library.

The 2007 Harvard study confirmed that older professors tend to be more liberal than younger ones are and that faculties are growing more moderate as new hires come in. But just because there are fewer gray-haired professors pushing Noam Chomsky on their students doesn't mean that the climate of universities is becoming less liberal. Instead, that climate may actually be getting more liberal, but in ways that reflect the social movements of today, rather than of the past.

For example, a 2007–2008 survey asked twenty-two thousand faculty members about their goals in teaching undergraduates. About 75 percent said it was "very important" or "essential" to "enhance students' knowledge of and appreciation for other racial/ethnic groups"—up from 57 percent of faculty who held this view only three years earlier. More than half of the faculty said it was essential to "Instill in students a commitment to community service"—up from around a third of faculty members three years earlier.[12] In other words, the norms of diversity and community service are spreading fast, even though "tenured radicals" may be hanging up their berets to retire.

The surge in service initiatives at universities is especially striking. In 1969, top leaders in the service world—representing VISTA, the Peace Corps, and other organizations—met in Atlanta to plot ways to make community service a central feature of higher education. The idea was to put college students on the forefront of social change efforts. The push got off to a slow start in the 1970s and the 1980s, but the dream of these planners is finally coming to fruition— and more so with every passing year. It got a big boost in 1985, when the presidents of three elite universities—Brown, Stanford, and Georgetown—came together to create Campus Compact, partly in response to the materialistic currents of the Reagan era. The Compact quickly became the leading national organization promoting service on campuses. In 1988, it had 2 state offices and 133 member institutions; now it has 33 offices and 1,100 members. Most of these schools have full-time service coordinators, and they need them. In 1999, students at Campus Compact schools engaged in an estimated 29 million hours of community service; by 2006, that number had risen to 316 million hours. Homelessness and hunger were among the issues most frequently addressed by service work.[13]

Environmentalism is spreading even faster on elite campuses. Since 2007, more than six hundred colleges and universities have pledged to eventually become carbon-neutral, and more are doing so every month. The Sustainability Endowment Institute releases an annual report card that rates hundreds of colleges and universities on how green they are, looking at a host of factors, such as whether the school has a sustainability office, whether new buildings are green, whether it is committed to reducing its carbon footprint, whether it recycles, and so on. In 2007, only four schools received an A minus. Two years later, sixteen schools received this grade. Guess which schools tended to have the best records? The wealthier, more prestigious universities. The schools that ranked among the top ten included Columbia, Dickinson, Harvard, Middlebury, Oberlin, and Brown. Among other things, all of these schools have full-time sustainability staffs, and several—such as Oberlin, Dartmouth, and Amherst—have "endowment sustainability leaders," who are working to ensure that the schools' investments are in line with their sustainability values.

Beyond these standouts, the institute finds striking evidence of a rapid greening in higher education. More than half of the three hundred schools it surveyed in 2009 now have full-time sustainability staffs; 57 percent have adopted campus-wide green building policies; 52 percent have made a commitment to reduce their carbon emissions; more than a third are now producing renewable energy on campus; two-thirds have hybrid or alternative-energy vehicles; and a majority host "sustainability competitions" on campus that encourage students to adopt green practices.

Much of this is very new, and it is changing the college experience for millions of students—especially those at the most elite universities. Coupled with the sustainability focus at private schools, it is now nearly impossible for prep-educated Ivy Leaguers to get credentialed without being bombarded by the message that they need to reduce their carbon footprint.

THE HEIRS

M ANY OF TODAY'S RICH KIDS—prepped and polished from their toddler days onward—will not only be the power players of tomorrow in fields such as business, law, and media; they will also be leading philanthropists and political donors as fortunes are handed down to the next generation. How much money are we talking about? *A lot.*

As a result of the long boom years that began in the 1980s, some thirty thousand U.S. households now have assets greater than $30 million, according to an estimate in the 2009 *World Wealth Report*, a study put out annually by Merrill Lynch and Capgemini, an international consulting firm. This estimate was made at the end of 2008, after the crash but before the stock market bounced back the following year. Although data on the wealthy aren't further segmented, it seems safe to estimate that at least a few thousand households have assets in the hundreds of millions of dollars—not including America's hundreds of billionaires.

As this money moves down the generational ladder, large chunks of it will be captured by estate taxes or charitable bequests. But there will be plenty left over, and thousands of Americans will inherit fortunes that are large enough to affect politics and philanthropy.

The United States has always had inherited wealth, but never on so large a scale. Even the most paranoid populists probably don't grasp the size of the new hereditary wealth elite that has been spawned by recent boom times. This is the stuff of Jeffersonian nightmares, only with Prada thrown in. In all likelihood, though, the coming tide of inherited wealth will move the upper class—and American life—to the left. In fact, it's already happening.

There are simple reasons for this. One, as we have just seen, is how children of the affluent are being educated. Regardless of their parents' politics, they are likely to be exposed to liberal ideas in private schools and universities—or even inculcated with these ideas.

Many of today's rich kids are also growing up in the most liberal places in the country, which have been epicenters of the boom: the New York metro area; Los Angeles; Chicago; the affluent suburbs of Washington, D.C.; the Bay Area; Austin; and Boston. These parts of the United States aren't merely liberal; some are among the last places where more radical values persist—where antiwar protesters can be found in the parks, local cafés serve vegan entrees and fair trade coffee, documentaries show in independent theaters, boutiques sell organic hemp clothing, alternative weekly papers expose official corruption, and gays and lesbians are openly out in large numbers.

Most of all, though, the residents in these places are highly educated, and this is a signature trait of wealthy kids in the information age: many grow up seeing postgraduate degrees as the norm. Their parents are loaded up with credentials, and, early on, they are tracked to do the same. This stands in stark contrast to the earlier periods, where there was often little stress on getting a top-notch education, and certainly not for women. (F. Scott Fitzgerald famously called Princeton the "pleasantest country club in America.") Now more rich kids are overachievers, just like Mommy and Daddy, and, as much as anything, members of today's upper class are reinforcing their position through massive investments in the education of their children. This is cementing in place a new overclass, which is bad, but the upside is that America's inherited wealthy of today aren't a bunch of ignorant dandies. Many are joining the cream of America's multicultural educated elite and—whatever their upbringing—may come to embrace the liberal values so common to this group.

Another trait of heirs that can tilt them leftward is more timeless: they are removed from the process of wealth creation. They grow up affluent but have never been employers making FICA payments or arguing with the Environmental Protection Agency. The linchpin ideas that draw the business rich to become conservatives—about cutting taxes and red tape—may have little or no traction with heirs. Instead of a reflex to defend hard-earned wealth, heirs may feel guilt about being loaded for doing nothing.

Finally, and related, it almost goes without saying that heirs are the ultimate "postmaterialists"—people who grow up economically secure and who have the luxury of focusing on concerns beyond survival. Although hardship leads people to embrace hierarchical authority and traditional morality, a lifelong assumption of financial well-being—and what Ronald Inglehart calls "existential security"— induces people to prioritize self-expression and secular-rational approaches to the world.

These generalizations about heirs are more than idle speculation. In fact, heirs are central players in the progressive movement, as we've seen in the pages of this book. Office furniture heir John Hunting put nearly his entire inherited fortune into environmental causes and is now busy giving what is left to Democratic candidates and liberal 527s. Jon Stryker has used his inherited wealth to become America's largest backer of gay rights causes, not to mention spending millions to move Michigan's politics to the left. Alida Messinger, the daughter of John D. Rockefeller III, is one of the most generous financial backers of the Democratic Party, 527s, and environmental causes. Josh Mailman, the heir to his father's conglomerate fortune, has been a pioneering figure in the corporate responsibility movement. The lucrative world of New York real estate has by itself produced a number of activist heirs, including Patricia Bauman, who funds a wide array of progressive groups, and Adam Rose, who has put big money into the Democratic Party and gay rights. Steve Bing, a major donor to the Democratic Party and environmental causes, inherited a vast New York real estate fortune that had its genesis in the boom times of the 1920s.

Other liberal money has come from less likely sources. Helen and Swanee Hunt both inherited tens of millions of dollars from their father, H. L. Hunt, a Texan oilman who was famous in earlier times for trying to corner the silver market and at one point was ranked as the richest person in the United States. Hunt was notoriously conservative, funding the John Birch Society and operating right-wing radio stations. Helen and Swanee had different plans. Like many who grow up amid affluence, they gravitated toward postmaterialist pursuits as they came of age: Swanee majored in philosophy at college and then went on to get two master's degrees in religion and psychology. Helen got degrees in liberal arts and counseling and eventually a PhD in theology. In 1981, after their father died, the sisters set up the Hunt Alternatives Fund and began to put their money into a variety of liberal groups. Swanee emerged as one of the biggest donors to the Democratic Party in the 1990s. Among the Hunt sisters' recent ventures is Women Moving Millions, a fund-raising effort aimed at channeling substantial amounts of money into women's issues. As of 2009, the fund had raised more than $181 million.

The Democracy Alliance has a number of heirs. The organization is chaired by Taco Bell heir Rob McKay, and members include Pat Stryker—Jon's sister—who like him inherited enough stock in the Stryker medical company from her grandfather to become a billionaire. By the time she joined the Democracy Alliance, Stryker had already emerged as a leading funder of liberal 527s and of progressive politics in Colorado, where her money had helped oust a Republican majority from the state legislature.

Alida Messinger didn't join the Democracy Alliance, but her cousin Anne Bartley, Winthrop Rockefeller's daughter, was an early and enthusiastic member. Bartley's activist work goes back decades. Among the so-called cousins—those Rockefellers who were the children of the "brothers" of Nelson Rockefeller's generation—Bartley has not been the biggest spender on progressive causes, but like several other cousins, she has devoted much of her life to organizations on the left.

The children of older liberal billionaires have also emerged as players in their own right, such as Jonathan Soros (the son of George), Jonathan Lewis (the son of Peter), and Steven Phillips, who is the son-in-law of Herb and Marion Sandler and a member of the Democracy Alliance. Elsewhere, campaign finance records show that James Simons's children have become major donors to the Democratic Party. Audrey and Nathaniel Simons, who works at his father's hedge fund, have both given the max at times to Democratic fund-raising committees—and there is a lot more where that came from.

Many liberal heirs do more than simply write checks. Some, like Rob McKay, occupy key leadership roles in progressive politics and are full-time activists. McKay's wealth comes from the Taco Bell fast-food chain, which his father helped build in Orange County, California, and led as the CEO. When McKay was a kid, he went scouting for new restaurant locations with his father, driving through neighborhoods to see what the houses looked like and what other retail operations were nearby. His friends ribbed him about getting free tacos. McKay's parents were Republican, and Orange County was an epicenter in the 1970s of a new conservative politics fueled by Sun Belt money and votes. Among McKay's earliest political memories was Ronald Reagan's sweeping victory in 1980.

McKay shared his parents' Republican politics, an outlook he held during his first two years at Occidental College, an expensive private college in Los Angeles. He recalled sitting on the floor of a dorm hallway late at night invoking the "domino theory" to defend U.S. policies in El Salvador. The first time he could vote, in 1984, he cast a ballot to reelect Reagan. But Occidental was a very liberal campus, and—in predictable fashion—McKay soon veered to the left. After college, he got a job at the Chicago Coalition for the Homeless and saw the role of private wealth in supporting social justice. "That's when the lightbulb went off: Gee, our family could be doing this, too."

After Taco Bell was sold to Pepsi in 1978, McKay's father invested in other holdings, growing his fortune. McKay's parents were open to the idea of starting a family foundation, but they didn't want to do it themselves. So, after getting a master's degree at the University of California, McKay took on the job of heading up the family foundation.

As a philanthropist, McKay would follow a familiar path. After years of making grants, mostly at the community level, his eyes were drawn upstream to more systemic problems and larger structures of power. McKay's first step toward a more activist political role came when he started to back the emerging living wage movement in California. McKay did more than simply fund living wage campaigns across the state; he also started one in San Francisco in 1998 after seeing the city's mayor, Willie Brown, quoted in the newspaper as saying that he would sign any living wage ordinance that reached his desk. McKay swung into action, pulling together a meeting of labor leaders and saying he would put up the money for a campaign if they did the organizing.

The campaign thrust McKay into city politics, and he found that he enjoyed tussling with local players like the colorful Brown. The effort succeeded in 2000, raising the minimum wage in companies that did business with the city to $11.03. Two years later, McKay spent $1.5 million on a state ballot initiative to allow voters to register and vote on Election Day. The initiative failed, but McKay found it invigorating to be part of a statewide campaign and get attacked by right-wingers. So when the call came from George Soros to join a July 2003 strategy meeting about ousting Bush, McKay eagerly attended. He not only committed $1 million to the effort, but also joined the board of Americans Coming Together. After the election, McKay was an early convert to the Democracy Alliance and, like Rob Stein and others, believed that the group filled a critical vacuum in terms of providing a community to wealthy donors. "A lot of these people felt a lot more isolated than we knew," McKay said. "Rich people are people, too, and actually like community. . . . The chance to be in a room with peers, to be able to think strategically, gave a number of people the impetus to do more than they did previously."

In June 2005, not long after he joined the Democracy Alliance, McKay penned a call to action by members of his class in the Huffington Post. "I don't know precisely where I fall among the richest

Americans—somewhere near the top 1 percent—but I think it's important that we 'people of wealth' start outing ourselves. We need to call attention to ourselves for the sole purpose of fighting Bush's tax cuts." McKay argued that "charity is not enough. We need to support—with our money, our connections and our public endorsements—advocacy."

Plenty of other heirs share this view, including a much younger generation that is only starting to come into their wealth. While Rob McKay is a Gen Xer, and other leading liberal heirs such as the Hunt sisters are boomers, it is the Millennial heirs—those born in the early 1980s onward—who stand to inherit the greatest fortunes of any generation in history. These heirs are more likely to have come of age in the liberal provinces of the new economy with highly educated professional parents.

Exactly how much money will flow to Millennial heirs is hard to say. The Center for Wealth and Philanthropy at Boston College has estimated that $41 trillion will be transferred to heirs by 2052 (or $25 trillion, after estate taxes and bequests) and that two-thirds of this money will be handed down within the top 7 percent of wealthiest households in the United States. Scholars at the Center say the recession will not diminish these numbers. Most of this money will go not to boomers but to Millennials or Xers. While the center estimated that only $6 trillion will in turn go to charity, this is actually a vast amount of money, given that all of the foundations in the United States had assets of some $600 billion in 2008.[1]

Beyond the swollen river of money headed toward this generation, the other trend that seems clear is the relative liberalism of the Millennial generation. In 2008, Obama won 66 percent of the Millennial vote—a margin 16 points greater than his victory among boomers. Obama's landslide among Millennials wasn't surprising, given that Millennials tend to identify as Democrats and liberals at higher rates than any other generation does, view government activism in favorable terms, support stronger environmental protections, and are tolerant on issues of gay rights. Morley Winograd and Michael D. Hais, the coauthors of the *Millennial Makeover*, argue that the Millennials may be the most progressive generation in U.S. history, and, in contrast to the boomers, they are far more unified ideologically. At the same time, Winograd and Hais note a major difference in the progressive ideology of boomers and Millennials. Whereas boomers on the left attacked key societal institutions as "incompetent and morally bankrupt," Millennials are more civic-minded and believe in institutions. (Late Gen Xers share many of the same views.)

So it isn't only that rich kids are growing up in deep-blue America and getting educated in LEED-certified buildings; it's also that they are part of a demographic cohort that makes the sixties generation look conservative by contrast. Some of these rich kids are so radical that they don't even want to be rich.

Take, for instance, Karen Pittelman, who is the granddaughter of the New York real estate baron Leonard Litwin. Pittelman grew up in a Jewish family on New York's Upper East Side, a city where her grandfather owns twenty-three buildings spread around Manhattan and is worth more than a billion dollars. Politics was seldom dis-cussed around the dinner table and money even less so. Pittelman went to Horace Mann, the pricey and exclusive prep school in Riverdale, New York. She had her first stirrings of political con-sciousness in an advanced placement American history class when the teacher assigned the works of Eric Foner, the liberal historian.

Pittelman's real awakening came when she went to college at Brown University, easily the most liberal of the Ivy League schools. Many of Pittelman's professors were clearly on the left. She wanted to be a writer and, through her literature courses, was exposed to the works of forgotten radical poets from the 1920s and the 1930s. Pittelman turned more liberal and, as that happened, felt increas-ingly ambivalent about her family's wealth. It started to seem wrong to her. It also felt embarrassing. This was during the late 1990s, and her professors, as well as activists on campus, were talking about sweatshops, corporate power, and the evils of globalization. "It was all in terms of us versus them," said Pittelman, "and you didn't want to be them." She never mentioned her family wealth but, over time, discovered that there were a lot of other "secret rich kids" at Brown.

Pittelman was never sure how much wealth she actually had of her own. Although her parents gave her money when she needed it, things were vague beyond that. During her senior year, Pittelman asked her parents directly and discovered that her grandfather had set up a trust for her. She was worth $3 million. "I had had no idea," she said.

That news set off a lot of soul searching, which grew more intense after she graduated from Brown and pondered her beliefs, along with what kind of person she wanted to be. "I didn't believe that 10 percent of the people should control 70 percent of the wealth," Pittelman said. "I didn't believe in the way the distribution of wealth works in this country. And that somebody should be able to have that much when so many people had so little. I didn't want to be part of that."

With her boyfriend, she took off across the country, putting serious distance between herself and the East Coast world of privilege in which she'd grown up. They spent time in Iowa and then Milwaukee, before heading down to New Mexico, where they hung out in a town aptly named Truth or Consequences.

"Around the time I hit New Mexico, I realized it didn't matter where I went; who I was was coming with me." Pittelman wondered whether she had to worry about her position of privilege or confront it in such a way that it squared with her beliefs. And, eventually, she felt that there was little choice but to take action. "By the time I got back, I was pretty resolved that what I wanted to do was dissolve the trust and give it away." All of it.

This idea did not go over so well with her family. It felt like a rejection to them, and it came at a sensitive time, when Pittelman was already establishing a life separate from her parents. "They thought I was being impetuous and that I didn't know what I really wanted," Pittelman said.

Her parents' response was a firm no. They said that the trust couldn't be dissolved, that it was legally "irrevocable." But Pittelman persisted, talking to lawyers, and it turned out that there was a chink in the legalese: in fact, the trust could be dissolved if its original creator, her grandfather, and its trustee, her mother, agreed to allow this to happen. Pittelman's grandfather was past eighty but still very much alive, an elder statesman among New York real estate titans.

Pittelman worked on both him and her mother for more than a year. "I couldn't give up. It felt to me that I couldn't be the person I wanted to be if I didn't take this action. I couldn't be complicit in something I didn't believe in."

Eventually, both her grandfather and her mother relented. When the day finally came to sign the papers at the family's law firm, lawyers crowded in to watch the proceedings. They had never before seen a trust dissolved.

Pittelman promised that the money would go into a foundation, but she was vague about what kind of foundation. "I think my parents imagined I would establish the Karen Pittelman Foundation or something," she said. Instead, she had very specific plans to put her money under the direct control of community activists. Pittelman, who was living in Boston by this time, had a number of conversations about where her money was needed. Eventually, she decided that the most marginalized group in the city—those with the least power and the fewest resources—were low-income women, particularly women of color and immigrants. When her trust was dissolved, she set up the Chahara Foundation and recruited a board of directors—seven women—drawn from the group she wanted to empower. She was initially involved in the foundation's start-up but quickly stepped away. "I wanted to transfer power to the people on the front lines, and I didn't want to define it more than that."

The Chahara Foundation made grants to a variety of activist groups and service organizations working with the poorest women in Boston. Single mothers. Battered wives. Immigrants with AIDS. The foundation was small, and its directors made the decision to spend down the assets, which included not only the initial $3 million but other funds that Pittelman later contributed. By 2009, most of the money was gone.

This might have been the end of the story, allowing Pittelman to get on with her writing career. But somewhere along the line, a local activist convinced Pittelman that if social change were to happen, everyone needed to "organize where they came from." For Pittelman, that meant reaching out to young heirs like herself. By this time, Pittelman had discovered an organization called Resource

Generation, which worked to engage young people of wealth who were involved in social change, and she became one of its first staffers. Pittelman also published a book in 2006 titled *Classified: How to Stop Hiding Your Privilege and Use It for Social Change* and coauthored another book, *Creating Change through Family Philanthropy: The Next Generation.*

Her books have a small but important audience. There are now so many people like Pittelman—"cool rich kids," as one young liberal heir dubbed them—that several groups have cropped up to offer them guidance. Resource Generation is the most prominent of these. Based in New York, it offers workshops, trainings, conferences, and local dinners to help young people of wealth become engaged in social justice philanthropy. As of 2009, the group was actively working with 750 young people of wealth across the United States.

Resource Generation was founded in the late 1990s by a group of affluent Boston activists who included Tracy Hewat, an heiress to one of America's oldest fortunes. The group started after a national conference for wealthy young people was canceled because not enough participants had signed up. Hewat blamed the turnout on the negative perception of rich kids. "The stereotype of young wealthy men and women was so awful—petulant, greedy, unmotivated," she later told the *Boston Phoenix.* "No one wanted to fly across the country to go to a conference with people they thought would be like that." Resource Generation set out to change this image and find like-minded young and well-off progressives. They started by holding monthly dinners around the Boston area, where people could share feelings and ideas in a safe space—that is, with others who could empathize with the burdens and anxieties that can accompany wealth.

After a few years in operation under Hewat's direction, holding dinners and recruiting at liberal colleges such as Hampshire and Tufts, Resource Generation had 250 constituents and a two-person staff. At the end of the group's first national conference in 1999, which drew 45 participants, everyone filled out a questionnaire that included a statement about his or her future net worth—which collectively came to $600 million. In other words, Resource Generation was drawing heirs who were the real deal. The group managed to overcome negative stereotypes to the point that it kept growing and attracting new constituents.

Resource Generation isn't for socialite heirs who aspire to hit the black-tie circuit. It's a pretty hard-core group, and Pittelman isn't the only member who has turned over her trust fund to grassroots activists. The organization embraces "social change philanthropy," a radical approach to giving that focuses on marginalized communities, seeks to address the root causes of problems, and includes community leaders in its grantmaking. (The Chahara Foundation embodies this approach.)

Research by the scholar Laura Wernick has found that heirs who get involved in Resource Generation tend to dramatically increase their annual giving by as much as ten times. They also retarget their money away from direct service to social justice organizations. Even more important, many get involved in trying to change how their family foundations operate. There are now tens of thousands of family foundations in the United States, most of which engage in innocuous giving to traditional charitable causes. A key goal of Resource Generation is to train young heirs to capture these entities and put this money, which will eventually total many billions of dollars, into activist causes. It is a quiet battle—few Americans even know it is going on—but one that will have profound consequences.

Rich heirs. Left-wing politics. New funds for social change. This collage will be familiar to keen students of the 1960s, when an earlier economic boom produced an upsurge of wealth that coincided with an earthquake in America's politics and culture. Much of what Resource Generation is doing today was done before, decades ago, by an earlier wave of liberal young people of wealth—some with famous family names—and these efforts are still shaping U.S. politics.

Stewart Rawlings Mott was among the most well-known liberal heirs of the era. Mott was the son of Charles Stewart Mott, who for many years was the largest shareholder of General Motors. After graduating from Columbia University in 1961, Stewart stirred up his first controversy when he returned to Flint, Michigan, and established a Planned Parenthood birth control clinic. Soon he was fighting with his father as he tried to push the family foundation—the Charles Stewart Mott Foundation—in a more liberal direction. In 1966, he left Flint for New York City, where he first lived on a Chinese junk on the Hudson River before buying a Manhattan penthouse. He established his own foundation and began to attract wide attention for his support of left-wing causes, along with his flamboyant lifestyle. He was among the main financiers of Eugene McCarthy's antiwar candidacy in 1968 and appeared at a G.M. annual meeting to criticize the company for not opposing the war in Vietnam. In 1972, Mott ranked as one of the largest political donors in the country, thanks to his $400,000 contribution to the McGovern campaign (which earned him a place on President Richard Nixon's "enemy list" with the notation "Nothing but big money for radic-lib candidates").[2]

Through his organization, People's Politics, Mott supported progressive work on women's issues, race, civil liberties, and good governance. In the wake of Vietnam, he focused on reforming the Pentagon by bankrolling the Project on Military Procurement, as well as the Center for Defense Information. Mott also founded the Fund for Constitutional Government, a group that sought to bring greater accountability to Washington and still operates today. Over the years, Mott's mansion in Northwest Washington was the scene of endless parties and fund-raisers on behalf of every possible liberal cause. Mott never forgot his roots, though, and took pride in driving a Volkswagen, not a G.M.-made car. Mott also once gave $1,000 to a neighborhood group in Detroit that was battling G.M. to stop the construction of a new auto plant.

Mott was about as good a rich friend as liberal activists could hope for, and when he died in 2008, Ralph Nader—the former G.M. nemesis and a frequent beneficiary of Mott's largesse—commented that Mott "was about the most versatile, imaginative philanthropist of his time." What Nader admired most about Mott was that he was a "pioneer," willing to take on issues that the big foundations weren't yet ready to touch, in this way pushing the envelope of liberal philanthropy.[3]

George Pillsbury was another key figure in the wealthy liberal circles of this era. Pillsbury's name was even more famous than Mott's, because it graced flour packages in many U.S. homes, although Pillsbury was not nearly as rich. Pillsbury inherited $400,000 while still at Yale and promptly focused on giving away nearly all of this money to left-wing causes. "My view," he would say later, "is that this money should rightfully have been going to employees of the Pillsbury Corporation over the years but was skimmed off and ended up in trust funds for people such as myself. I felt it was not my money."[4] Along the way, Pillsbury crossed paths with other young trust-funders—including Mark Dayton, whom he had known growing up. "We were all drawn in by the social movements of the times," Pillsbury said. "It was hard to be untouched by what was going on." He was especially influenced by Obie Benz, an heir to the Daimler-Benz auto company fortune, as well as to the Sunbeam bread fortune. After graduating from Middlebury, Benz had moved to San Francisco, where he started the Vanguard Public Foundation in 1972, which raised money from wealthy young people to fund cutting-edge activism and direct services to poor and marginalized groups. Pillsbury found the model inspiring and decided to draw on his network to create a similar pass-through foundation. Thus was born the Haymarket People's Fund in 1974, which was initially funded by Pillsbury and a half-dozen wealthy donors. By 1977, Haymarket had emerged as an important source of cash for activist organizations, funding 110 groups that year to the tune of nearly $300,000.

The creation of the Vanguard Public Foundation and the Haymarket People's Fund generated a sense of purpose and belonging among liberal heirs. "The late sixties and early seventies was a very hard time to be wealthy and young," Alida Rockefeller Messinger recalled. "Many of our peer group were speaking out against the wealthy and against people like ourselves. They believed that the more money you had, the guiltier you were for the problems of the world." Messinger joined up with Vanguard and became one of its first volunteer staff members. "It was an incredible education for a young person.

It was like a training session in social change philanthropy." She then got involved at the national level with other young heirs, moving in one of the more rarefied precincts of liberal politics. "We were all in our early twenties with inherited money and a strong desire to give back to society," she said. "That became the core of a group of young progressive donors from all over the country that grew and evolved over the years."

The expanding movement of young rich donors committed to "change, not charity," led to the creation in the late 1970s of other pass-through foundations: the Liberty Hill Foundation in Los Angeles (created by George's sister, Sarah Pillsbury) and the North Star Fund in New York. In 1979, George Pillsbury and others created an umbrella organization, the Funding Exchange (FEX), which included all of these groups. By 2009, the Funding Exchange encompassed fifteen foundations and a national office that together channeled $15 million annually to progressive groups. Again and again over the years, the Funding Exchange was the "first on the scene" in backing causes that were too radical for mainstream foundations, such as antiglobalization activism, the living wage movement, gay and lesbian rights, and environmental justice organizing by poor communities.

Even as the Funding Exchange network grew in size during the 1980s and the 1990s, a far larger progressive funding octopus emerged in San Francisco: the Tides Foundation. Tides was founded in 1976 by Drummond Pike, the son of a California investment banker who had fallen in with a group of activist heirs in 1970 as associate director of the Youth Project in Washington. The Youth Project had spun out of the Center for Community Change and was set up to channel money from young wealthy donors to progressive groups fighting for social change. Among its funders was Alan S. Davis, the son of the insurance mogul Leonard Davis, who later recruited Pike to run his Shalan Foundation. Not long after Pike had taken that job, he was approached by a wealthy young couple from New Mexico who wanted to donate anonymously to social justice organizations and needed a foundation to handle their money. Pike created the Tides Foundation to help them, working with Jane Bagley Lehman, a Greenwich-born heir to the R. J. Reynolds tobacco fortune.

Tides grew rapidly to become the premier pass-through fund for wealthy West Coast liberals who didn't want to start their own family foundations. By 2009, Tides was handling $75 million a year for wealthy donors—most of which went to fund social change work that focused on everything from Asian American rights to global warming to youth justice.

The wealthy left-wing heirs of the sixties generation built a funding machine that has transformed activism in the United States, nurturing a vast universe of social change groups that might not otherwise exist. Today, an even wealthier generation of liberal heirs—determined to "leverage privilege"—is setting out to do much the same thing. These efforts are likely to mobilize liberal money on a scale that dwarfs anything seen so far.

There are rich ironies at play here. In the name of redistributing wealth and power, a tiny group of the most privileged members of U.S. society will help decide which social justice groups—and causes—will thrive in the next half century and which will wither. Karen Pittelman is unusual in her desire to transfer her assets directly to community activists. Many liberal heirs are more like Rob McKay—they want to play a hands-on role in giving away their money. Inevitably, the growing flood of such heirs into social justice work will have a crowding effect on ordinary people who are already in that civic space. Just as self-financed politicians can block the upward movement of lifelong public servants, so, too, can trust-fund activists use their superior resources and connections to snag plum positions within nonprofits. We are used to this phenomenon in other sectors—the way that rich kids can afford to take prestigious unpaid internships in publishing or Hollywood or finance that burnish their résumés or can use Daddy's Rolodex to get their foot in the door of elite institutions. But it is different when these same advantages come into play in a sector that is explicitly aimed at democratizing U.S. society and reducing inequalities.

The leaders of Resource Generation, like the founders of Haymarket and Vanguard decades earlier, suggest that social change philanthropy is all about putting grassroots activists and low-income communities in the driver's seat. Surely, this is the idea. But even in this model, many of the biggest decisions are still being made upstream as wealthy donors decide what issues they want to take up in the first place and which activists, exactly, they wish to empower.

To some degree, of course, none of this can be helped—not given the current nature of our economic system. Irony and contradiction are simply part of the terrain in the world of the liberal rich.

A Benign Plutocracy?

T HE VILLAGE OF DOBBS FERRY, New York, just up the Hudson from Manhattan, is fairly typical of Westchester County. About half of the adult residents are college grads and a quarter have post-graduate degrees. Median household income is around $85,000 a year—lower than more upscale towns nearby but still way above the national average. Homes often run more than $1 million. And, of course, Dobbs Ferry is strongly Democratic. It went for Barack Obama, John Kerry, and every other Democratic presidential candidate of the last two decades. Political donations from the town overwhelmingly favor Democrats.

Dobbs Ferry draws a lot of two-income professional couples, people such as Edward and Karen Zuckerberg, both in the medical field. (Edward is a dentist in town.) The couple has gotten a lot of attention lately because their son, Mark, who was born and raised in Dobbs Ferry, started Facebook. Mark went to public schools in the area before spending his senior year at Phillips Andover Academy and then going to Harvard.

Mark Zuckerberg hasn't given many hints as to his politics, but his basic stats—professional parents, blue-state upbringing, elite education, years spent in the Bay Area—all point to probable liberal leanings. Zuckerberg is still very young—he was born in 1984—and given how busy he's been with work, he may not even have well-formed political beliefs. He started programming in middle school, and he's been operating at a feverish pace since launching Facebook from his Harvard dorm room in early 2004. Zuckerberg reportedly owns about 30 percent of the company, and *Forbes* pegged his fortune at $4 billion in 2010. Someday, if Facebook goes public and if it can actually earn a profit, Zuckerberg is likely to be worth far more. Looking further ahead, the day will come when Zuckerberg starts to tire of business and will want to do something useful with his pile of money. And although it's impossible to say what he might do, there is a good chance that he won't be bankrolling right-wing think tanks or school vouchers.

Zuckerberg's fortune is just one of many that will be harnessed for public purposes in future years. Although the United States seems at the end of its second Gilded Age, we are still at the beginning of a golden era of philanthropy that taps the wealth created during this period. Some of today's largest new fortunes have barely been touched for charitable or political causes—like the money of the Google Guys ($17.5 billion each in 2010), or the great wealth of people such as Steve Ballmer ($14.5 billion), Jeff Bezos ($12.3 billion), Abigail Johnson ($11.5 billion), James Simons ($8.5 billion), Steven Cohen ($6.4 billion), and on and on. By the time many of these people do get around to large-scale charity, their fortunes will likely be even bigger than they are today.

Together, the Forbes 400 had a net worth of $1.5 trillion in 2008, a number that fell sharply after the crash but is now rebounding and will continue to go up as time goes on. (The Forbes 400 were worth just $250 million in 1988, and $750 million in 1998.) The wealth of these four hundred people is twice as great as the total assets of the seventy-five thousand U.S. grant-making foundations that now exist, a pool of funds that took more than a century to grow to its current size.

Meanwhile, even after the crash, there are still thousands of Americans worth tens or hundreds of millions of dollars. Many of these people, too, can be expected to turn to philanthropy and otherwise step up their civic involvements in the future.

If the economy turns around, and we enter another boom period, we can expect the ranks of the rich to grow again, although almost certainly at a slower pace. New fortunes will emerge, while the existing rich will get richer. Should the wealth of the Forbes 400 increase at only half the rate in the next twenty years as in the last twenty, the combined assets of this group will be three times what they are today, or nearly $4.5 trillion.

New policies can reduce inequality, but they won't make much of a dent in the rise of vast fortunes. The basic drivers of great wealth seem here to stay, such as the large amounts of capital sloshing around the world, technological innovation, and a huge global market for successful new products and services.

Facebook shows these trends in action. Most of its growth has been in overseas users, and even amid the worst downturn since the 1930s, Facebook attracted a $200 million investment from a Russian Internet company. Absent radical redistribution, beyond anything now contemplated by even the most liberal Democrats, tomorrow's Mark Zuckerbergs will still be insanely rich.

And many will be a lot like Zuckerberg. As manufacturing continues its decline and natural resources dwindle, the makeover of the rich will be ongoing. Take a look at the Forbes 400 today and you'll still find plenty of old-economy tycoons, many of whom are quite old—men such as George Kaiser, the sixty-seven-year-old oil magnate ($10 billion), and Charles Koch, seventy-three, who amassed $17.5 billion in energy and chemicals. Fortunes built through oil and manufacturing still made up about 15 percent of the list in 2009. That ratio will continue its steady decline. Likewise, although the Forbes 400—and the super-wealthy class as a whole—now includes many people without college degrees, this group will grow proportionately smaller, too, as the rich continue to become much more educated. Another trend—the would-be wealthy flocking to liberal metro areas—is also likely to be ongoing, along with its acculturating effects. Nationally, the rich may remain largely Republican, as is the case today, but economic and demographic changes will continue to increase the ranks of those disposed toward liberalism.

Right-wingers with enormous resources at their disposal will not disappear by any means, and some could be very influential. For instance, one of Facebook's earliest backers, Peter Thiel, is a libertarian and sits on the board of the conservative Hoover Institution. Thiel is already a billionaire; when Facebook goes public or is sold, Thiel—who is in his early forties—will become far richer. He has become a major donor to the Republican Party in recent years and, in a hint of things to come, Thiel reportedly gave $1 million to the anti-immigration group NumbersUSA.

The conservative infrastructure was built largely by old-economy fortunes during the 1980s and the 1990s. But right-wing policy mavens are now tapping new sources of money, especially from Wall Street. Bruce Kovner, a hedge fund star with a $3.5 billion fortune— he made $640 million in 2008 alone—has been among the biggest backers of the American Enterprise Institute and the Manhattan Institute. Both groups have attracted a number of other large donors from the finance world. The chair of the Manhattan Institute, Paul Singer, who runs one of the oldest hedge funds on Wall Street, has spent millions backing conservative causes and candidates in the last decade. Denver tycoon Philip Anschutz subsidizes the right-wing *Weekly Standard* among other ventures and has barely scratched the surface of his $6 billion fortune. The Koch brothers have given tens of millions of dollars to libertarian causes over the past three decades, which amounts to a pittance compared to their current combined net worth of $32 billion. The Walmart heirs, who collectively have some $80 billion at their disposal, have only just gotten started with philanthropy that leans to the right.

In all, don't expect the fierce battles within the upper class to go away. The mega-rich will still fund competing politicians, think tanks, media outlets, and activist groups.

Is the rise of the liberal rich a good thing? That depends on where you sit and what you worry about.

If you're conservative, it is hard to see anything positive here. Right-wingers have complained since the days of Edmund Burke about members of the upper class who attack the foundations of their own wealth and privilege. What's happening today is not like previous periods, when young aristocrats turned into Marxists. But if today's class traitors are quite moderate, the scope of defection is far wider and the resources at stake are much greater. Much of this book will confirm the right's worst fears about ties between coastal wealth elites and left-wing activists. Never before has so much money been available for advancing liberal ideals. This trend, along with the intellectual exhaustion of conservatism, poses a deep threat to the right's influence.

For liberals, the rise of wealthy allies is complicated, provoking both hope and misgivings. At some level, what's not to like? A Democratic president and congressional majority—elected partly thanks to rich donors—are fighting to enact a long-dormant liberal wish list. New organizations such as the Center for American Progress and Media Matters, both funded by the super-wealthy, are providing key support for Democratic efforts. Progressive organizations working on the environment, gay rights, civil liberties, and global humanitarian relief are larger than ever thanks to wealthy donors. Even if it's wrong to talk about anything like a realignment of class interests, enough rich have moved leftward to change what is politically possible in the United States.

The left's traditional prism of class politics, positing a unified upper class as the enemy, is no longer operative. The world has changed, and it is silly to pretend that it hasn't.

Yet there is something to the old critique. Although some rich liberals are bankrolling the push for economic justice, this group more typically prioritizes social and environmental causes. As affluent liberal donors and voters rise in influence, progressive politics may more closely mirror their priorities—in ways both good and bad.

Definitely, the news is good if you're a polar bear, and the Democratic Party is sure to focus more on the environment in coming years, thanks to the clout of the eco rich. Environmental groups will also keep growing in size and influence. That's important, because any chance of arresting climate change hinges on a much greater U.S. push to change its ways—which will happen only if far more power is mobilized behind environmental causes. The spread of eco values in America's upper class may be the most fateful trend highlighted in this book. On the other hand, don't expect inner-city kids with asthma to get much attention. Activists from poor communities of color have long complained about an environmental movement dominated by affluent donors and white upper-middle-class leaders. Issues such as climate change and wilderness preservation have been high on the movement's agenda, but the devastating effects of pollution in poor communities caused by incinerators or toxic waste dumps have often gotten short shrift. This doesn't seem likely to change.

Likewise, the rise of the liberal rich is good for civil rights in some ways, if not in others. Gays and lesbians are the big winners. The sea change in upper-class attitudes, along with the big bucks of wealthy gay donors, has been pivotal to historic victories for LGBT rights. Wealthy liberals also remain in the forefront in the struggle for reproductive rights and gender equality, and some are now using their fortunes to spread this battle to developing countries.

The picture is more mixed on racial equality. Although multiculturalism has become axiomatic in large swaths of the upper class, this enlightenment has so far mainly benefited nonwhites who already have a foothold in the meritocracy—especially Asian Americans. The troubling nexus between race and economic hardship is barely on the radar. Nor is there much appetite for attacking outright racial discrimination, even as evidence abounds that the old-fashioned civil rights movement has lots of unfinished business. And while the liberal rich are all for open borders when it comes to IT experts from Madras, you won't find many crusading to stop abuses of migrant workers or to help poor immigrants get Medicaid. Obama is a perfect fit for many rich liberals: his skin color is immaterial, given his talents, and, for the most part, he doesn't raise a ruckus about structural racism.

As for economic equity, I've argued in this book that rich liberals are changing their views here as the gap between the haves and have-nots has widened to near-record levels. Obama has won upper-class support for redistributory tax policies, just as Bill Clinton did in the 1990s. And creating more educational opportunities for poor kids has become one of the hottest causes among the rich. Still, don't mistake the liberal rich for progressive populists. Most believe in globalization, free trade, and outsized rewards to winners. Warren Buffett delivered a reminder of enduring class lines when, in March 2009, he opposed the "card check" labor rights bill pending before Congress.

Even if many of the Democrats' biggest Wall Street and corporate donors "don't have their hand out," as one bundler claimed about them, relying on this money is a recipe for moderation on economic policy. That was seen in the selection of Obama's economic team, which is decidedly centrist, and in events that have transpired since—such as a bailout strategy that largely stayed the course set by the Bush administration and a watered-down approach to financial regulation. The fact that key Democrats in Congress have colluded with the finance industry to derail certain reforms is stark evidence of what happens when this sector underwrites a party that is supposed to work for ordinary people. In May 2009, for instance, a measure that would have allowed bankruptcy judges to modify the mortgages of struggling homeowners was killed in the Senate, with Democratic help—leading Senator Dick Durbin to comment that banks are "still the most powerful lobby on Capitol Hill. And they frankly own the place."[1]

The familiar left narrative about big money and compromised Democrats offers damning insights about Obama's Washington. It is also an incomplete story. As discussed earlier, the biggest Democratic opponents of progressive reform have been members of Congress from middle-income or downscale areas of the country that largely went for Bush in the 2004 election. Among the more reliable supporters of reform have been Democrats from the wealthiest districts, places heavily populated with elites from finance and corporate America. When the House voted on a sweeping financial regulation bill in December 2009, all of the Democratic members from upscale districts lined up behind bill. The twenty-seven Democrats who voted no mostly represented downscale, largely white districts in states that Bush won in 2004. Likewise, most of the thirty-four House Democrats who voted against the healthcare bill in March 2010 were from less affluent districts in states that Bush had won.

In both cases, Democrats who voted against these historic reforms received slightly more campaign money from industry than did Democrats who supported the measures. Such contributions may well have affected their votes. The bigger factor, however, is surely that these Democrats were running scared of moderate voters who distrust government and were turning against the Obama agenda.

Many of the compromises by Obama and congressional Democrats can be better explained by the need to appease centrists from conservative states or districts than by the influence of special-interest money. It is possible that Senator Ben Nelson, who famously helped gut liberal provisions of the Senate's healthcare bill, was motivated by his financial ties to the insurance industry (although many Democratic senators, including Harry Reid, have gotten far more money from insurers than Nelson has). Weighing more heavily on Nelson, though, was probably the fact that John McCain won Nebraska by 15 points in 2008 and Bush won the state by 33 points in 2004. As might be expected of any Democrat hoping to survive in this terrain, Nelson has been a centrist since taking office in 2001.

Ultimately, the healthcare bill that emerged from the U.S. Senate was so weak in large part because that chamber gives a disproportionately greater voice to thinly populated heartland states that are less affluent and more conservative. This pattern can be seen again and again on other issues. Well-to-do voters have their strongest voice in the House while downscale white voters have an influence well beyond their numbers thanks to the Senate.

Of course, the question is not whether money *or* moderate white voters have been the main roadblocks to reform. Both have been culprits, and the two factors work in concert: special interest donors often target Democrats from moderate districts because their votes are most up for grabs.

In any case, the compromises by Obama and top Democrats should not obscure the pledges these leaders have kept, even after a record haul from wealthy campaign contributors in 2008. Obama did push income tax hikes on the rich, and has mounted a bold effort to tax offshore corporate profits. House Democrats tried to stick the rich with much of the tab for healthcare reform with an extraordinary 5.4 percent surtax on the highest income earners in the nation. Senate Democrats also embraced higher taxes on the rich to pay for reform, although to a smaller degree. And Democrats enacted a bill reining in credit card issuers, among other measures.

Obama is no FDR, but he has pushed reform in ways that have shocked some of his well-heeled big bundlers. A hedge fund manager who was a major Obama fund-raiser, speaking anonymously to a reporter, said, "I'm appalled at the anti–Wall Street rhetoric. It was okay on the campaign, but now it's the real world. I'm surprised that Obama is turning out to be so left-wing. He's a real class warrior."[2] Microsoft's Steve Ballmer, who along with his wife contributed $100,000 to Obama's inauguration committee, was openly critical of Obama's offshore crackdown, a proposal that also reportedly angered Google's high command and other Democratic donors in the tech world.

This discontent cannot be ignored by the White House. If Obama faces a tough reelection bid, he will need the same crew of donors from corporations and finance to prevail, and they might not be there for him if he moves too far left. By the same token, though, Obama could lose support from other wealthy donors if he tacks too much to the center. For instance, Obama would imperil his large funding base in Hollywood if he moderated his stances on social issues like abortion. The very largest backers of Obama's 2008 election push— namely, top 527 funders such as Steve Bing and George Soros— might also keep their checkbooks closed in 2012 if Obama morphs into a centrist.

Do Obama's legions of small donors mitigate the influence of big money? Not really, because the role of such donors was never as important as Team Obama claimed. Obama relied on major donors from the start of his presidential bid, and, as much as anything, he is president because of his early competitive showing in the "money primary," in which he snared major backers and made himself a plausible contender for the White House. These people played a pivotal role not only at the outset of Obama's run, but during the campaign. Only a quarter of all of Obama's money came from donors who contributed no more than $200 apiece to his campaign, which is not much different from Bush's tally in 2004. A third of his donations came from donors who contributed at least $2,300—a level of giving that is out of reach for most Americans.[3]

The role of major donors looms even larger if you include money raised for the Democratic National Convention, for 527 groups that campaigned for Obama, and for the inauguration. Donors who gave the maximum were dominant in all three of these areas. If you add up this money, along with the campaign funds pulled in by bundlers or contributed by big donors, it turns out that Obama's much-vaunted small donors didn't contribute anything close to a majority of his funds. People writing very large checks were instrumental in putting Obama in the White House. If he wants to stay there, he may have little choice but to heed their views.

That's not right. The outsized influence of rich people over electoral outcomes—whatever their ideology—undermines the ideal of one person, one vote. In an electoral system that feeds on vast sums of money, the politically active wealthy operate as "supercitizens." A single well-placed bundler who lines up significant early money for a candidate like Obama can wield as much influence over outcomes as primary voters in an entire city.

Affluent supercitizens don't derive their clout merely from giving and raising money. They also participate more in nearly every kind of political activity. They are more likely to contact an elected representative, more likely to organize a petition drive, more likely to write a letter to a newspaper editor, more likely to volunteer for a campaign, and so on. The effect of these efforts, on top of campaign contributions, is such that the voices of the affluent easily overpower the voices of ordinary citizens.

Things have become so bad that "the preferences of people in the bottom third of the income distribution have *no* apparent impact on the behavior of their elected officials."[4] Or at least that is a conclusion of *Unequal Democracy*, the authoritative study of politics in the new Gilded Age by the political scientist Larry Bartels. Another major study by the political scientist Martin Gilens eachoed this point: "Influence over actual policy outcomes appears to be reserved almost exclusively for those at the top of the income distribution."[5]

The influx of wealthy liberals into politics may serve to mitigate the downsides of such quasi-plutocratic rule by helping to elect Democrats who care about those at the bottom of the economic ladder, and that's already apparent in policies enacted by Obama and the Democratic Congress. This is not the same as granting a political voice to the lower classes, however. Indeed, the recent emergence of legions of new prosperous do-gooders, each anxious to write a bigger check than the next liberal billionaire, actually has the opposite effect.

The irony of the liberal rich is that because they believe in government and social activism, they are likely to have a much bigger civic footprint and, inevitably, they will often crowd out the nonrich. The growing number of self-financed progressive politicians, such as Jon Corzine and Jared Polis, stands as a stark example of this effect: both men steamrolled over veteran public servants in their rise to power. These days, even the most talented politicians must face the demoralizing possibility of seeing their careers ended by rich amateurs. The fact that such amateurs may have the best intentions or can think outside the box doesn't make this any less disturbing. One effect of the proliferation of people such as Corzine and Polis is that elected officials must spend even more time raising money from special interests so that they will have a big-enough war chest should some rich candidate come after them.

The footprint of leading philanthropists is even greater. Wealthy donors such as Bill Gates and George Soros give on a level that can and does change the course of public policy. In a 2006 survey, educational experts named Bill Gates as the single most influential person in the world of education policy during the last decade—more so than George W. Bush, who enacted No Child Left Behind. Even if you're pleased that Gates has spent $2 billion to reform public schools, you can also see that something is very wrong here: in a democracy, public policy is supposed to be set by elected representatives, not by individuals who happen to be very good at trading stocks or writing software.

Anywhere the rich get involved in civic life, they inevitably bring more resources to the table than ordinary Americans can, and they speak with a louder voice. This is true at every level. It is a good thing, for instance, that more wealthy heirs are doing community service in prep schools and choosing careers in the nonprofit sector, but it's a bad thing when these young people use their superior resources to gain an edge by taking unpaid internships or low-paid entry-level jobs. Rich kids, as it happens, can more easily afford to save the world than can middle-class kids, and guess who ends up with the better résumés?

In the *Republic*, Plato imagined a leadership group called the Guardians who could govern society in a totally selfless fashion. That ideal has long fascinated liberal elites, stretching back to the early days of an Establishment filled with Dean Acheson types who had grown up studying the Greek philosophers at places such as the Groton School. Although Plato envisioned the Guardians as eschewing all material desires and living at a remove from worldly concerns, the modern version of his ideal has looked a little different: first, you make a boatload of money or are born to it, and then—keeping your multiple homes and perhaps your private jet—you turn to doing some good in the world.

If oligarchy is government by the rich, for the rich, the contemporary Platonic ideal is about something else: rule by the rich on behalf of the common good, as they define it. This new noblesse oblige is spreading fast, and although it is a big step forward from the "greed is good" ethos, it is still deeply troubling.

There are books about American life that describe what is happening, and books that suggest what should happen. This has mainly been the former kind of book. Obviously, however, the trends described so far have weighty implications for those trying to change the direction of public policy and politics.

Republican strategists can take away a simple message from my findings: the GOP needs to move to the center if it hopes to again command the loyalties of the upper class. The "to-do" list for Republicans here is long and getting longer. It includes moderating the party's stance on social issues, creating distance from the Christian right, standing up to nut jobs like Rush Limbaugh, showing the door to climate change deniers, abandoning Calvin Coolidge–era economic ideas, squelching the GOP's xenophobic wing, and learning to like at least some of the things that government does, such as investing in infrastructure and higher education.

If the GOP takes steps in this direction and nominates a moderate technocrat such as Minnesota Governor Tim Pawlenty in 2012, or even Mitt Romney, it should be able to recover some of the ground it has lost among affluent voters and donors. Of course, all of this would demobilize the GOP's large conservative base, whether it's Tea Party activists or evangelicals, which is why Republicans may face minority status for some years to come.

Democrats face a different challenge, which is to solidify their cross-class coalition and forge an enduring political majority. This seems eminently feasible. For decades, the hardest part about melding affluent voters into the Democratic coalition was that their cultural liberalism rankled socially conservative working-class voters who formed the Democratic base. This tension has diminished over time as many working-class voters in the South have moved into the Republican camp and as the culture war has waned amid demographic changes. It is hard to see a rift over abortion or gay marriage fracturing the Democratic coalition that brought Obama to power in 2008. And there should be nothing to stop Democratic leaders from expanding this coalition even as the party remains quite liberal on social and environmental issues.

Economic equity is the much harder circle for Democrats to square. Many liberals have long pushed the Democrats to mount a frontal assault on inequality by embracing a new anticorporate populism and a fierce politics of redistribution. This might pull in disaffected working-class whites who think the whole system is stacked against them, but would just as surely alienate new allies in the affluent professional class. This isn't a great gamble, especially since it's hard to translate populist rhetoric into material benefits for working-class voters without expanding government, which these voters often see as part of the system that is against them. The opposition among many heartland white voters to an expanded government role in healthcare is a case in point.

To maintain and broaden the winning 2008 coalition, Democrats need an equity strategy that is congruent with the values of both affluent voters and those of modest means. The findings of this book offer insights about where there is the most overlap. To start with, wealthy Obama voters would look favorably on major new

investments in education at all levels, including universal pre-kinder-
garten and much bigger subsidies for college. Few things would do
more to promote an egalitarian society than to create real educational
opportunity for all Americans, and the coastal upper class would get
behind such an effort. Affluent voters would also support a bold new
push to promote shared economic growth through large-scale investments in infrastructure, basic scientific research, and clean energy.
Ensuring U.S. competitiveness by dominating the industries of tomorrow is a long-standing preoccupation of cosmopolitan wealth elites.
Blue collar workers would be among the prime beneficiaries of such
investment-driven growth policies.

Beyond these two major strategies for equity, Obama's wealthy
backers are likely to stick with the Democrats even if the president
and Congress make more use of fiscal policy as a vehicle for redistribution. The evidence suggests that many wealthy people are not
so worried about paying higher taxes. As long as economic growth
resumes, the Democrats can probably get away with further tax hikes
on the rich. Such increases would ideally be used to directly fund the
equity strategies mentioned above. Sophisticated voters and donors
in the upper class may well reason that they will get wealthier in the
long run in a better educated America that invests more heavily in
the foundations of prosperity.

In some policy areas—such as trade, regulation, and labor—it will
be trickier for Democrats to find happy solutions that please both the
upper and lower classes. The rich like globalization, as mentioned,
and they don't much like unions or regulation. But Democrats can
probably forge viable compromises in all of these areas. For instance,
even a substantial hike in the minimum wage would probably be
a nonissue to many of Obama's big donors from knowledge economy
industries or to affluent metro professionals. Nor would expanded
tax credits for childcare, a guarantee of paid family leave, and universal portable pensions be likely to ruffle upper-class feathers. These
policies aren't a substitute for stronger unions, but they are something
in a country with legions of low-wage workers—including many
downscale white women in Sarah Palin country—who live in poverty, cannot afford childcare, have no paid time off from their jobs,

and cannot save for retirement. On trade, Democrats could promote sweeping new policies to retrain and support displaced workers so that the losers of globalization don't face such adverse consequences. Denmark, which combines open trade with large-scale "flexicurity" aid for transitioning workers, offers a promising model how to have the best of both worlds.

It won't be easy to maintain and build on the 2008 coalition while trying to make the United States a more equal society. Beyond smart win-win policies, a key to success will be the tone of Democratic leaders. If they are future-oriented and manifestly committed to enlarging the economic pie through pro-growth investments, they'll be able to push the envelope to also reslice that pie.

Some readers will fume at the very idea that the Democratic Party should mold its agenda to accommodate the upper class. I don't see much choice, given how important affluent voters and donors have become in the progressive coalition. Anyway, the ineluctable truth of our times is that Democrats simply cannot build a more equitable society without some cooperation from the upper class. Even if so many lower- and middle-income whites didn't routinely vote against their own economic interests, it would still be very difficult to force the wealthy to more generously share the fruits of capitalism.

The stars aren't exactly aligned in favor of the public interest. Globalization has given capital a huge edge, allowing corporations to slip free of regulatory oversight in the United States by simply moving their operations overseas, to countries that don't protect workers or the environment. Labor unions are in steep decline, to the point that less than 8 percent of workers in the private sector belong to a union. The campaign finance system is in shambles, allowing the rich, in effect, to pour as much money as they want into the political process. Meanwhile, the wealthy have more control over the nation's wealth assets than at any time since the 1920s. In 1979, the top 1 percent of households owned 25 percent of all assets in the country, such as stocks and real estate; by 2008, that figure had risen to 39 percent. Corporate leaders and the wealthy have also more tightly consolidated control over media ownership, with a handful of conglomerates owning a greater share of the nation's newspapers, cable companies, Internet providers, and radio and television stations. Overall, corporations and the wealthy are more powerful and less accountable than they've been at any time since the presidency of Herbert Hoover.

Liberals should keep dreaming about reviving organized labor or turning NASCAR dads against the Republican Party. In time, these dreams may come true and empower a popular movement for redistribution. Right now, though, class warfare is a losing proposition. Our better hope is that a creative new progressive politics can enlist the growing ranks of rich liberals in proactive efforts to reduce inequality and diminish their own privilege.

This has happened before, post–World War II, when income gaps narrowed and the middle class greatly expanded—a period that economist sometimes call the "Great Compression." The raw power of organized labor, which included a third of all workers in 1955, helped account for much of the social leveling that occurred in this era. But another factor was that affluent Americans and corporate leaders supported many of the liberal policies that fired economic growth and created the modern middle class, such as huge investments in higher education, infrastructure, and scientific research, as well as generous tax subsidies for home ownership. Until the 1970s, when growth stalled, many in the upper class also backed a steady expansion of the social safety net. For instance, a 1971 survey of 120 top business leaders found high levels of support for President Richard Nixon's Family Assistance Plan, an antipoverty measure that would be considered quite radical by today's standards. The same survey found that the executives overwhelmingly supported Keynesian economic ideas. (Then, as now, business leaders from the South and smaller towns were more conservative than those from the Northeast and big cities, who tended to be particularly liberal. And, then as now, those business leaders who had attended elite prep schools and Ivy League universities tended to be more liberal than those who had not.)[6]

As noted, the mainstream corporate elite embraced so-called equity norms during the postwar period. They eschewed conspicuous consumption and didn't push for outsized compensation, in part because it would have put them out of step with the culture. Most of the mansions in the United States were built before 1929 and after 1980, and the reason is not just that people couldn't afford them during the mid-twentieth century. It is that such grandiosity was out of fashion in an era where the everyman was king.

Another shift toward equity norms, albeit on a smaller scale, seems perfectly possible in the coming years. This time around it might be related to the spread of ecological values that valorize reduced consumption. Or maybe, as I speculated earlier, it could be an outgrowth of the social responsibility movement in business.

Even if the liberal rich do remain part of the Democratic coalition and cooperate in bold efforts to reduce inequity, vast fortunes will persist. If a top hedge fund manager takes home $500 million in a good year instead of $1 billion, he will still be fantastically rich. He will still be able to wield disproportionate influence over policy choices by bankrolling politicians and advocates.

The outsized clout of the rich is profoundly subversive of democracy and should worry those on both the left and the right. More than ever, the United States needs to take steps to limit the influence of the wealthy over the political choices that affect the lives of all Americans. For starters, this means major reforms in the area of campaign finance and elections.

Even before the Supreme Court's January 2010 ruling in the Citizens United case, allowing more money into politics, campaign finance reform was virtually dead. Caps on individual donations to candidates or party committees have not stopped an ever-swelling river of funds from flooding into elections. In 2004 and 2008, the super-rich spent as much money as they wanted through 527s to support the candidates of their choice—and some, such as Soros, spent on a scale never before seen in this democracy or any other. State ballot initiatives also offer a vehicle for unlimited expenditures, as witnessed most dramatically when Steve Bing sank $49 million into backing a 2006 initiative in California. The biggest individual expenditures of all have been by self-financed candidates. It's bad enough when someone spends $80 million buying his or her way into City Hall in New York or the U.S. Senate. Worse will be the day when a candidate spends $800 million to try to buy his or her way into the White House.

There are several ways to stem the flood of money into politics. Public financing of campaigns can help offset contributions by rich donors or the millions that affluent candidates may spend of their own money. But such systems tend to break down when the sums of money involved get really enormous. Obama rejected public financing and swamped McCain by raising hundreds of millions of dollars—even while McCain took public funds. Fernando Ferrer received $9 million in public funds when he ran against Michael Bloomberg in 2005—money that didn't go very far against Bloomberg's $85 million in spending. If public financing is to work in cases like these, it will require far greater sums of money to ensure that publicly financed candidates can keep up with deep-pocketed opponents. And, of course, public financing must be widely in place, as opposed to only in select states.

Giving candidates free television and radio time is another way to level the playing field. An original intent of federal communications laws was to ensure that broadcasters serve the public interest in return for access to the airwaves, which Americans collectively own. This principle should be revitalized, and broadcasters should be required, at election time, to make available ample free airtime to candidates. Such a step would deprive big-spending candidates of a vital edge, given that television advertising is often a campaign's single biggest expense.

These measures would make a difference. But ultimately, the only way to really get money out of politics is to amend the Constitution. Right now, laws can't block the super-rich from spending a fortune in politics because such spending has been defined by the Supreme Court as a form of free speech. A constitutional amendment could explicitly exempt campaign spending from this protection, and several bills of this kind have been introduced in Congress.

Pulling more ordinary people into civic life can also help offset the outsized influence of the rich over our democracy. Voter turnout has gone up in the last two presidential elections, but the United States still has one of the lowest turnout rates among advanced democracies. One way to expand participation is through shifting the burden of voter registration from individuals to the government, so that all citizens are registered automatically, and these records are updated when they move. If people arrive at a polling place to discover that they aren't registered, they should be able to sign up to vote then and there, which is now allowed in only nine states. Making Election Day a holiday or moving it to the weekend would also boost turnout.

Expanding funds for community service is another way to get more people involved in civic life, especially young people. Right now, the best service opportunities are available to the most privileged kids because private schools and wealthy universities can most afford strong service programs. These kids go on to have an edge in competing for positions in government and the nonprofit sector. More resources for service programs, as well as more paid opportunities for service, would help level the field. The expansion of AmeriCorps passed by Congress in 2009 is a step in the right direction.

Changes are needed in other areas, too, such as philanthropy. Too often, the rich use tax-deductible giving to improve their own communities and cultural institutions. Charitable gifts that actually help the poorest members of society have been declining as a proportion of total grant-making. Giving that reaches ethnic minorities is low and is growing at a much slower rate than overall giving. Rural areas receive few charitable funds in comparison to urban areas. Smaller community organizations, led by people of color, often find it impossible to raise enough money.

A strong civil society sector fueled by philanthropy is one of the great things about the United States. But this system raises troubling questions about equity and democracy, especially as private fortunes get bigger and bigger. Tax-deductible donations don't only support charity for the poor or the arts; they also bankroll sharply ideological groups such as the Heritage Foundation and the Center for American Progress or large-scale experiments to revamp public education.

It is disturbing how much influence a single mega-rich individual can have over public policy—all subsidized by the taxpayer. It's especially scary when the wealthy don't know what they are doing. Many philanthropists have taken a hands-on role in using their money to advance change, brimming with confidence that the smarts and creativity that made them a success in business will translate into social problem solving. But just because you're good at developing software or betting on the market doesn't mean you'll know how to raise test scores in America's urban school districts or bring clean water to Africa's rural villages. The history of philanthropy is littered with disastrous mistakes or plain failures. Most recently, Bill Gates has acknowledged that his vast investment in public schools, with a big focus on creating new small schools, has not yielded the desired results. Many educators view his experiment as a debacle. Some data on charter schools—a major focus of Eli Broad's giving and also that of Gates and other donors—find that these schools aren't necessarily any better than regular schools. At least one important study, released in 2009 by Stanford University, found that students in these schools were actually doing worse than students in traditional schools.[7]

The chance of misfires points to one obvious step that wealthy donors should take, which is to closely evaluate their own work and encourage others to evaluate it. Every initiative should include resources for evaluation. Donors should also put money into collaborative efforts at learning in philanthropy, so that everyone looks over one another's shoulders and shares lessons and best practices.[8]

Another key is to make sure that the intended beneficiaries of philanthropy have a real say in how the money is spent. A startling number of rich donors set up foundations with boards of advisers and directors consisting of people very much like themselves. In their desire to think outside the box and bring fresh solutions to problems, they can get stuck in another box of their own making. All foundations should have leadership that is inclusive of those groups they purport to serve.

Philanthropists should also do everything possible to empower the beneficiaries of their giving. Too often, donors keep their grantees on a short leash, doling out small grants for specific projects and leaving recipients constantly begging for more—not to mention wasting valuable time writing grant proposals. A better approach is to write larger checks for general support and take a more hands-off approach. If an organization has impact, keep funding it. If not, pull the plug. And if you really like an organization, you should consider helping it achieve financial independence by endowing it.

A more radical step is for donors to cede control early on to those they are hoping to help, as Karen Pittelman did with the Chahara Foundation. Pittelman said it is striking how often rich donors "don't question the idea that they should be in charge." In her view, the wealthy need to take a big step back so that their money doesn't only address specific problems, but also changes patterns of power and allows new leaders to find their voices.

Much has changed since Theodore Roosevelt was ostracized from his class for supporting such ideas as the income tax, women's suffrage, and the right to strike. The rich are now a class divided, with an influential slice embracing liberalism. That shift has helped fuel a push for social change at home, kick-start a new crusade against poverty abroad, and put Democrats in control of Washington.

This may all be a good thing, depending on your outlook, but it doesn't change stark truths about money and power. A benign plutocracy is still a plutocracy. The Supreme Court justice Louis Brandeis once commented that "We can have democracy in this country, or we can have great wealth concentrated in the hands of a few, but we can't have both." That point rings true today, whatever the politics of the rich.

Ordinary people can do much to steer the United States away from plutocracy. But our chances of escaping this fate will be greater if the wealthy class has leaders who are actively working to curb their own power. That means embracing the policy reforms and self-restraints already mentioned; it also means a big change in outlook. Even the smartest, best-intentioned people of wealth need to engage the world with humility—not only because they may screw up in their philanthropy or even because they may fail to empower the people they are trying to help. There is a larger principle at stake, which is egalitarianism.

Since America's founding, its most exciting, most radical ideal has been the presumption that all people are equal and that no one— because of birth or wealth—is intrinsically superior to anyone else. Although that ideal has continually evolved to include more groups, to the point where we now have an African American president, it is deeply threatened by the rise of a large class of affluent supercitizens.

How the United States deals with this threat will largely depend on the norms that hold sway among the rich themselves, because, realistically, it is neither possible nor desirable to create total economic equality. Even with serious reforms, concentrations of wealth will always exist, and there will always be affluent people with more financial and civic resources. Egalitarianism cannot be imposed on the rich. Instead, if the United States is to remain the United States, the upper class must uphold this spirit voluntarily.

A new era of civic equality may be hard to imagine right now. But with the right trends in place—with pushing from ordinary people and continued changes by wealthy people—a new egalitarian era may lie in the not-so-distant future.

ACKNOWLEDGMENTS

My biggest debt in writing this book is to those individuals who agreed to be interviewed and enabled me to better understand the world of the liberal rich through their firsthand experiences. They were generous with their time and candid in their reflections. This book could not been written without their help.

I also owe a huge debt to my colleagues at Demos, the think tank where I work. Demos is a special place in the way that it accommodates staff who wish to take time off to research and write books. Demos president Miles Rapoport has been a great friend and ally not just to me, but to many other authors who have brought book projects to fruition under Demos's auspices. Other colleagues at Demos have helped me in different ways with this project, either as sounding boards for my ideas or in working on the book's publicity campaign. They include Benjamin Barber, Lew Daly, Tamara Draut, Jinny Khanduja, Gennady Kolker, Robert Kuttner, Jim Lardner, Donna Parson, and Tim Rusch.

Andrew Stuart, my literary agent of ten years, was a big supporter of this project from its earliest inception and helped me sharpen my ideas as the book evolved. My editor, Eric Nelson, took a leap of faith in signing up this project and then gave me the time and space to write a book that turned out to be very different from the one I had originally promised. Eric also brought a keen editorial eye to the manuscript and pushed me to sharpen my arguments at every turn. My production editor at Wiley, Lisa Burstiner, helped improve the writing throughout the book.

A lot happened in my personal life during the time I wrote this book. I became a father for the first time and moved twice. I suppose it's remarkable that the book got written at all. But ultimately everything worked out because I have an amazing wife and partner, Wendy Paris.

NOTES

Introduction: The New Class Traitors

1. John Hughes, "Dulles Closes Runway to Handle Influx of Inaugural-Bound Jets," Bloomberg News, January 17, 2009.

2. Christopher Hayes, "The Choice," *Nation*, February 18, 2008.

3. "Reality Check: Obama Received about the Same Percentage from Small Donors in 2008 as Bush in 2004," Campaign Finance Institute, November 24, 2008.

4. James MacGregor Burns and Susan Dunn, *The Three Roosevelts: Patrician Leaders Who Transformed America* (New York: Grove Press, 2001), 126, 309.

5. "Political Ideology: 'Conservative' Label Prevails in the South," August 14, 2009, www.gallup.com/poll/122333/political-ideology-conservative-label-prevails-south.aspx. The wealth of the state is measured by median household income.

6. Exit polls are from www.cnn.com/ELECTION/2008/results/polls.main/. Results among voters who earn more than $200,000 are unavailable in many poorer states; the claim that Obama lost upper-income voters is based on results of voters who earn more than $100,000 a year. On trends over time, see Larry Bartels, *Unequal Democracy: The Political Economy of the New Gilded Age* (Princeton, NJ: Princeton University Press, 2008), 72–75, 96. See also Nolan McCarty, Keith T. Poole, and Howard Rosenthal, *Polarized America: The Dance of Ideology and Unequal Riches* (Cambridge, MA: MIT Press, 2006).

7. *2009 World Wealth Report*, Capgemini and Merrill Lynch Global Wealth Management, June 24, 2009, 3; "U.S. Millionaires Grow 16% to

7.8 Million in 2009, Spectrum Group Reports," Spectium Group, March 9, 2010.

8. Emmanuel Saez, "Striking It Richer: The Evolution of Top Incomes in the United States" (update with 2007 estimates), August 5, 2009, http://elsa.berkeley.edu/~saez/saez-UStopincomes-2007.pdf. See also, "Testimony of Robert Greenstein, Executive Director, Center on Budget and Policy Priorities, before the Subcommittee on Workforce Protections," Center on Budget and Policy Priorities, July 31, 2008.

1. Educated, Rich, and Liberal

1. Rudolph Bush and Dan X. McGraw, "Bushes Confirm Purchase of Dallas Home in Preston Hollow," *Dallas Morning News*, December 5, 2008.

2. Bill Bishop, *The Big Sort: Why the Clustering of Like-Minded America Is Tearing Us Apart* (Boston: Houghton Mifflin, 2008), 134.

3. Robert Hanley, "Nixons Are Preparing to Buy $1 Million House in Saddle River," *New York Times*, June 12, 1981.

4. Andrew Gelman et al., "Rich State, Poor State, Red State, Blue State: What's the Matter with Connecticut," *Quarterly Journal of Political Science* 2 (2007): 345–367. See also an expanded explanation in Andrew Gelman, *Red State, Blue State, Rich State, Poor State* (Princeton, NJ: Princeton University Press, 2008).

5. Gerald Prante, "IRS Data Reveal Which Congressional Districts Pay the Highest Federal Income Taxes," Tax Foundation, January 17, 2007.

6. Michael Franc, "Who Will Pay for President Obama's Tax Increases?" Heritage Foundation, May 18, 2009.

7. Data compiled from tables in "Who Will Pay for President Obama's Tax Increases?" Heritage Foundation, May 18, 2009; and 2008 congressional ratings by Americans for Democratic Action, found in *ADA Today*, 64, no. 1 (Spring 2009): 10–21.

8. "Gross Domestic Product by Industry," Bureau of Economic Analysis, Department of Commerce, 2008.

9. Chuck Collins, Mike Lapham, and Scott Klinger, "I Didn't Do It Alone: Society's Contribution to Wealth and Success," United for a Fair Economy, August 2004, 1–2, 17.

10. Jennifer Cheeseman Day and Eric C. Newburger, "The Big Payoff: Educational Attainment and Synthetic Estimates of Work-Life Earnings," U.S. Census Bureau, July 2002, 4. The connection between

income and education can also be seen in data from the National Election Studies and the General Social Survey.

11. On the number of college graduates on the Forbes 400 List, see Peter W. Bernstein and Annalyn Swan, eds., *All the Money in the World* (New York: Alfred Knopf, 2007), 32. On the top five universities, see Andrew Farrell, "The Billionaire Universities," *Forbes*, May 19, 2008. On MBA's, see Duncan Greenberg, "Billionaire Clusters," *Forbes*, April 1, 2009.

12. David Francis, "Changing Demographics of U.S. Science-Engineering PhDs," Digest, National Bureau of Economic Research, January 2005.

13. See "Percent of People 25 Years and Over Who Have Completed a Bachelor's Degree," U.S. Census Bureau, 2003.

14. Figures are from CNN exit polls at www.cnn.com.

15. John B. Judis and Ruy Teixeira, *The Emerging Democratic Majority* (New York: Scribner, 2002), 46; and Ronald Inglehart, *Modernization and Post-Modernization: Cultural, Economic, and Political Change in 43 Societies* (Princeton, NJ: Princeton University Press, 1997).

16. Richard Florida, *Who's Your City: How the Creative Economy Is Making Where to Live the Most Important Decision of Your Life* (New York: Basic Books, 2008), 96.

17. Bishop, *The Big Sort*, 154.

2. What's the Matter with Connecticut?

1. Adam Lashinsky, "California's Hedge Fund King," *Fortune*, September 29, 2008, 146.

2. Dane Hamilton, "Renaissance Hedge Fund: Only Scientists Need Apply," Reuters, May 22, 2007.

3. Eric Lipton and Raymond Hernandez, "The Reckoning: A Champion of Wall Street Reaps Benefits," *New York Times*, December 14, 2008.

4. Mike Brewster, *Unaccountable: How the Accounting Industry Forfeited a Public Trust* (Hoboken, NJ: John Wiley & Sons, 2003), 205.

5. Keith T. Poole, "The Decline and Rise of Party Polarization in Congress during the Twentieth Century," *Extensions* (Fall 2005); and Jacob Hacker and Paul Pierson, *Off Center: The Republican Revolution and the Erosion of American Democracy* (New Haven, CT: Yale University Press, 2006).

6. *ADA Today* 63, no. 1 (February 2008).

7. *New York Times*/CBS News Poll, 2004 Democratic Convention Delegates, June 16–July 17, 2004. See also Morris P. Fiorina with Samuel J. Abrams, *Disconnect: The Breakdown of Representation in American Politics* (Norman: University of Oklahoma Press, 2009), 8.

8. Fiorina, *Disconnect*, 15.

9. Larry Bartels, *Unequal Democracy: The Political Economy of the New Gilded Age* (Princeton, NJ: Princeton University Press, 2008), 29–63.

10. Kevin Drawbaugh, "Obama, Edwards Bash Lobbyists over Private Equity Taxes," Reuters, October 9, 2007.

11. Svea Herbst-Bayliss, "Hedge Fund Managers Throw Weight behind Obama," Reuters, July 11, 2008.

12. Lloyd Grove, "The World According to: Alan Patricof," December 4, 2007, www.portfolio.com/views/columns/the-world-according-to/2007/12/04/An-Interview-With-Alan-Patricof/.

13. Barack Obama, *The Audacity of Hope: Thoughts on Reclaiming the American Dream* (New York: Crown Publishers, 2006), 114.

14. Julianna Goldman and Ian Katz, "Obama Doesn't 'Begrudge' Bonuses for Blankfein, Dimon," Bloomberg.com, February 10, 2010, www.bloomberg.com/apps/news?pid=20601087&sid=aKGZkktzkAlA.

15. Peter Francia et al., "Limousine Liberals and Corporate Conservatives: The Financial Constituencies of the Democratic and Republican Parties," *Social Science Quarterly* 86, no. 4 (November 2005): 761–777; Nolan McCarty, Keith T. Poole, and Howard Rosenthal, *Polarized America: The Dance of Ideology and Unequal Riches* (Cambridge, MA: MIT Press, 2006), 153–155.

3. The Eco Rich

1. Kevin J. Delaney, Lynn Lunsford, and Mark Maremont, "Wide-Flying Moguls: Google Duo's New Jet Is a Boeing 767-200," *Wall Street Journal*, November 4, 2005.

2. Hank Stuever, "Question Celebrity," *Washington Post*, April 29, 2007.

3. Laura MacInnis, "Private Jet Operator Faces Climate Change Heat," Reuters, January 26, 2007.

4. "Warren Buffett's Private Jet Company Makes Carbon Offsets Obligatory," *International Herald Tribune*, September 13, 2007.

5. Jamie Cheng, "When Flying in a Private Jet, Fly Carbon Neutral," *Helium Report*, January 10, 2008; and "Responsible Travel Cancels Carbon Offset Program," *USA Today*, November 25, 2009.

6. "Plane Stupid Shuts Down (Part of) City Airport," www .oneclimate.net/2009/06/10/plane-stupid-shuts-down-part-of-city-airport/, June 10, 2009.

7. Dina Boghdady, "Can Big Be Green? Some High-End Builders Have a Surprising Answer to the Question," *Washington Post*, February 16, 2008, F01.

8. Patricia Sellers, "The First Certifiably Green Mansion," *Fortune*, March 19, 2007.

9. Andrew Miga, "Kerry's New Book Hails Everyday People Saving the Environment," *Boston Globe*, March 10, 2007.

10. Amanda Little, "John Kerry and Teresa Heinz Kerry Chat about Their New Environmental Book," www.grist.org/article/kerry6, March 29, 2007.

11. Ronald Inglehart, "Globalization and Postmodern Values," *Washington Quarterly* 23, no. 1 (2000).

12. Center for American Progress, www.americanprogress.org/issues/2009/03/pdf/political_ideology.pdf, March 2009, 4. When broken down by income, the data for this survey show low-income Americans even supporting renewable energy and a strong response to climate change by slightly higher margins than upper-middle class Americans.

13. Eric Alterman, "The Hollywood Campaign," *Atlantic*, September 2004.

14. Kenneth R. Weiss, "Math Whiz Donates Hundreds of Millions: Conservation Causes Benefit," *Los Angeles Times*, November 7, 2004.

15. Glen Elsasser, "The Greenhouse Effect," *Chicago Tribune*, September 22, 1996.

16. Susan Carey Dempsey, "Sharing the Lessons of a Foundation Spend-Out," www.onphilanthropy.com/site/News2?page=NewsArticle &id=7825, May 29, 2009.

17. "The Generosity Index," *Conde Nast Portfolio*, January 2008, 74.

18. Duff McDonald, "Robert Wilson's Chore," www.portfolio.com/executives/features/2007/12/17/Robert-Wilson-Q-and-A/, December 17, 2007.

19. "Goldman Sachs Announces Transfer of Unique Chilean Wilderness to WCS," Wildlife Conservation Society, December 2004.

20. Andrew C. Revkin, "Gore Group Plans Ad Blitz on Global Warming," *New York Times*, April 1, 2008.

21. "Environmentalism, Millennial-Style," *Time*, March 10, 2009.

4. Wealth and the Culture War

1. "Interview with Jon Stryker: A Journey to Inclusive Philanthropy," *Global Giving Matters*, Summer 2008.

2. Paul G. Schervish and Andrew Herman, "Money and Hyperagency: The Worldly Empowerment of Wealth," Social Welfare Research Institute, Boston College, May 1991, 6.

3. "State of American Political Ideology, 2009," Center for American Progress, March 2009.

4. Exit polls on ballot measures can be found at www.cnn.com.

5. Data were compiled using tables on numbers of taxpayers in congressional districts with incomes of more than $200,000 from "Who Will Pay for President Obama's Tax Cuts?" and "Congressional Scorecard: Measuring Support for Equality in the 110th Congress," Human Rights Campaign.

6. G. William Domhoff, *Fat Cats and Democrats: The Role of the Big Rich in the Party of the Common Man* (Englewood Cliffs, NJ: Prentice-Hall, 1972), 128–131.

7. Sam Roberts, "Westchester Adds Housing to Desegregation Pact," *New York Times*, August 11, 2009.

8. William Henry and Elaine Lafferty, "Not Marching Together," *Time*, May 3, 1993.

9. Craig A. Rimmerman, *From Identity to Politics: The Lesbian and Gay Movements in the United States* (Philadelphia: Temple University Press, 2001), 90–92.

10. Robert Frank, *Richistan: A Journey through the American Wealth Boom and the Lives of the New Rich* (New York: Crown, 2007), 197.

11. Paul G. Schervish, "Why the Wealthy Give: Factors Which Mobilize Philanthropy among High Net-Worth Individuals," in Adrian Sargeant and Walter Wymer, *The Routledge Companion to Nonprofit Marketing* (New York: Routledge, 2008), 178.

12. Kerry Eleveld, "There Is a Gay Agenda: Winning Elections," Salon, November 29, 2006.

5. The One-World Wealthy

1. Lauren Foster, "Understanding Global Philanthropy 2007: A Businesslike Approach to Charity," *Financial Times*, December 11, 2007.

2. Stephanie Hanes, "Greg Carr's Big Gamble," *Smithsonian*, May 2007.

3. Michelle O'Keeffe, "Computer Millionaire Helps Just a Little Byte," *Sunday Mirror*, September 15, 2002.

4. Nicole Lewis, "The Audacity of Hope," *Chronicle of Philanthropy*, February 22, 2007.

5. Ibid.

6. "Bill Gates—2002 World Economic Forum," www.gatesfoundation .org/speeches-commentary/Pages/bill-gates-2002-world-economic-forum .aspx.

7. Ibid.

8. Ibid.

9. Ibid.

10. "Remarks by Bill Gates: Global Foundation Address, September 12, 2000," www.gatesfoundation.org/speeches-commentary/Pages/bill-gates-2000-global-foundation.aspx.

11. "William J. Brennan, Jr., Defense of Freedom Award Recipient, 2004," Media Law Resource Center, 2004.

12. "Nuclear Weapons: The Greatest Peril to Civilization," *YaleGlobal*, March 25, 2008.

13. David Rohde, "Ted Turner Plans a $1 Billion Gift for U.N. Agencies," *New York Times*, September 19, 1997.

14. Ted Turner, *Call Me Ted* (New York: Grand Central Publishing, 2008), 405.

6. "Please Raise My Taxes"

1. Karlyn Bowman, ed., "Public Opinion on Taxes," American Enterprise Institute, June 26, 2008.

2. Jeff Zeleny, "Investors Speculate in Obama," *Chicago Tribune*, November 28, 2005.

3. John McCormick, "Buffett Is Obama Meal Ticket," *Chicago Tribune*, August 16, 2007.

4. Warren Buffett, "Dividend Voodoo," *Washington Post*, May 20, 2003, A19.

5. Andrew Lee and Joel Friedman, "Administration Continues to Rely on Misleading Use of 'Averages' to Describe Tax-Cut Benefits," Center for Budget and Policy Priorities, May 28, 2003.

6. Berkshire Hathaway, Inc., *Annual Report*, 2003.

7. "Warren Buffett: The Rich Must Pay More Taxes," Monsterandcritics .com, November 17, 2007, www.monstersandcritics.com/news/usa/news/ article_1374472.php/Warren_Buffett_The_rich_must_pay_more_taxes.

8. Tomoeh Murakami Tse, "Buffett Slams Tax System Disparities," *Washington Post*, June 27, 2007, D3.

9. Adam Lashinsky, "California's Hedge Fund King," *Fortune*, September 29, 2008, 146.

10. "BET Founder on Obama's Tax Plans," www.foxnews.com, August 29, 2008, www.foxnews.com/story/0,2933,413302,00.html.

11. Joe Nocera, "Facing Crisis, Congress Makes Sense," *New York Times*, November 14, 2008.

12. Reed Hastings, "Please Raise My Taxes," *New York Times*, February 6, 2009.

13. Edgar M. Bronfman, "Raise My Taxes," Huffington Post, December 5, 2008.

14. Robert Frank, "The Rich Support McCain, the Super-Rich Support Obama," Wall Street Journal Online, October 13, 2008, http://blogs.wsj.com/wealth/2008/10/13/the-rich-support-mccain-the-super-rich-support-obama/.

15. Ed Kopko, "Debate Over," *Chief Executive*, September/October 2008.

16. "Wealth in America 2006," Northern Trust, December 2005.

17. Allen Salkin, "You Try to Live on 500k in This Town," *New York Times*, February 8, 2009.

18. Kenneth Gilpin, "Clinton's Economic Plan Finding Respect from Corporate America," *New York Times,* March 1, 1993, A1.

19. Chuck Collins, Mike Lapham, and Scott Klinger, "I Didn't Do It Alone: Society's Contribution to Individual Wealth and Success," Responsible Wealth, a project of United for a Fair Economy, August 2004, 17–18.

20. "Wealth Tax Views in Notable Talks," *New York Times*, December 14, 1906.

21. Remarks by Microsoft chairman Bill Gates before the Committee on Science and Technology, House of Representatives, March 12, 2008.

22. The campaign against the estate tax is recounted in "Spending Millions to Save Billions: The Campaign of the Super Wealthy to Kill the Estate Tax," Public Citizen and United for a Fair Economy, April 2006.

23. Larry Bartels, *Unequal Democracy: The Political Economy of the Gilded Age* (New York: Russell Sage Foundation, 2008), 217.

24. Kimberly French, "From Riches to Responsibility—Defending the Estate Tax," *UU World*, March/April 2003.

25. Lynda Richardson, "Rich, Yes, but Even More Different: Liberal and Fun," *New York Times*, February 27, 2001, B2.

26. Keith Naughton, "Billionaire Backlash," *Newsweek*, February 26, 2001, 48.

27. David Cay Johnston, "Dozens of Rich Americans Join in Fight to Retain the Estate Tax," *New York Times*, February 14, 2001, A1.

7. The Billionaire Backlash

1. "Factor Investigation: George Soros," April 24, 2007, FoxNews .com, www.foxnews.com/story/0,2933,268045,00.html.

2. William Shawcross, "Turning Dollars into Change," *Time*, September 1, 1999.

3. Edward Robinson, "George Soros Bankrolls Voter Hunt in Swing States," Bloomberg News, September 28, 2004; and Laura Blumenfeld, "Billionaire Soros Takes on Bush," *Washington Post*, November 11, 2003.

4. Jane Mayer, "The Money Man: Can George Soros's Millions Insure the Defeat of President Bush?" *New Yorker*, October 18, 2006.

5. Ibid., 26.

6. Ibid., 39.

7. Jim Rutenberg, "New Internet Site Turns Critical Eyes and Ears to the Right," *New York Times*, May 3, 2004.

8. Tom Bawden, "Buffett Blasts System That Lets Him Pay Less Tax Than Secretary," Times Online, June 28, 2007.

9. Paul Andrews, "Gates Reveals Aim for a Philanthropic Future," *Seattle Times*, April 26, 1996.

10. Matthew Bishop and Michael Green, *Philanthrocapitalism: How the Rich Can Save the World* (New York: Bloomsbury, 2008), 51.

11. Andrew Carnegie, "Wealth," *North American Review* 148, no. 391 (June 1889): 653–665.

12. G. William Domhoff, *Fat Cats and Democrats: The Role of the Big Rich in the Party of the Common Man* (Englewood Cliffs, NJ: Prentice-Hall, 1972), 175.

8. Left-Coast Money

1. "Top Wealthholders with Gross Assets of $300,000 or More, by State of Residence: 1982," Table 724, *Statistical Abstract of the United States*, 1988.

2. Robert Frank, "California Boasts Most Millionaires," May 5, 2008, http://blogs.wsj.com/wealth/2008/05/05/california-boasts-most-millionaires/.

3. Mike Snider, "DVD Feels First Sting of Slipping Sales," *USA Today*, January 7, 2008.

4. Jerry Ropelato, "Internet Pornography Statistics, Top Ten Reviews." See also, "Adult Entertainment in America: A State of the Industry Report," Free Speech Coalition, 2006.

5. "Cable and Premium TV—Summary: 1975 to 2007," Table 1105, *Statistical Abstract of the United States*, 2009; and "Industry Statistics," National Cable and Telecommunications Association, 2009.

6. "Industry Facts," Entertainment Software Association, 2009.

7. "2007 Year-End Shipment Statistics," Recording Industry Association of America, 2009.

8. "The Celebrity 100," Forbes online, June 11, 2008, www.forbes.com/lists/2009/53/celebrity-09_The-Celebrity-100_Rank_4.html.

9. Bob Thomas, *Clown Prince of Hollywood: The Antic Life and Times of Jack L. Warner* (New York: McGraw-Hill, 1990), 306.

10. Ronald Brownstein, "Inside the California Money Machine," *Los Angeles Times*, October 23, 1988.

11. Michael Fleeman, "Clinton Becomes the Toast of Hollywood Presidential Donors," Associated Press, February 25, 1992.

12. Richard Florida, *The Rise of the Creative Class* (New York: Basic Books, 2002), 13.

13. Madeleine Schwartz, "Welcome to the Reel World," *Harvard Crimson*, February 5, 2009.

14. David Postman, "RealNetworks CEO Donates Big Bucks to Politics," *Seattle Times*, July 26, 2004.

15. "Green Economy Offers New Opportunities for Growth in Silicon Valley," *2009 Silicon Valley Index*, February 17, 2009, www.jointventure.org/index.php?option=com_content&view=article&id=74:the-2009-silicon-valley-index&catid=39:silicon-valley-index&Itemid=52.

16. Lori Olszewski, "Some Prop. 39 Backers Have Deep Pockets," *San Francisco Chronicle*, October 23, 2000.

17. Paul Festa, "High-Tech Advocates Clash over School Vouchers, Skilled Labor," CNET News, September 22, 2000, http://news.cnet.com/High-tech-advocates-clash-over-school-vouchers,-skilled-labor/2100-1023_3-246068.html.

18. Neil Gross and Solon Simmons, "The Social and Political Views of American Professors," Harvard University, Working Paper, September 24, 2007.

19. John Markoff, *What the Doormouse Said: How the 60s Counterculture Shaped the Personal Computer Industry* (New York: Viking, 2005).

9. Patrician Politicians

1. Robert Frank, "A Richistani Runs for Office," Wall Street Journal Online, May 23, 2007, http://blogs.wsj.com/wealth/2007/05/23/a-richistani-runs-for-office/.

2. Lynn Bartels, "Money Pours into Effort to Influence Ethics Measure," *Rocky Mountain News*, April 18, 2007.

3. Jennifer Steen, "Maybe You Can Buy an Election, but Not with Your Own Money," *Washington Post*, June 25, 2000, B01.

4. E. Digby Baltzell, *The Protestant Establishment: Aristocracy and Class in America* (New Haven, CT: Yale University Press, 1964), 179.

5. Ibid., 302.

6. Craig Horowitz, "The Deal He Made," *New York*, July 10, 2006.

7. Morris P. Fiorina with Samuel J. Abrams, *Disconnect: The Breakdown of Representation in American Politics* (Norman: University of Oklahoma Press, 2009), 17.

10. The Corporate Liberal

1. Interview with Peter Bernstein and Annalyn Swan, Random House, www.randomhouse.com/catalog/display.pperl?isbn=9780307266125& view=auqa.

2. "The Social Responsibility of Business Is to Increase Its Profits," *New York Times Magazine*, September 13, 1970.

3. Jeffrey Hollender, *What Matters Most: How a Small Group of Pioneers Is Teaching Social Responsibility to Big Business and Why Big Business Is Listening* (New York: Basic Books, 2004), 10.

4. Ibid., 11–12.

5. Russell Mokhiber and Robert Weissman, "Hijacked: Business for Social Responsibility," *Sounding Circle*, November 4, 2005.

6. Lynn Sharp Paine, *Value Shift: Why Companies Must Merge Social and Financial Imperatives to Achieve Superior Performance* (New York: McGraw Hill, 2003), x.

7. J. Figg, "Consumers Indict Irresponsible Companies," *Internal Auditor*, December 22, 1999.

8. "The Impact of CSR on the General Public: A Nationwide Poll on Corporate Social Responsibility," FGI Research, Inc., May 2007.

9. Bill Baue, "Two Sides of the Same Coin: Surveys Track Growth of Interest in CSR and SRI," February 1, 2006, www.socialfunds.com/news/article.cgi/1918.html.

10. Ibid.

11. "Corporate Equality Index: A Report Card on Gay, Lesbian, Bisexual and Transgender Equality in Corporate America," Human Rights Campaign, September 2008.

12. Sergey Brin, "Our Position on California's No on 8 Campaign," Official Google Blog, September 26, 2008, http://googleblog.blogspot.com/2008/09/our-position-on-californias-no-on-8.html.

13. "The CRO's 100 Best Corporate Citizens 2009," www.thecro.com/100best09.

14. "Gay Consumers' Brand Loyalty Linked to Corporate Philanthropy and Advertising," Witeck-Combs Communications, July 22, 2002.

15. "Corporate Profit as Share of G.D.P. Rising, Wage Share at New Low," August 26, 2008, www.nytimes.com/imagepages/2006/08/28/business/28wages_chart.html.

11. A (Very) Liberal Education

1. "Trends in Private Education: An Interview with the NAIS President-Elect," http://privateschool.about.com/library/weekly/aa062501a.htm.

2. National Association of Independent Schools, "Non-NAIS Member Schools Facts at a Glance 2006–2007"; and "NAIS Member Schools Facts at a Glance 2007–2008," www.nais.org.

3. E. Digby Baltzell, *The Protestant Establishment: Aristocracy and Class in America* (New Haven, CT: Yale University Press, 1964), 344.

4. "Percent Students of Color," www.boardingschoolreview .com/highest_percentage_students_color/sort/1.

5. The difference between private and public schools was cited on the Web site of the National Association of Independent Schools in a letter by GLSEN executive director, Kevin Jennings. See www.nais.org/ equity/index.cfm?itemnumber=148941&sn.ItemNumber=142552&tn .ItemNumber=149077. On harassment by income level, see "The 2007 National School Climate Survey: The Experiences of Lesbian, Gay, Bisexual and Transgender Students," Gay, Lesbian and Straight Education Network, 2005, 74.

6. Patrick F. Bassett, "Independent Perspective: Developing Sustainable Schools," *Independent Schools*, Spring 2005.

7. William Snider, "Private-School Apartheid Protest Asked," *Education Week*, December 18, 1985.

8. "Independent Schools and Global Education," NAIS Presentation, ACPA/NASPA Joint Meeting, Orlando, Florida, April 2, 2007.

9. "Community Service and Service Learning Initiatives in Independent Schools," NAIS, December 20, 2001.

10. William G. Bowen, Martin A. Kurzweil, and Eugene M. Tobin, *Equity and Excellence in American Higher Education* (Charlottesville: University of Virginia Press, 2005).

11. Neil Gross and Solon Simmons, "The Social and Political Views of American Professors," Harvard University, Working Paper, September 24, 2007.

12. "The American College Teacher: National Norms for 2007–2008," Higher Education Research Institute, UCLA, March 2009, 1.

13. "2006 Service Statistics: Highlights and Trends of Campus Compact's Annual Membership Survey," *Campus Compact*, 2007.

12. The Heirs

1. John J. Havens and Paul G. Schervish, "Why the $41 Trillion Wealth Transfer Estimate Is Still Valid: A Review of Challenges and Questions," *Journal of Gift Planning* 7, no. 1 (January 2003): 11–15, 47–50.

2. Adam Bernstein, "Flamboyant Philanthropist and GM Heir Stewart Mott," *Washington Post*, June 14, 2008, B6.

3. "Ralph Nader's Statement on Stewart Mott and Tim Russert," PR Newswire, June 13, 2008.

4. Susan Ostrander, *Money for Change: Social Movement Philanthropy at Haymarket* (Philadelphia: Temple University Press, 1995), 9.

Conclusion: A Benign Plutocracy?

1. Victoria McGrane, "Durbin Goes after Bankers . . . Again," *Politico,* May 13, 2009.

2. Leonard Doyle, "Barack Obama's Rich Supporters Fear His Tax Plans Show He's a Class Warrior," *London Telegraph*, May 9, 2009.

3. "Reality Check: Obama Received about the Same Percentage from Small Donors in 2008 as Bush in 2004," Campaign Finance Institute, November 24, 2008.

4. Larry Bartels, *Unequal Democracy: The Political Economy of the New Gilded Age* (New York: Russell Sage Foundation, 2008), 285.

5. Martin Gilens, "Inequality and Democratic Responsiveness," *Public Opinion Quarterly* 69:778–796.

6. Alan H. Barton, "Determinants of Economic Attitudes in the American Business Elite," *AJS Journal*, 91, no. 1 (1985): 54–87.

7. Zach Miners, "Charter Schools Might Not Be Better," *U.S. News and World Report*, June 17, 2009.

8. This idea and others in this section draw from Michael Edwards, *Just Another Emperor? The Myths and Realities of Philanthrocapitalism* (New York: Demos and the Young Foundation, 2008), 85–90.

INDEX